AF512021

# Fundamental of Machine Learning & Deep Learning

## ABOUT THE AUTHORS

**Dr. Anisha Kumari** is currently working as an Assistant Professor in the Department of Computer Science and Engineering at Kalinga Institute of Industrial Technology (KIIT), Bhubaneswar, India. She earned her Ph.D. in Computer Science and Engineering from the National Institute of Technology (NIT), Rourkela. She completed her M.Tech. in Computer Science and Engineering from Veer Surendra Sai University of Technology (VSSUT), Burla, Odisha.Her primary research interests include cloud computing, serverless computing, and performance modeling in emerging technologies. She has published numerous research articles in reputed journals, conferences, and book chapters. Additionally, she holds six patents in various domains of computer science.

**Dr. Ranjan Kumar Behera** is currently working as an Assistant Professor in the Department of Computer Science and Engineering at the Indian Institute of Information Technology (IIIT), Ranchi. Previously, he served as an Assistant Professor at prestigious institutions such as Birla Institute of Technology (BIT) Mesra, XIM University, Bhubaneswar, and Veer Surendra Sai University of Technology (VSSUT), Burla, Odisha. He obtained his Ph.D. in Computer Science and Engineering from NIT Rourkela, India, and completed his M.Tech. in Computer Science and Engineering from NIT Hamirpur in 2014. His research interests include big data analytics in social networks, sentiment analysis, cloud computing, and serverless computing. He has published numerous articles in reputed journals, conferences, and book chapters and holds six patents in various fields of computer science.

**Dr. Kirti Kumari** is currently an Assistant Professor in the Department of Computer Science and Engineering at the Indian Institute of Information Technology (IIIT), Ranchi, Jharkhand, India. Before joining IIIT Ranchi, she worked as an Assistant Professor in the Department of Computer Science and Engineering at Siksha 'O' Anusandhan (Deemed to be University), Bhubaneswar, Odisha. She earned her Ph.D. in Computer Science and Engineering from NIT Patna, her M.Tech. in Computer Science and Engineering from M.S. Ramaiah Institute of Technology, Bangalore, and her B.Tech. in Computer Science and Engineering from Bhagalpur College of Engineering (Government of Bihar), Bhagalpur. Her research focuses on cyberbullying, cyberaggression, hate speech, depression detection, and hope speech. She is actively engaged in the fields of Natural Language Processing (NLP), Machine Learning, Deep Learning, and Social Network Analysis.

# Fundamental of Machine Learning & Deep Learning

Dr. Anisha Kumari
Dr. Ranjan Kumar Behera
Dr. Kirti Kumari

ACADEMIC ENCLAVE

*First Edition, 2025*

ISBN: 978-93-48642-92-9

*Published by*
**ACADEMIC ENCLAVE™**
House No. 10/15, Ground Floor,
Block-A, Street No. 14/3, Kamal Vihar,
Kamal Pur, Burari, Delhi-110084
*Email: info@academicenclave.com*
*Mobile: +91-7042423166*
*Website: www.academicenclave.com*

Printed at Replika Press Pvt. Ltd.

# Preface

Machine learning and deep learning have emerged as transformative forces, revolutionized industries and driving innovation across diverse domains such as healthcare, finance, and autonomous systems. Fundamentals of Machine Learning & Deep Learning offers a comprehensive and structured introduction to these dynamic fields, catering to both beginners and seasoned professionals seeking to deepen their expertise. The book begins by establishing a strong theoretical foundation with Bayesian Decision Theory and fundamental machine learning concepts, gradually progressing to advanced topics such as neural networks, ensemble learning, and deep learning applications. Each chapter strikes a balance between theoretical depth and practical implementation, ensuring readers can seamlessly connect concepts to real-world scenarios. Core topics, including classification and regression algorithms, component analysis, and clustering techniques, are presented with clarity and reinforced with illustrative examples. The advanced sections delve into cutting-edge areas such as deep learning optimization techniques, convolutional neural networks (CNNs), and hybrid models integrating supervised and unsupervised learning approaches. Whether you are a student, researcher, or industry professional, this book serves as a reliable guide to mastering both foundational principles and advanced methodologies in machine learning and deep learning. By the end, readers will have developed a solid grasp of the underlying principles and practical applications, ranging from traditional linear models to state-of-the-art deep neural networks. This holistic approach ensures not just conceptual understanding but also the ability to apply knowledge effectively in solving complex, real-world challenges.

**Dr. Anisha Kumari**

**Dr. Ranjan Kumar Behera**

**Dr. Kirti Kumari**

# Contents

CHAPTER - 1

# Bayesian Decision Theory and Machine Learning Basics

## Bayesian Decision Theory

Bayesian Decision Theory is a powerful statistical framework that facilitates decision-making under uncertainty by employing probabilistic reasoning. At its core, it systematically integrates prior knowledge about event probabilities (prior probabilities) with observed data (likelihood) to compute posterior probabilities using Bayes' theorem. This approach enables a structured assessment of uncertainty, allowing for more informed and rational decision-making. A key strength of Bayesian Decision Theory lies in its ability to minimize risk by considering both the likelihood of various outcomes and the associated costs or rewards of each decision. This is achieved through the incorporation of a loss function, which quantifies the penalty for incorrect decisions. The optimal decision is then determined by minimizing the expected loss, striking a balance between the probability of an event occurring and the potential consequences of errors. This makes the framework particularly effective for applications requiring high-stakes decision-making, such as classification, diagnostics, and risk assessment. In practice, Bayesian Decision Theory finds widespread application in domains where uncertainty and probabilistic reasoning are critical. These include medical diagnosis, spam detection, pattern recognition, financial risk management, and machine learning. By accounting for both prior knowledge and newly observed evidence, it ensures that decisions are not only data-driven but also contextually relevant. However, its effectiveness depends on the accuracy of prior probabilities and likelihood estimates. Additionally, in high-dimensional or complex scenarios, the computational demands can be significant, necessitating advanced techniques for efficient implementation.

Below is Figure 1.1 showing how Bayesian Decision Theory classifies data points based on posterior probabilities and decision boundaries.

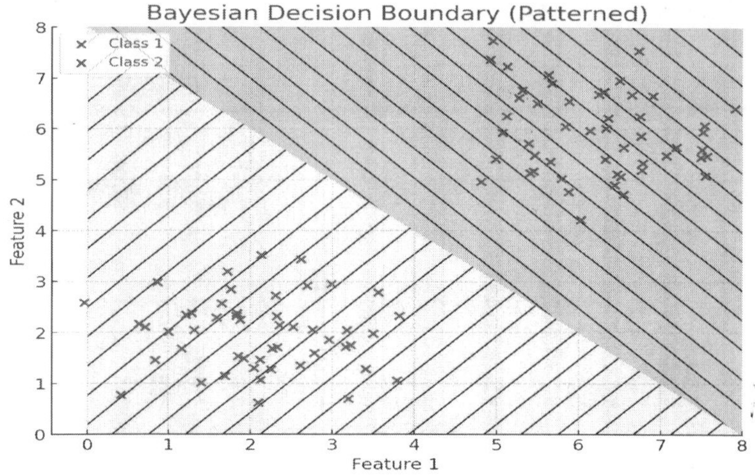


**Figure 1.1: Bayesian Decision Boundaries**

This figure demonstrates:

- **Decision Boundaries:** When the posterior probabilities of the two classes are equal, the decision boundary is represented by the curve that divides the red and blue regions.
- **Regions:** Regions that are red and blue indicate where the decision rule allocates data points to the appropriate classes.
- A fundamental component of contemporary machine learning and pattern recognition methods, Bayesian Decision Theory offers an ideal framework for probabilistic decision-making. Let me know if you'd like further explanations or the generated figure!

## Important Components

**Prior Probability (**P(wi)**)**: Represents the probability of a specific class or hypothesis before any data is observed. For example, in a binary classification task, $P(w_1)$ and $P(w_2)$ represent the likelihood of belonging to class $w_1$ or $w_2$ respectively.

Likelihood ($P(x|w_i)$): Describes the probability of observing the data (x) given that it belongs to a particular class ($w_i$).

Posterior Probability ($P(w_i|x)$): Combines prior probabilities and likelihood using Bayes' theorem:

$$P(w_i|x) = \frac{P(x|w_i)P(w_i)}{P(x)}$$

This is the probability of class $w_i$ given the data x.

Loss or Risk Function: Decision-making often involves minimizing risk. The risk is calculated as:

$$R(w_i|x) = \sum_j L(w_i, w_j)P(w_j|x)$$

Where $L(w_i, w_j)$ is the loss incurred for deciding $w_i$ when the true class is $w_j$.

## Bayesian Decision Rule

According to the Bayesian decision rule, the class with the highest posterior probability or the lowest expected loss is chosen. For example, in a simple classification task:

$$\text{Decide } w_i \text{ if } P(w_i|x) > P(w_j|x), \forall j \neq i$$

By utilizing the probability distributions of the classes, this decision rule guarantees the best possible classification performance.

## Applications

Bayesian Decision Theory is applied in:

- Pattern Recognition: Classifying images, texts, or audio data.
- Medical Diagnosis: Estimating the probability of a disease based on test results and symptoms.
- Spam Detection: Determining whether an email is spam.
- Robotics and Automation: Providing direction for decision-making in uncertain circumstances.

## Normal Distribution

The Normal Distribution, also referred to as the Gaussian Distribution, is a fundamental probability distribution in statistics and machine learning. It represents how data points are symmetrically distributed around a central mean ($\mu$), forming a characteristic bell-shaped curve. This distribution is widely utilized due to its prevalence in natural phenomena, measurement errors, and numerous statistical models, where data often tend to cluster around the mean with predictable variability. Its mathematical properties make it a cornerstone for inferential statistics, hypothesis testing, and various machine learning algorithms.

Figure 1.2 illustrates a normal distribution with a mean ($\mu$) of 0 and a standard deviation ($\sigma$) of 1. The shaded regions represent 68% and 95% of the data within one and two standard deviations from the mean, respectively.

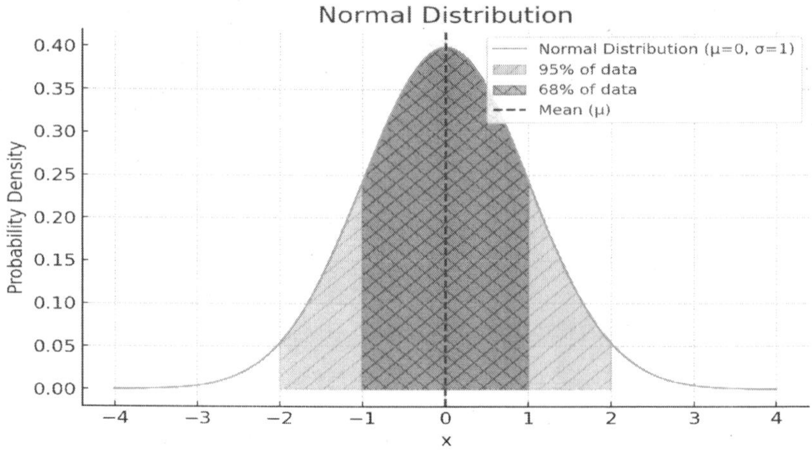


**Figure 1.2: Normal Distribution with a Mean.**

## Properties of the Normal Distribution

The normal distribution is mathematically defined by its probability density function (PDF):

$$f(x) = \frac{1}{\sqrt{2\pi\sigma^2}} e^{-\frac{(x-\mu)^2}{2\sigma^2}}$$

Where:

- x: The data point or variable
- μ: The mean (center) of the distribution
- σ: The standard deviation (spread) of the distribution
- $\sigma^2$: The variance ($\sigma^2=(\sigma)^2$)

Key properties:

1. Symmetry: The curve is symmetric around the mean $\mu$.
2. Mean = Median = Mode: The central point is the same for all three.
3. Bell Shape: The curve tails off symmetrically on both sides of the mean.
4. 68-95-99.7 Rule:
   - About 68% of data falls within [μ−σ,μ+σ].
   - About 95% of data falls within [μ−2σ,μ+2σ].
   - About 99.7% of data falls within [μ−3σ,μ+3σ].

## Importance & Application of Normal Distribution

The normal distribution is a cornerstone of statistics and machine learning, serving as both a foundational theoretical concept and a critical tool for diverse applications. Its significance is underscored by the Central Limit Theorem (CLT), which states that, regardless of the original data distribution, the means of sufficiently large random samples tend to follow a normal distribution. This property makes the normal distribution indispensable for statistical modeling and data analysis, as many natural and social phenomena such as human heights, test scores, and measurement errors exhibit a normal pattern. Beyond its theoretical importance, the normal distribution plays a pivotal role in inferential statistics, forming the backbone of confidence interval estimation, hypothesis testing, and regression analysis. Its influence extends across multiple domains. In machine learning, many algorithms such as Naïve Bayes, Linear Regression, and Principal Component Analysis (PCA)rely on assumptions of normality to function optimally. In quality control, it aids in assessing manufacturing variability, ensuring that products meet industry standards. In finance, it is widely used to model stock returns, evaluate risk, and optimize investment portfolios. The ubiquity and versatility of the normal distribution make it an indispensable tool across disciplines, reinforcing its status as a fundamental concept in both theoretical and applied statistics.

## Machine Perception Extraction

Machine perception extraction refers to the process of enabling machines to sense, interpret, and process sensory information from their environment. This involves analyzing visual, auditory, and tactile data to derive meaningful insights, mimicking human sensory perception. By leveraging advanced algorithms and artificial intelligence, machines can interact with and respond to their surroundings effectively. This capability is crucial in domains such as computer vision, speech recognition, and robotics, where accurate sensory interpretation is essential. In computer vision, for instance, machines extract and analyze features from images or videos to recognize objects, faces, and scenes. Techniques like convolutional neural networks (CNNs) allow systems to detect edges, colours, and textures, enabling precise visual interpretation. Similarly, in speech recognition, auditory signals are transformed into textual data by identifying patterns in sound waves using methods like spectrogram analysis and Mel Frequency Cepstral Coefficients (MFCCs).By integrating these technologies, machine perception extraction plays a pivotal role in developing intelligent systems capable of real-time decision-making and adaptive interactions in complex environments.

The tactile domain plays a crucial role in empowering machines, particularly robots, to perceive, interpret, and respond to physical interactions with their environment. Equipped with advanced sensors, robotic arms can detect variations in pressure, texture, and temperature, allowing them to grasp, manipulate, and interact with objects with remarkable precision. This capability is especially critical in high-stakes industries such as healthcare, where surgical robots perform delicate procedures, and logistics, where automated systems efficiently sort and handle packages. However, extracting meaningful insights from machine perception presents significant challenges due to the complexity and variability of sensory data. Factors such as noise, missing information, and high dimensionality can hinder accurate interpretation. To address these issues, high-quality sensor inputs, robust preprocessing techniques, and cutting-edge machine learning algorithms are essential. Despite these hurdles, rapid advancements in deep learning and sensor technologies have dramatically enhanced the accuracy, efficiency, and adaptability of machine perception systems. These innovations continue to push the boundaries of robotic capabilities, bringing us closer to a future where machines seamlessly integrate into diverse real-world applications.

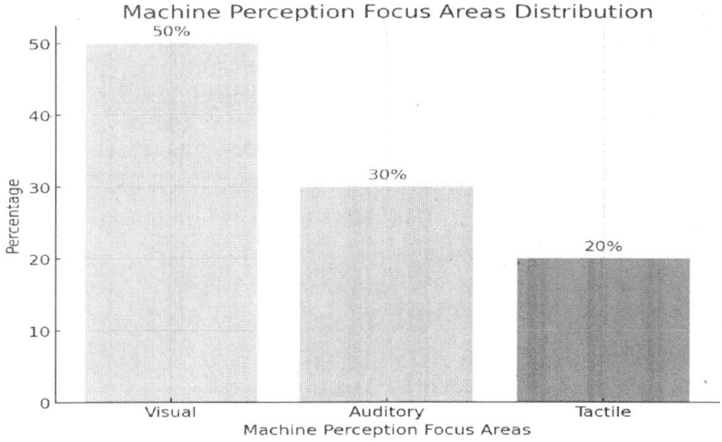


**Figure 1.3: Machine Perception Focus Area.**

Figure 1.3 illustrates the distribution of focus areas in machine perception, highlighting three primary domains: visual (50%), auditory (30%), and tactile (20%). These represent the relative emphasis placed on enabling machines to process visual, auditory, and physical sensory data for perception and decision-making tasks.

## Methods for Feature Extraction

Feature extraction is the process of deriving meaningful and distinctive characteristics from data across various modalities, enabling efficient analysis and pattern recognition. In image processing, techniques such as edge detection (e.g., Canny and Sobel filters), color histogram analysis, and feature descriptors (e.g., Scale-Invariant Feature Transform (SIFT) and Speeded-Up Robust Features (SURF)) are widely employed to capture visual patterns and structures. For audio analysis, methods like spectrogram representation, Mel Frequency Cepstral Coefficients (MFCCs), and zero-crossing rate are instrumental in identifying key sound features and distinguishing different audio signals. In natural language processing (NLP), approaches such as Bag of Words (BoW) and word embeddings (e.g., Word2Vec, GloVe) facilitate the extraction of semantic and syntactic information from text, enhancing text-based analysis. Furthermore, multi-sensor fusion integrates data from multiple sources, such as audio, video, and other sensor modalities, to extract richer, complementary features, thereby improving the accuracy and robustness of advanced applications in fields like machine learning, artificial intelligence, and pattern recognition(Figure 1.4).

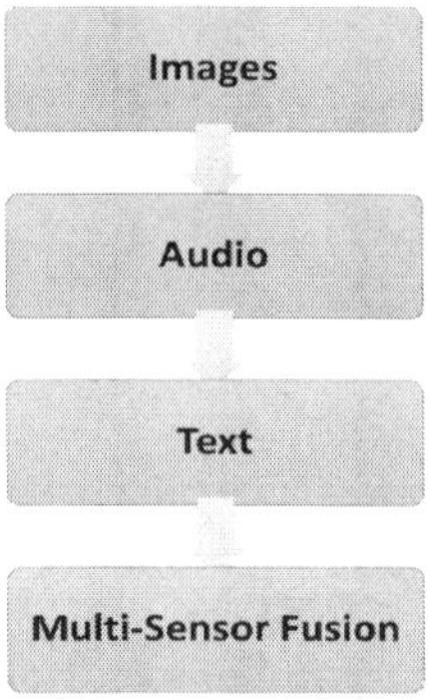


**Figure 1.4:Feature Extraction.**

## Classification &Clustering

Classification and clustering are fundamental techniques in machine learning that facilitate data organization and analysis. Although both methods involve grouping data, they serve distinct purposes, employ different methodologies, and are applied in varied contexts. The following provides an in-depth exploration of each concept, highlighting their key differences and practical applications(Figure 1.5).

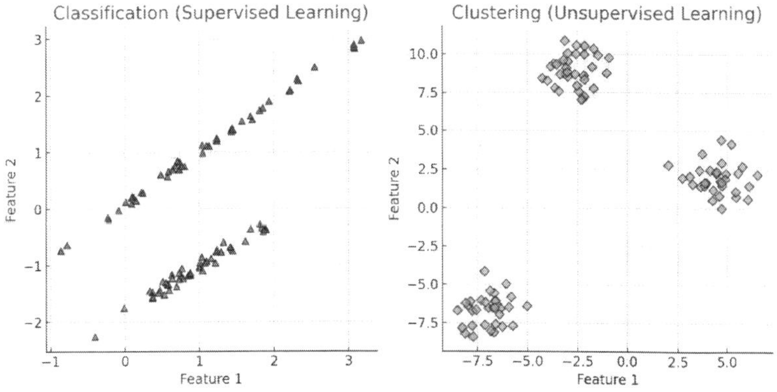


**Figure 1.5: Differences between Classification and Clustering.**

Figure 1.5 visually contrasts classification and clustering techniques. In the classification plot, labeled data points are assigned to two predefined categories using supervised learning, which relies on prior knowledge to guide the categorization process. In contrast, the clustering plot exemplifies unsupervised learning, where data points are grouped into three distinct clusters based solely on inherent similarities, without any predefined labels or prior training.

## 1. Classification

Classification is a supervised learning technique aimed at categorizing data points into predefined classes or labels based on their features. Since the class labels are known in advance, the process relies on a training dataset containing labeled examples to learn patterns and relationships. This trained model can then accurately classify new, unseen data based on the learned associations.

### Steps in Classification:

- Training Phase:

Each data point has a class label attached to it in the labeled dataset that is supplied. Equations such as Neural Networks, Decision Trees, and Logistic Regression are used to teach the model a mapping between features and their corresponding labels.

- Prediction Phase:

Unseen data points are categorized using the trained model into one of the predetermined classes.

### Applications of Classification:

- Email Spam Detection: Identifying whether an email is spam or not.
- Medical Diagnosis: Using a patient's symptoms to determine whether they have a disease.
- Sentiment Analysis: Categorizing text into positive, negative, or neutral sentiment.

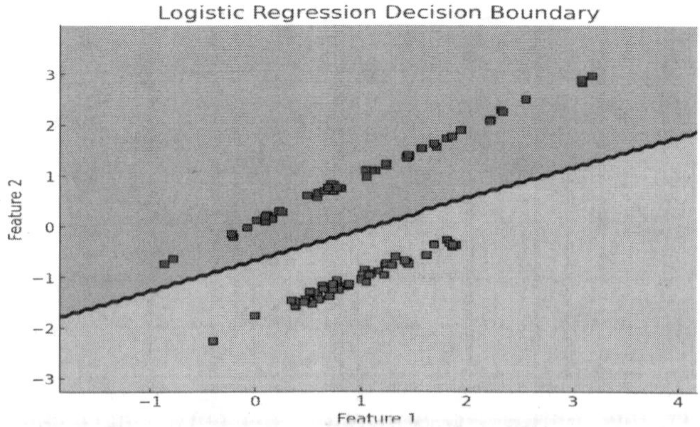


**Figure 1.6: Logistic Regression.**

Based on probabilities calculated using a sigmoid function, the dataset is split into two regions by the linear decision boundary for logistic regression. The straight boundary in Figure 1.6 demonstrates how well it performs for linearly separable data.

## Common Algorithms for Classification:

### 1. Logistic Regression

Logistic Regression is a widely used supervised learning algorithm designed for binary classification tasks. It estimates the probability of a given data point belonging to a particular class by applying the sigmoid function, which maps outputs to a range between 0 and 1. The algorithm constructs a decision boundary using a linear combination of input features, effectively distinguishing between classes. Despite its simplicity, Logistic Regression is highly effective for datasets that are linearly separable. It optimizes the log-loss (cross-entropy) function to maximize the likelihood of accurate classification. Due to its interpretability and efficiency, it finds extensive applications in areas such as spam email detection, credit risk assessment, and medical diagnosis, where probabilistic predictions are essential.

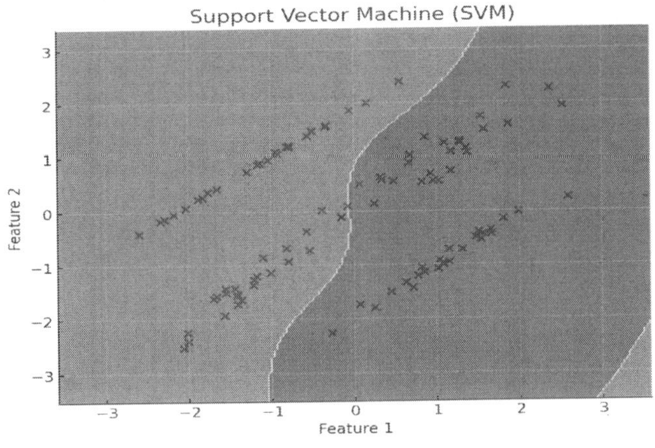


**Figure 1.7: SVM Boundary**

Based on the support vectors, the SVM decision boundary maximizes the difference between the two classes. An example of a linear SVM boundary with the maximum margin between classes is shown in Figure 1.7.

### 2. Support Vector Machines (SVM)

Support Vector Machines (SVM) are powerful supervised learning algorithms designed to find the optimal hyperplane that maximally separates data points into distinct classes. This separation is achieved by maximizing the margin between the closest data points, known as support vectors, which play a crucial role in defining the decision boundary. SVM can be extended to handle non-linearly separable data using kernel functions such as the Radial Basis Function (RBF) and polynomial kernels, effectively transforming the input space to improve classification. Renowned for its robustness against outliers and effectiveness in high-dimensional spaces, SVM is widely applied in fields such as image recognition, bioinformatics, and text classification, where precise and reliable pattern recognition is essential.

### 3. Decision Trees

Decision Trees classify data by recursively partitioning it into branches based on feature thresholds, creating a structured, tree-like model. Each internal node represents a decision rule, guiding the data split, while the leaf nodes correspond to class labels or final outcomes. The tree is built by selecting features that either maximize information gain or minimize impurity, typically measured using metrics such as the Gini Index or Entropy. Decision Trees are highly interpretable and perform well on smaller datasets. However, without proper pruning or regularization techniques, they are prone to overfitting. They find applications in diverse domains, including fraud detection, customer segmentation, medical diagnosis, and risk assessment.

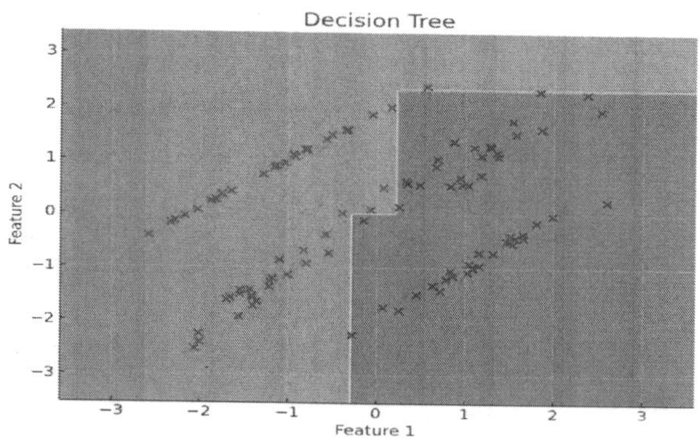


**Figure 1.8: Decision Tree.**

A non-linear decision boundary produced by a decision tree is depicted in Figure 1.8. Although the tree divides the feature space into regions according to thresholds, optimizing for class separation, the boundaries are rectangular.

### 4. Random Forests

Random Forests are a powerful ensemble learning technique that leverages multiple decision trees to enhance predictive accuracy and mitigate overfitting. Each tree in the forest is independently trained on a randomly selected subset of the dataset, using a unique combination of features. The final prediction is derived through majority voting for classification tasks or by averaging the outputs for regression. Known for their robustness to noise and ability to effectively handle high-dimensional data, Random Forests are extensively applied across various domains, including credit risk assessment, stock market forecasting, medical diagnostics, and remote sensing.

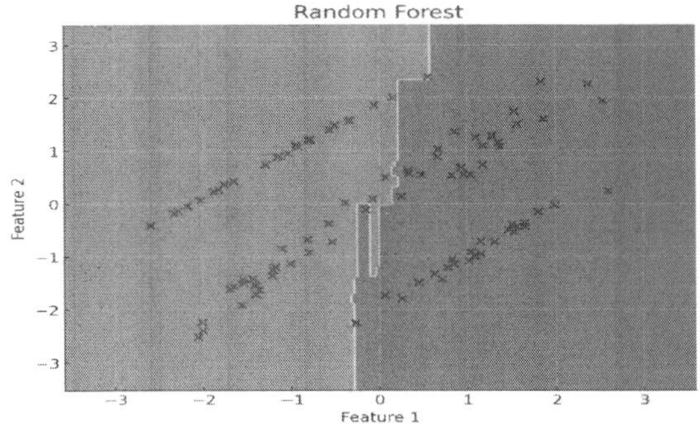


**Figure 1.9: Random Forests.**

Multiple Decision Trees are combined in Random Forests to produce intricate decision boundaries. In Figure 1.9, irregular boundaries are used to demonstrate how the ensemble approach manages data variability more effectively than individual trees.

## 5. Naïve Bayes

Naïve Bayes is a powerful probabilistic classifier founded on Bayes' theorem. It operates under the simplifying assumption that features are conditionally independent, which significantly reduces computational complexity. Despite this seemingly unrealistic assumption, Naïve Bayes consistently delivers strong performance, particularly in text-based applications. Its speed and efficiency make it an ideal choice for tasks such as spam detection, sentiment analysis, and document classification, where rapid and reliable predictions are essential.

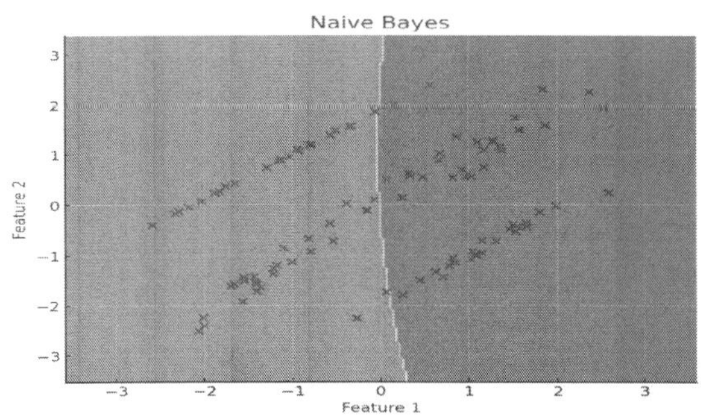


**Figure 1.10: Decision Boundary for Naïve Bayes.**

Naïve Bayes uses a probabilistic decision boundary that presumes feature independence. In Figure 1.10, class probabilities based on Gaussian distributions for the features are represented by a smooth, curved boundary.

## 2. Clustering

Clustering is a powerful unsupervised learning technique that automatically groups data points into clusters based on their inherent similarities. Unlike classification, which relies on labeled data for training, clustering operates without predefined categories. Instead, it uncovers hidden patterns and natural structures within the dataset, making it particularly useful for exploratory data analysis, anomaly detection, and segmentation tasks.

### Steps in Clustering:

- Initialization:

Data points are analysed to find clusters or natural groupings. Finding the closeness of two points is frequently done using a similarity metric, such as the Euclidean distance.

- Cluster Formation:

Points that are similar are grouped together, and points that are different are placed in different groups. Until a predetermined stopping criterion is satisfied, algorithms iteratively modify clusters.

### Applications of Clustering:

- Customer Segmentation: Grouping customers based on purchasing behavior.
- Image Segmentation: Dividing an image into regions based on pixel similarity.
- Anomaly Detection: Identifying outliers or unusual patterns in data.

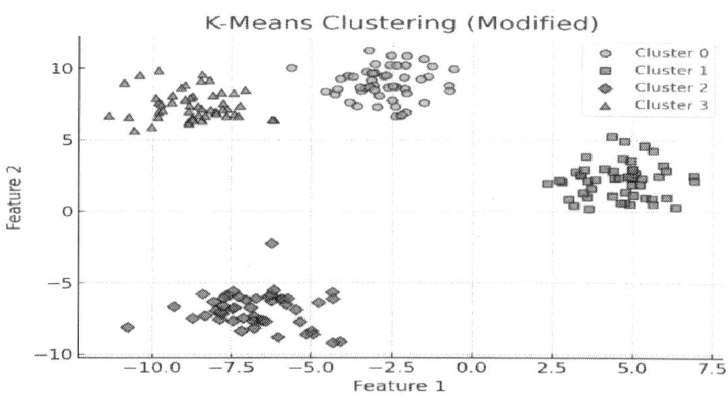


**Figure 1.11: K-Means Clustering.**

Figure 1.11 illustrates the clusters generated by the K-Means algorithm, where data points are assigned to clusters based on their proximity to the nearest centroid. Each cluster is distinctly coloured for clarity, and the decision boundaries between clusters are linear, reflecting the inherent partitioning mechanism of K-Means. This algorithm performs effectively when clusters are approximately spherical and of similar size, ensuring optimal separation and organization of data points.

## Common Algorithms for Clustering:

### 1. K-Means Clustering

K-Means is a widely used unsupervised learning algorithm that clusters data intok distinct groups. It begins by randomly initializingk cluster centroids and then iteratively refines them by assigning each data point to the nearest centroid based on Euclidean distance. After each assignment, the centroids are recalculated as the mean of their assigned points, and this process continues until convergence—either when the centroids stabilize or a predefined stopping criterion is met. K-Means is valued for its simplicity, scalability, and efficiency, particularly in cases where clusters are well-separated and roughly spherical. However, it has limitations, such as sensitivity to outliers and the necessity of specifying the number of clusters in advance.

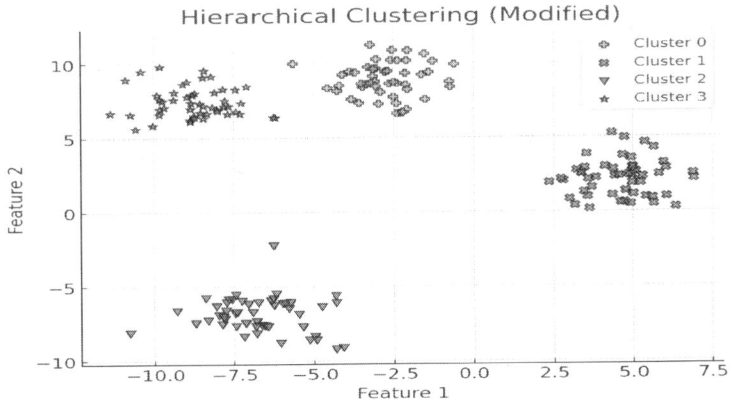


**Figure 1.12: Hierarchical Clustering.**

Figure 1.12 illustrates hierarchical clustering, employing a bottom-up (agglomerative) approach to form clusters. In this method, individual data points are progressively merged based on similarity, creating a hierarchy of nested groupings. The resulting dendrogram provides valuable insights into the underlying data structure, enabling a clear visualization of relationships and cluster formations.

## 2. Hierarchical Clustering

Hierarchical clustering constructs a hierarchy of clusters using either a bottom-up (agglomerative) or top-down (divisive) approach. In the agglomerative method, each data point initially forms its own cluster, and clusters are iteratively merged based on a specified linkage criterion, such as single, complete, or average linkage. This process continues until all data points belong to a single cluster. The resulting dendrogram visually represents the nested clustering structure, providing insights into data relationships. While hierarchical clustering is valuable for data exploration and visualization, its computational complexity increases significantly with larger datasets, making it less scalable for big data applications.

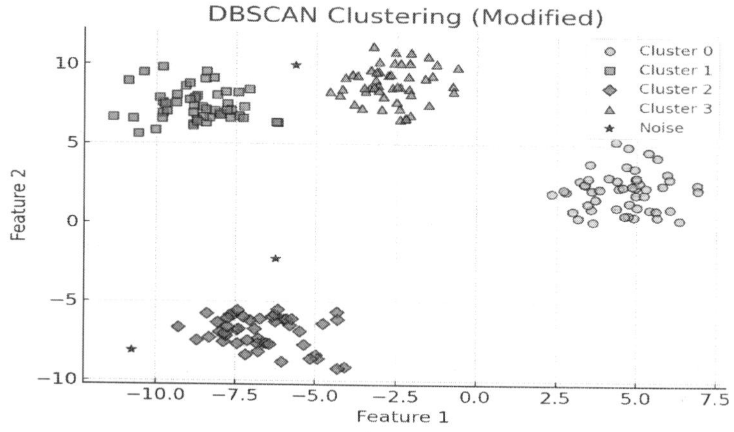


**Figure 1.13: Clusters based on Data Density.**

Figure 1.13 visually represents the clustering results of the DBSCAN algorithm, which identifies clusters based on data density. In this approach, densely packed points are grouped into clusters, while sparsely populated regions are designated as outliers. DBSCAN excels in detecting clusters of arbitrary shapes and is particularly effective in handling datasets with significant noise.

## 3. DBSCAN (Density-Based Spatial Clustering)

DBSCAN (Density-Based Spatial Clustering of Applications with Noise) identifies clusters by analyzing the density distribution of data points within a given region. It groups closely packed points within a specified distance ($\epsilon$) while designating points in sparse regions as outliers. Unlike traditional clustering methods, DBSCAN does not require the number of clusters to be predefined and is capable of detecting clusters of arbitrary shapes. This makes it particularly effective for datasets containing noise and varying cluster densities. However, its performance can be hindered when clusters exhibit significantly different densities or when the selection of $\epsilon$ and the minimum number of points is not well-optimized.

## 4. Gaussian Mixture Models (GMM)

The Gaussian Mixture Model (GMM) is a probabilistic clustering algorithm that assumes data points are generated from a combination of multiple Gaussian distributions. Each cluster is represented by a distinct Gaussian component, defined by its mean and variance. The algorithm employs the Expectation-Maximization (EM) technique to iteratively refine cluster assignments by estimating the probability of each data point belonging to different clusters. Unlike K-Means, which enforces rigid spherical clusters, GMM offers greater flexibility by accommodating clusters of varying shapes and sizes. However, careful initialization is crucial to prevent convergence to suboptimal solutions.

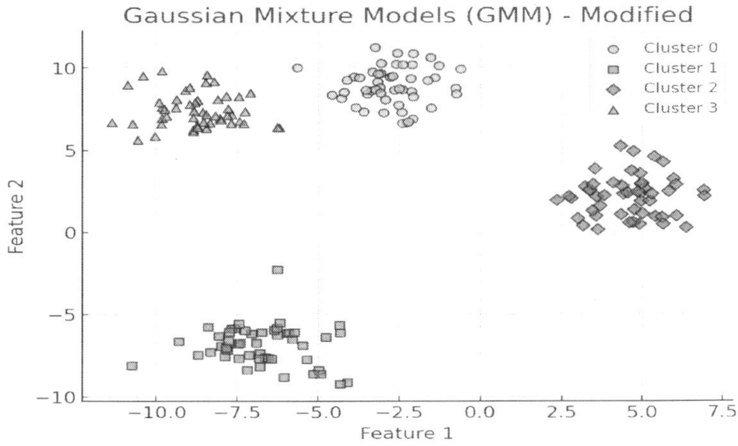


**Figure 1.14: Gaussian Distributions.**

Figure 1.14 illustrates the Gaussian Mixture Model (GMM), where clusters are represented as Gaussian distributions with diverse shapes and sizes. Unlike K-Means, which assigns data points to clusters deterministically, GMM uses probabilistic assignments, leading to more flexible and smoother cluster boundaries. This approach makes GMM particularly well-suited for complex, non-linear, and overlapping data distributions.

Below Table 1.1. Explain the differences between classification and clustering:

**Table 1.1: Differences between Classification and Clustering.**

| Feature | Classification | Clustering |
|---|---|---|
| **Definition** | A supervised learning technique that categorizes data into predefined classes. | An unsupervised learning technique that groups data based on similarities. |
| **Type of Learning** | Supervised learning (requires labeled data). | Unsupervised learning (does not require labeled data). |
| **Labeling** | Requires predefined labels for training data. | No predefined labels; groups are discovered from data. |
| **Goal** | To predict the category of new data points based on training data. | To find hidden patterns and structure in data. |
| **Examples** | Email spam detection (spam or not spam), disease classification (cancer or non-cancer). | Customer segmentation, document clustering, anomaly detection. |
| **Algorithm Examples** | Decision Trees, Naïve Bayes, Support Vector Machine (SVM), Neural Networks. | K-Means, Hierarchical Clustering, DBSCAN, Gaussian Mixture Models. |
| **Output** | A specific class label for each data point. | A cluster label or grouping of data points. |
| **Training Data Requirement** | Needs labeled data for training. | Works with unlabeled data. |
| **Use Case** | Used when the classes are known and need to be predicted. | Used when the structure of data is unknown and needs exploration. |

## Linear and Logistic Regression

### Linear Regression

Linear Regression is a fundamental supervised learning algorithm designed for predicting continuous target variables. It operates under the assumption of a linear relationship between independent variables ($X$) and the dependent variable ($Y$). The primary objective of linear regression is to determine the optimal line that best fits the data by minimizing the difference between predicted and actual values, typically using methods like the Least Squares approach. This model is widely used in various domains, including finance, healthcare, and social sciences, for trend analysis, forecasting, and data-driven decision-making.

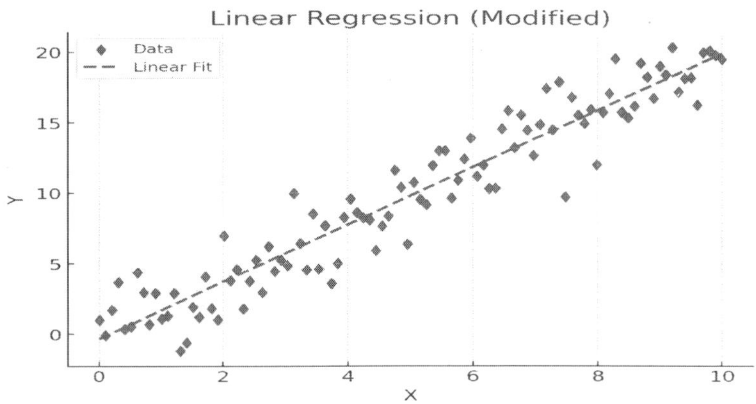


**Figure 1.15: linear Relationship between the Input $X$ and the Target $Y$.**

Figure 1.15 depicts a linear relationship between the input variableX and the target variableY, where a straight line represents the optimal fit. Linear regression is a predictive modeling technique that estimates continuous values by minimizing the discrepancy between the observed data points and the fitted line, ensuring the best possible representation of the underlying trend.

### Formula

The hypothesis for linear regression is:

$$Y = \beta_0 + \beta_1 X_1 + \beta_2 X_2 + \cdots + \beta_n X_n + \epsilon$$

**Where:**

- $Y$: Dependent variable (target).
- $X_i$: Independent variables (features).
- $\beta_i$: Coefficients (weights).
- $\epsilon$: Error term.

**Objective**

The objective is to minimize the Mean Squared Error (MSE):

$$MSE = \frac{1}{n}\sum_{i=1}^{n}(Y_i - \hat{Y}_i)^2$$

Where $\hat{Y}_i$ is the predicted value.

**Applications**

- Predicting house prices based on area and location.
- Estimating sales figures based on advertising budget.
- Forecasting weather conditions

**Logistic Regression**

Logistic Regression is a supervised learning algorithm designed for both binary and multi-class classification tasks. Unlike linear regression, which predicts continuous values, logistic regression estimates the probability of an instance belonging to a particular class. It employs the sigmoid function to transform these probabilities into class labels, ensuring outputs fall within the range of 0 to 1, making it particularly effective for classification problems.

**Figure 1.16: Sigmoid Curve.**

Figure 1.16 illustrates a sigmoid curve that transforms input valuesX into probabilities ranging from 0 to 1. Logistic regression leverages this function for binary classification, where a probability threshold of 0.5 typically serves as the decision boundary, distinguishing between the two classes.

**Formula**

The hypothesis for logistic regression is:

$$P(Y = 1|X) = \sigma(Z) = \frac{1}{1 + e^{-Z}}$$

**Where:**

- $Z=\beta_0+\beta_1X_1+\beta_2X_2+\cdots+\beta_nX_nZ$
- σ(Z): Sigmoid function.

The model predicts class probabilities (P) between 0 and 1, and the decision boundary is typically set at P=0.5.

If P≥0.5, predict class 1; otherwise, predict class 0.

### Objective

Logistic regression optimizes the Log-Loss (Cross-Entropy Loss):

$$Loss = -\frac{1}{n}\sum_{i=1}^{n}\left[Y_i \log(\hat{P}_i) + (1 - Y_i)\log(1 - \hat{P}_i)\right]$$

Where $\hat{P}_i$ is the predicted probability.

### Applications

- Spam detection (spam vs. not spam).
- Disease diagnosis (e.g., predicting diabetes presence).
- Customer churn prediction (retain vs. leave).

### *Linear Regression Example*

**Problem**: Calculate the size of a house (in square feet) to predict its price.

### *Dataset (Table 1.3)*:

**Table 1.3: Dataset**

| House Size (sq. ft.) | Price ($1000s) |
|---|---|
| 800 | 150 |
| 1000 | 200 |
| 1200 | 250 |
| 1500 | 300 |
| 1800 | 350 |

### *Linear Regression Model:*

- Input: House size (X).
- Output: Price (Y).

- Hypothesis: $Y=\beta_0+\beta_1 X$.

Once the model has been trained, we could potentially get the equation:

$$Y=50+0.2X$$

For a house size of 1400 sq. ft., the predicted price would be:

$$Y=50+0.2(1400)=330 \text{ (in \$1000s)}.$$

Differences between Linear and Logistic Regression explain in below Table 1.2:

**Table 1.2: Differences between Linear and Logistic Regression**

| Feature | Linear Regression | Logistic Regression |
|---|---|---|
| **Type of Problem** | Used for regression (continuous output) | Used for classification (categorical output) |
| **Output Nature** | Produces continuous values | Produces probabilities (0 to 1) and maps them to classes |
| **Equation Form** | $Y = b_0 + b_1X_1 + b_2X_2 + \ldots + b_nX_n$ | $P(Y) = \frac{1}{1+e^{-(b_0+b_1X_1+\ldots+b_nX_n)}}$ |
| **Dependent Variable** | Continuous (e.g., price, age, salary) | Categorical (e.g., spam/not spam, disease/no disease) |
| **Algorithm Used** | Uses least squares method (minimizes mean squared error) | Uses maximum likelihood estimation (MLE) |
| **Prediction Output** | Direct numerical values | Probability values, often classified into binary or multiple categories |
| **Linearity Assumption** | Assumes a linear relationship between independent and dependent variables | Assumes a linear relationship between independent variables and log-odds (logit function) |
| **Error Measurement** | Uses Mean Squared Error (MSE) or Root Mean Squared Error (RMSE) | Uses Cross-Entropy or Log Loss |
| **Decision Boundary** | Can take any value from −∞-\infty−∞ to +∞+\infty+∞ | S-shaped (sigmoid) curve for binary classification |
| **Application Examples** | Predicting house prices, stock prices, sales forecasting | Email spam detection, disease prediction, fraud detection |

## Types of Learning

Machine learning is centered around equipping systems with the ability to learn from data and enhance their performance over time without the need for explicit programming. The learning process in machine learning is classified based on how algorithms interact with data and the nature of feedback they receive. The three primary learning paradigms are Supervised Learning, Unsupervised Learning, and Reinforcement Learning. Each of these learning methods is tailored for specific challenges and applications, driving advancements in fields ranging from healthcare and finance to artificial intelligence and automation.

## Supervised Learning

Supervised learning is a machine learning approach in which a model learns to establish a mapping function between input variables ($X$) and their corresponding known outputs ($Y$). This process relies on a training dataset comprising labeled examples, where each input is paired with its correct output. Through iterative optimization, the model continuously refines its parameters to minimize the discrepancy between its predictions and the actual target values, enhancing its accuracy and generalization capabilities.

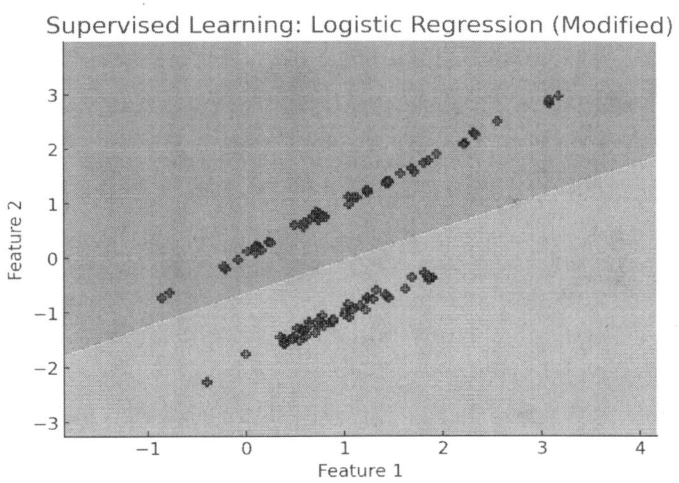


**Figure 1.17: Concept of Supervised Learning Using a Logistic Regression Model.**

Figure 1.17 illustrates the concept of Supervised Learning through the application of a Logistic Regression model, showcasing its functionality in making predictions based on labeled data.

- **Data Points:** The points, which are represented by various colors (such as red and blue), are samples from two classes.
- **Decision Boundary:** The decision boundary produced by the Logistic Regression model is represented by the curved line in the center. By

forecasting probabilities and allocating points to the class with a probability greater than 50%, it distinguishes between the two classes.

- **Goal:** To train the model to accurately classify unseen data, labeled data is used to teach it the relationship between features and their corresponding class labels.

### Characteristics

- **Labeled Data:** Each input feature (like a house's size) is paired with an output label (like the price of the house) in supervised learning datasets.
- **Goal:** The model reduces the discrepancy between the labels in the training data and its predictions.
- **Training Process:** Labeled examples are provided to the model, which iteratively modifies its parameters (such as weights) to lower the error.

## Types of Supervised Learning

**Regression:** Forecasts continuous values.

Example: Using characteristics like area, location, and number of rooms to forecast home prices.

Common Algorithms: Linear Regression, Polynomial Regression.

**Classification:** Forecasts distinct class labels.

Example: Email spam detection (whether it's spam or not).

Common Algorithms: Logistic Regression, Support Vector Machines (SVM), Decision Trees.

### Common Algorithms

- Linear Regression: It establishes that input features and continuous output have a linear relationship.
- Logistic Regression: Probability models for problems involving binary or multi-class classification.
- Decision Trees: it divides data into branches according to feature thresholds for regression or classification.
- Support Vector Machines (SVM): Determines the best hyperplane to divide classes.
- Neural Networks: It uses several layers to handle intricate patterns and non-linear relationships.

### Applications

- Healthcare: Using patient symptoms to predict diseases (e.g., diabetes detection).

- Finance: Predicting loan approval using a customer's credit history.
- Marketing: Customer churn prediction.
- Natural Language Processing (NLP): Sentiment analysis, spam detection.
- Computer Vision: Image recognition, object detection.

***Example***

Email Spam Detection:

- Input: Email text, subject line, sender information.
- Output: Spam (1) or Not Spam (0).
- Algorithm: Logistic Regression.
- Training: The model is trained on a dataset of labeled emails (spam and not spam).
- Prediction: For a new email, the model predicts whether it is spam or not based on learned patterns.

## Unsupervised Learning

Unsupervised learning is a branch of machine learning in which a model is trained on data without predefined labels or outputs. The primary objective is to uncover hidden structures, patterns, or relationships within the dataset. Unlike supervised learning, which relies on labeled data to map inputs to specific outputs, unsupervised learning autonomously explores the data, revealing natural groupings or latent structures. This makes it particularly valuable in scenarios where manual labeling is impractical, expensive, or infeasible. One of the most common applications of unsupervised learning is clustering, where similar data points are grouped into clusters based on shared characteristics. Algorithms such as K-Means and DBSCAN are widely employed in customer segmentation, anomaly detection, and image segmentation. Another crucial application is dimensionality reduction, where techniques like Principal Component Analysis (PCA) reduce the number of features while preserving essential information. This not only enhances computational efficiency but also facilitates the visualization and interpretation of high-dimensional data. Unsupervised learning plays a pivotal role in exploratory data analysis, allowing researchers and analysts to uncover valuable insights that might not be immediately apparent. However, its outcomes are often subjective and require domain expertise for accurate interpretation. Despite this challenge, it serves as the backbone for various applications, including recommendation systems, market basket analysis, and biological data analysis. By identifying hidden patterns and structures, unsupervised learning provides a foundation for data-driven decision-making across diverse industries.

Table 1.4: Comparison Table

| Feature | Supervised Learning | Unsupervised Learning | Reinforcement Learning |
|---|---|---|---|
| **Definition** | Learning from labeled data where the algorithm maps input to output | Learning from unlabeled data to find patterns or structures | Learning through trial and error by interacting with the environment |
| **Data Type** | Labeled Data (input-output pairs) | Unlabeled Data | No predefined dataset; learns from environment feedback |
| **Goal** | Predict output based on input data | Discover hidden patterns or structures in data | Maximize cumulative reward through actions |
| **Example Tasks** | Classification, Regression | Clustering, Association Rule Learning | Game Playing, Robotics, Dynamic Pricing |
| **Examples** | Spam detection, Fraud detection, Image classification | Customer segmentation, Market basket analysis, Anomaly detection | AlphaGo, Self-driving cars, Stock trading bots |
| **Training Approach** | Learns a function from input-output mapping | Identifies patterns, similarities, or structures | Learns through rewards and penalties from the environment |
| **Feedback** | Direct (labeled examples) | No direct feedback | Reward/Penalty based on action outcome |
| **Algorithms** | Decision Trees, SVM, Neural Networks, Linear Regression | K-Means, DBSCAN, PCA, Autoencoders | Q-learning, Deep Q Networks (DQN), Policy Gradient Methods |
| **Dependency on Labels** | Requires labeled data | Does not require labels | No predefined labels, learns through interaction |
| **Challenges** | Data labeling can be expensive | Interpretability, No clear evaluation metric | Requires significant computational resources and exploration |

## Reinforcement Learning

Reinforcement Learning (RL) is a powerful machine learning paradigm designed to train an agent to make optimal decisions in an interactive environment. Unlike supervised learning, which depends on labeled data, RL operates through a process of trial and error. The agent interacts with its environment, receives feedback in the form of rewards or penalties, and refines its decision-making strategy accordingly.

At the core of RL is the concept of a policya strategy that guides the agent in selecting actions to maximize cumulative rewards over time. The learning process follows a continuous cycle: the agent observes the current state of the environment, chooses an action based on its policy, transitions to a new state, and receives a reward signal that indicates the effectiveness of its choice. By continuously updating its policy, the agent improves its ability to make better decisions in the future. A crucial aspect of RL is the balance between exploration (experimenting with new actions to discover potentially better strategies) and exploitation (leveraging known strategies to maximize immediate rewards). Striking the right balance is essential for effective learning, especially in dynamic and complex environments.Reinforcement learning has demonstrated remarkable success in fields requiring sequential decision-making, such as robotics, game AI (e.g., AlphaGo), autonomous vehicles, and finance. Its ability to handle uncertain and evolving environments makes it invaluable in scenarios where explicitly programming optimal behavior is impractical. However, RL can be computationally intensive and highly sensitive to the design of the reward system—poorly structured rewards can lead to unintended or suboptimal behaviors. By harnessing the power of reinforcement learning, researchers and engineers continue to push the boundaries of artificial intelligence, creating systems capable of autonomous learning, adaptation, and decision-making in real-world applications. Comparison of Supervised Learning, Unsupervised Learning and Reinforcement Learning as explain in below Table 1.4:

## Bayesian Decision Theory Classifiers

Bayesian Decision Theory is a powerful statistical framework for decision-making in uncertain environments. It leverages probabilistic reasoning by integrating prior knowledge with observed evidence to classify data effectively. Utilizing probability distributions, Bayesian Decision Theory classifiers make optimal decisions that minimize risks or maximize rewards, following the principles of Bayes' theorem. This approach enables adaptive and informed decision-making across various fields, from machine learning to finance and medical diagnostics.

### Core Concept

Bayesian Decision Theory fundamentally revolves around estimating the posterior probability that a given data point belongs to each possible class and making a decision by selecting the class with the highest probability. This process is guided by Bayes' theorem, which serves as the mathematical foundation for updating prior knowledge with new evidence to achieve optimal classification:

$$P(C_k|x) = \frac{P(x|C_k)P(C_k)}{P(x)}$$

**Where:**

- $P(C_k|x)$: Posterior probability of class $C_k$ given data x.
- $P(x|C_k)$: Likelihood of data x given class $C_k$.
- $P(C_k)$: Prior probability of class CkC_kCk.
- P(x): Evidence or marginal likelihood of data x.

## Classification Rule

The class *Ck* with the highest posterior probability is given a data point *x* as the decision rule:

$$\text{Classify } x \text{ as } C_k \text{ if } P(C_k|x) > P(C_j|x) \text{ for all } j \neq k$$

The marginal likelihood $(x)$ is frequently ignored for practical implementation since it is constant across all classes and has no bearing on the comparison.

## Types of Bayesian Classifiers

### a). Naïve Bayes Classifier

Naïve Bayes operates under the assumption that features are conditionally independent given the class label. Although this assumption may not always hold in real-world scenarios, it significantly simplifies computations. Despite its simplicity, Naïve Bayes often delivers strong performance, particularly in high-dimensional datasets, making it a robust choice for various classification tasks.

***Example:***

Spam Detection: Word frequency is one feature used to determine whether an email is spam or not.

Formula:

$$P(C_k|x) \propto P(C_k)\prod_{i=1}^{n} P(x_i|C_k)$$

Where $x_i$ are individual features.

### b). Bayesian Network Classifier

A Bayesian network is a probabilistic graphical model that represents the conditional dependencies among a set of variables. Unlike the Naïve Bayes approach, which assumes independent features, a Bayesian network allows for complex interdependencies, providing a more flexible and accurate representation of real-world uncertainty.

***Example:***

**Medical Diagnosis:** Identifying diseases by their interdependencies and symptoms.

## Applications

- Text Classification: Naïve Bayes is frequently used for spam filtering and sentiment analysis.
- Medical Diagnosis: Diseases can be identified using Bayesian classifiers based on test results and symptoms.
- Pattern Recognition: Using probabilistic models to classify speech signals or images.
- Anomaly Detection: Detecting abnormalities in financial transactions or network activity.

## Discriminant Functions, and Decision Surfaces

Discriminant functions and decision surfaces are core principles in machine learning and pattern recognition, especially in classification tasks. These concepts facilitate the separation of data points belonging to different classes by analyzing their feature distributions. Discriminant functions define boundaries that optimize class distinction, while decision surfaces act as the geometric representation of these boundaries, ensuring accurate and efficient classification.

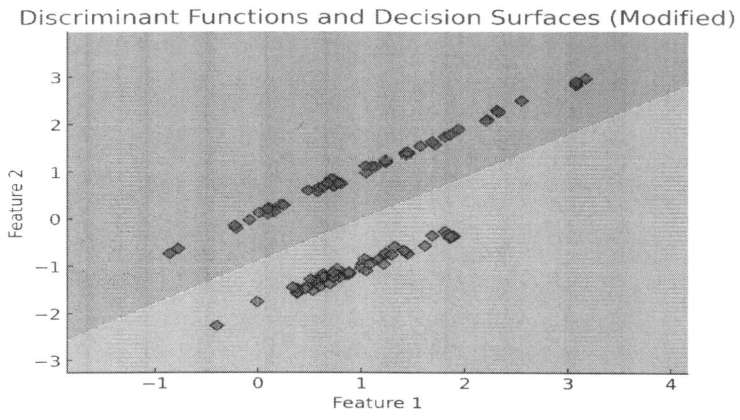


**Figure 1.18: Concept of Discriminant Functions and Decision Surfaces.**

Figure 1.18 uses a linear discriminant function implemented with logistic regression to demonstrate the idea of discriminant functions and decision surfaces.

***Below is a detailed explanation:***

## 1. Discriminant Functions

A discriminant function is a mathematical tool used for classifying data points into distinct categories. It computes a numerical score for each data point, quantifying its likelihood of belonging to a particular class. The classification process is determined by comparing these scores, with each data point assigned to the class with the highest score, ensuring an optimal decision boundary for accurate classification.

### Concepts:

Function Definition: For a two-class problem, the discriminant function is defined as:

$$g(x) = w^T x + b$$

**Where:**

- w: Weight vector (defines the orientation of the decision boundary).
- x: Input feature vector.
- b: Bias term (shifts the decision boundary).

### Decision Rule:

- Assign class 1 if g(x)>0.
- Assign class 2 if g(x)≤0.

**Multiple Classes**: For K classes, multiple discriminant functions $g_k(x)$ are used, and the data point is assigned to the class with the highest score:

$$\text{Classify } x \text{ as } C_k \text{ if } g_k(x) > g_j(x) \text{ for all } j \neq k.$$

### Types of Discriminant Functions:

Linear Discriminant Functions:

- Decision boundaries are hyperplanes.
- Example: Linear Discriminant Analysis (LDA).

### Non-Linear Discriminant Functions:

- Decision boundaries are curves or complex surfaces.
- Example: Quadratic Discriminant Analysis (QDA), Neural Networks.

## Decision Surfaces

A decision surface is a geometric representation of the boundary that distinguishes different classes within a feature space. It is formulated based on the discriminant function and serves as a fundamental component in classification tasks, guiding the assignment of data points to their respective categories. This boundary effectively partitions the feature space, ensuring optimal class separation and enhancing the accuracy of predictive models.

### Concepts:

Definition: The collection of points where the discriminant function equals zero is known as the decision surface.

$$g(x)=0$$

### Linear Decision Surfaces:

- Formed by linear discriminant functions.
- Represented by straight lines (in 2D) or hyperplanes (in higher dimensions).

### Non-Linear Decision Surfaces:

- Formed by non-linear discriminant functions.
- Represented by curves or complex shapes.

Multi-Class Problems: The decision surfaces for $K$ classes are generated by the intersections of several discriminant functions.

$$g_k(x) = g_j(x), \forall j \neq k.$$

## Applications of Decision Surfaces

- **Support Vector Machines (SVM):** Support Vector Machines (SVMs) are extensively employed in classification tasks to identify the optimal hyperplane that best separates data points belonging to distinct classes. The hyperplane, also referred to as the decision boundary, is strategically positioned to maximize the margin—the distance between the hyperplane and the closest data points, known as support vectors. By maximizing this margin, SVMs enhance the model's ability to generalize to unseen data, thereby improving classification accuracy and robustness.

This characteristic makes SVMs particularly effective for a wide range of applications, including text classification, image recognition, and bioinformatics.

- **Neural Networks:** Neural networks are highly sophisticated models capable of learning complex, non-linear decision boundaries with remarkable precision. By progressively transforming input data through multiple layers, they extract increasingly abstract and high-level representations, allowing the model to discern intricate patterns and subtle correlations. These dynamic decision surfaces are fundamental in applications such as object detection, facial recognition, and speech processing, where the underlying data relationships are inherently non-linear and multifaceted.
- **Clustering Algorithms:** In clustering, algorithms like K-Means and DBSCAN inherently construct decision boundaries that partition the feature space, grouping similar data points into distinct clusters. These boundaries define regions where data points exhibit greater similarity to their respective cluster centroids or neighboring points than to those in other clusters. Such clustering techniques are widely applied in customer segmentation, market basket analysis, and anomaly detection, where identifying underlying patterns and group dynamics is essential for informed decision-making.

## Univariate and Multivariate Normal Densities

The normal distribution is a key concept in probability and statistics, describing how data is distributed around the mean. It is characterized by its mean ($\mu$) and variance ($\sigma 2$). The normal density can be categorized into two forms: univariate (single variable) and multivariate (multiple variables) normal distributions.

### Probability Density Function (PDF):

$$f(x) = \frac{1}{\sqrt{2\pi\sigma^2}} e^{-\frac{(x-\mu)^2}{2\sigma^2}}$$

**Where:**

x: Random variable.

$\mu$: Mean of the distribution.

$\sigma^2$ : Variance of the distribution.

**Properties:**

- Symmetrical around the mean (μ).
- The area under the curve equals 1.

- ▶ 68% of data lies within one standard deviation ($\sigma$) of the mean, 95% within two, and 99.7% within three (68%–95%–99.7 rule)

### Applications:

Modeling test scores, measurement errors, or natural phenomena like heights and weights.

### Multivariate Normal Density

The multivariate normal density generalizes the univariate normal distribution to multiple variables, capturing their joint probability distribution. It not only defines the individual behavior of each variable but also incorporates their interdependencies through correlations, providing a comprehensive representation of their relationships.

### Probability Density Function (PDF):

$$f(x) = \frac{1}{(2\pi)^{n/2}|\Sigma|^{1/2}} e^{-\frac{1}{2}(x-\mu)^T\Sigma^{-1}(x-\mu)}$$

Where:

- $x$: Vector of $n$ random variables ($x = [x_1, x_2, \ldots, x_n]^T$).
- $\mu$: Mean vector ($\mu = [\mu_1, \mu_2, \ldots, \mu_n]^T$).
- $\Sigma$: Covariance matrix ($n \times n$), which captures variances and covariances.

### Properties:

- ▶ The distribution is characterized by a mean vector ($\mu$) and a covariance matrix ($\Sigma$).
- ▶ The distribution's form is determined by the covariance matrix's eigenvalues and eigenvectors.
- ▶ Higher dimensions exhibit an ellipsoid shape for multivariate densities.

### Applications:

- ▶ Financial modeling of interdependent variables, such as stock returns.
- ▶ Feature analysis in machine learning (e.g., Principal Component Analysis).

## Bayesian Belief Networks

Bayesian Belief Networks (BBNs), also referred to as Bayesian Networks (BNs), are probabilistic graphical models that utilize directed acyclic graphs (DAGs) to represent a set of variables and their conditional dependencies. By integrating principles from both probability theory and graph theory, BBNs provide a robust framework for modeling uncertainty, enabling efficient reasoning and decision-making in scenarios with incomplete or uncertain information. Their structured representation makes them valuable tools in diverse fields, including artificial intelligence, machine learning, diagnostics, and risk assessment.

## Structure of Bayesian Networks

- A Bayesian Network consists of:

**Nodes:** Explain random variables, which can be continuous or discrete in nature. A variable in the domain (such as symptoms, illnesses, or system states) is represented by each node.

Edges: Display the variables' conditional dependencies. When there is a directed edge connecting node $A$ to node $B$, it means that $A$ directly affects $B$.

Conditional Probability Tables (CPTs): With each node, the probability of the variable given its parent nodes is specified.

## Probabilistic Reasoning

Bayesian Networks leverage Bayes' theorem to calculate the posterior probabilities of variables based on observed evidence. They serve as a powerful framework for probabilistic reasoning under uncertainty, dynamically updating beliefs as new evidence becomes available, enabling more accurate and adaptive decision-making. The posterior probability is calculated as:

$$P(H|E) = \frac{P(E|H)P(H)}{P(E)}$$

***Where:***

H: Hypothesis or event of interest.

E: Evidence.

For instance, in a network modeling diseases and symptoms, observing evidence like "cough" can update the probability of having the flu.

Bayesian Belief Networks (BBNs) provide a powerful framework for reasoning under uncertainty, making them indispensable across diverse domains such as healthcare, artificial intelligence, and risk assessment. By effectively capturing probabilistic dependencies and causal relationships, BBNs enable sophisticated decision-making, predictive analytics, and inference, enhancing the accuracy and reliability of complex systems.

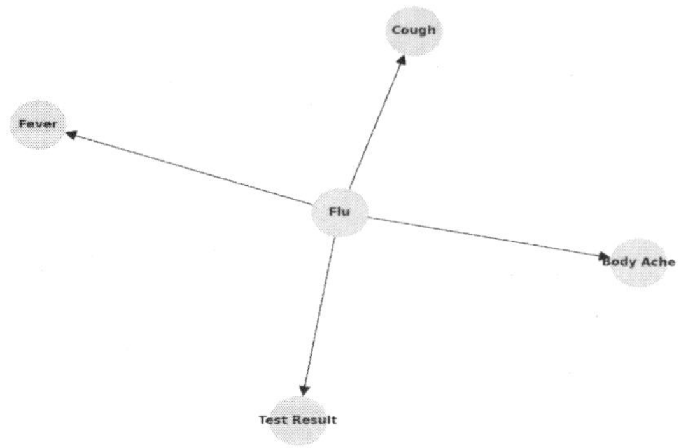


**Figure 1.19: Bayesian Belief Network.**

Figure 1.19 presents a Bayesian Belief Network, where each node represents a variable (e.g., Flu, Fever, Cough), and the directed edges signify conditional dependencies between them. For instance, the presence of the flu increases the probability of related symptoms such as fever, cough, and body ache, demonstrating how one variable can directly influence the likelihood of others within the network.

## Summary

Bayesian Decision Theory provides a structured approach to decision-making under uncertainty by integrating probabilistic reasoning with fundamental concepts such as prior and posterior probabilities. The normal distribution is a cornerstone of statistical modeling, supporting both univariate and multivariate analyses for effective data interpretation. Machine perception extraction encompasses critical tasks like classification (e.g., logistic regression) and clustering, enabling machines to process and interpret sensory data efficiently. The three primary learning paradigms supervised, unsupervised, and reinforcement learning—each cater to distinct applications, optimizing performance across various domains. Bayesian classifiers and discriminant functions leverage probability-based techniques to differentiate between classes, while decision surfaces graphically depict the boundaries that separate them. Expanding on these principles, Bayesian Belief Networks model dependencies within complex systems, facilitating advanced reasoning and inference under uncertainty.

## Exercise Questions:

- Define Bayesian Decision Theory and explain how it helps in classification tasks.
- Describe the difference between univariate and multivariate normal distributions with examples.
- What is the role of a decision surface in classification models? Provide a simple example.

- Explain the key differences between supervised, unsupervised, and reinforcement learning.
- Write the mathematical formula for the probability density function of a multivariate normal distribution and explain each component.
- How do discriminant functions and Bayesian classifiers differ in their approach to classification?
- Discuss how logistic regression and linear regression differ in terms of output and applications.
- Explain the importance of clustering in unsupervised learning and list two commonly used clustering algorithms.
- What are Bayesian Belief Networks, and how are they used in reasoning under uncertainty? Provide an example.
- Illustrate the concept of machine perception extraction and discuss its applications in real-world scenarios.

CHAPTER - 2

# Classification and Regression Algorithms

Machine learning is a powerful field of artificial intelligence that enables computers to learn patterns from data and make predictions. Among the different types of machine learning techniques, classification and regression algorithms are widely used for predictive modeling. These two types of algorithms help in solving different problems based on the nature of the output variable. While classification focuses on categorizing data into discrete labels, regression is used for predicting continuous values. Understanding these algorithms is crucial for various real-world applications, ranging from medical diagnosis to stock market forecasting. Classification algorithms are used when the target variable consists of predefined categories or classes. For example, classifying emails as spam or not spam, recognizing handwritten digits, and predicting customer churn are all classification problems. These algorithms work by learning decision boundaries from training data and applying them to new, unseen data to determine the correct category. Common classification techniques include decision trees, support vector machines, k-nearest neighbors, and deep learning models like convolutional neural networks.

On the other hand, regression algorithms are applied when the output is a continuous numerical value. These algorithms help in predicting trends, such as the price of a house based on its features or the temperature for the next day. Regression models establish a relationship between dependent and independent variables, allowing them to make accurate predictions. Linear regression, polynomial regression, ridge regression, and neural network-based regression models are some widely used techniques in this category. Both classification and regression algorithms rely on supervised learning, meaning they require labeled training data to learn patterns before making predictions on new data. However, their evaluation metrics differ: classification models are assessed using accuracy, precision, recall, and F1-score, while regression models are evaluated using metrics like mean absolute error

(MAE), mean squared error (MSE), and R-squared ($R^2$). The choice of an algorithm depends on the nature of the problem, the available data, and the desired accuracy.

In real-world applications, classification and regression play a vital role in fields such as healthcare, finance, marketing, and automation. Classification algorithms power medical image diagnosis, fraud detection, and sentiment analysis, while regression models are extensively used in economic forecasting, demand prediction, and risk assessment. The integration of advanced techniques like ensemble learning and deep learning has further enhanced the accuracy and efficiency of these algorithms. As the field of machine learning evolves, new hybrid models combining classification and regression techniques are emerging, allowing for more robust predictions. By selecting the right algorithm, tuning hyperparameters, and optimizing models with large datasets, data scientists can unlock valuable insights and drive innovation across industries. Understanding these algorithms is essential for anyone looking to build intelligent systems that can make data-driven decisions effectively.

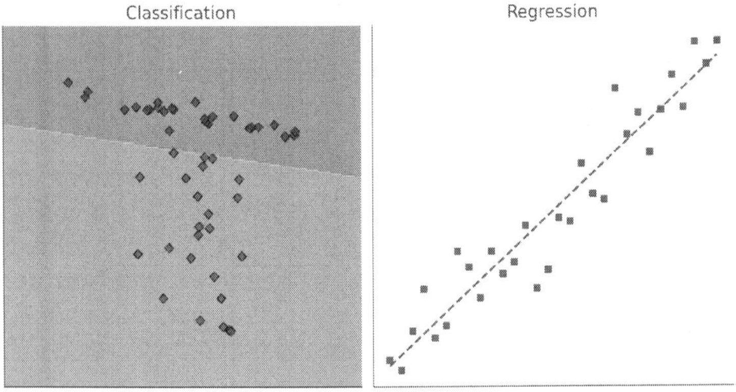


**Figure 2.1: Distinction between Classification and Regression in Machine Learning.**

To demonstrate the difference between machine learning's classification and regression, look at the following diagram(Figure 2.1):

- Data points are grouped into distinct classes, like "X" and "O," as shown in the classification on the left.
- Regression, which is displayed on the right, uses input features to predict numerical results using a continuous line.

## Classification Algorithms

Classification algorithms are fundamental to supervised learning in machine learning, designed to accurately predict discrete class labels based on input data. By analyzing patterns within training data, these algorithms develop decision-making models that can generalize and effectively classify new, unseen instances with high accuracy(Figure 2.2).

```
                  Classification Algorithms
                  /                        \
          Linear Models                Non-Linear Models
          /          \                 /        |        \
Logistic Regression   LDA       Tree-Based  Kernel-Based  Instance-Based
                                  /  \        /     \           |
                       Decision Trees  Random Forests  k-Nearest Neighbors
                                              /   \
                                   SVM            Kernel SVM
```

**Figure 2.2: Classification Algorithms.**

Here's a detailed explanation of common classification algorithms, their workings, and their use cases:

## 1. Logistic Regression

Introduction: Logistic Regression is a powerful statistical technique primarily used for binary classification tasks. Despite its name, it is not a regression algorithm but rather a classification method that estimates the probability of an instance belonging to one of two distinct categories. By applying the logistic (sigmoid) function, it transforms linear predictions into probability values between 0 and 1, enabling decision-making based on a predefined threshold. Logistic Regression is widely employed in various real-world applications, such as email filtering (spam vs. not spam), medical diagnosis (disease present vs. absent), and credit risk assessment (default vs. no default). Its simplicity, interpretability, and effectiveness make it a fundamental tool in machine learning and data science.

**How It Works:** Logistic Regression is a statistical method that models the relationship between input features and the probability of a specific class using the logistic (or sigmoid) function. This function transforms predicted values into a probability range between 0 and 1. During training, the algorithm iteratively adjusts the model's weights to minimize the log loss, which quantifies the discrepancy between predicted probabilities and actual class labels. Finally, based on a predefined decision threshold—typically set at 0.5—the model classifies instances into one of the possible categories.

**Applications:** Logistic Regression is widely used in various applications, including email spam detection, medical diagnostics (such as predicting whether a tumor is malignant or benign), credit risk assessment, and marketing analytics. In marketing campaigns, it helps classify customer responses, enabling businesses to optimize targeting strategies and improve engagement.

## 2. K-Nearest Neighbors (KNN)

**Introduction:** The K-Nearest Neighbors (KNN) algorithm is a non-parametric, instance-based machine learning technique used for both classification and regression tasks. Known for its simplicity and intuitive approach, KNN makes predictions by evaluating the similarity between data points, classifying or estimating values based on the majority or average of the nearest neighbors in the feature space.

**How It Works:** The K-Nearest Neighbors (KNN) algorithm does not construct an explicit model during training. Instead, it retains the entire dataset as a reference. When predicting the class of a new data point, KNN calculates its distance from all points in the training set using metrics such as Euclidean or Manhattan distance. It then identifies the *k* closest neighbors and assigns the class label that appears most frequently among thema process known as majority voting. The choice of *k* significantly influences the model's behavior, with smaller values capturing finer details and larger values producing smoother, more generalized predictions.

**Applications:** K-Nearest Neighbors (KNN) is widely utilized in various machine learning applications, including recommendation systems (e.g., personalized movie or product suggestions), image classification, and complex pattern recognition tasks such as handwriting digit recognition. Its versatility and ease of implementation make it a powerful tool for both supervised and unsupervised learning scenarios.

## 3. Decision Tree

**Introduction:** A Decision Tree is a structured, flowchart-like model where each internal node signifies a decision based on a specific feature, branches denote possible outcomes, and leaf nodes represent the final class labels or target values. Renowned for its versatility and interpretability, this algorithm efficiently handles both classification and regression tasks, making it a powerful tool for data-driven decision-making.

**How It Works:** The algorithm employs a recursive approach to partition the dataset based on feature values, progressively forming branches that lead to the most homogeneous subsets (pure classes). To determine the optimal split at each step, it evaluates criteria such as the Gini index, entropy (information gain), or variance reduction. This process iterates until predefined stopping conditionssuch as reaching a maximum tree depth or a minimum number of samples per leafare met, ensuring a balance between model complexity and generalization.

**Applications:** Decision Trees are used in healthcare (e.g., diagnosing diseases), finance (e.g., credit risk assessment), and customer segmentation.

## 4. Random Forest

**Introduction:** Random Forest is a powerful ensemble learning technique that constructs multiple Decision Trees and aggregates their predictions to enhance accuracy, stability, and generalization. By leveraging this collective decision-making approach, it significantly mitigates the risk of overfitting, a common drawback in individual Decision Trees, resulting in a more robust and reliable model.

**How It Works:** The algorithm constructs multiple Decision Trees by employing a technique called bagging, which involves randomly sampling data and selecting a subset of features at each split. To generate the final prediction, it aggregates the outputs of all trees—using majority voting for classification tasks and averaging for regression. This controlled randomness enhances the model's ability to generalize effectively while simultaneously reducing variance, thereby improving overall predictive performance.

**Applications:** Random Forest is frequently utilized in predictive analytics, medical diagnostics, and fraud detection in sectors like retail and insurance.

## 5. Support Vector Machine (SVM)

**Introduction:** Support Vector Machine (SVM) is a powerful and adaptable machine learning algorithm designed for both binary and multi-class classification tasks. It excels in handling high-dimensional datasets and is particularly effective when precise class separation is required. By leveraging the concept of hyperplanes, SVM optimally distinguishes between classes, making it a preferred choice for complex classification problems, including text categorization, image recognition, and bioinformatics.

**How It Works:** Support Vector Machines (SVM) determine the optimal hyperplane that maximizes the margin between different classes within the feature space, ensuring the best possible separation. The data points that lie closest to this hyperplane, known as support vectors, play a crucial role in defining the decision boundary. For datasets that exhibit non-linearity, SVM employs kernel functionssuch as the Radial Basis Function (RBF) and polynomial kernelsto transform the data into a higher-dimensional space, where a linear separation becomes feasible. This approach enhances the model's ability to classify complex patterns effectively.

**Applications:** Support Vector Machines (SVM) are widely utilized in various domains, including text classification, bioinformatics (such as cancer diagnosis and gene expression analysis), and handwriting recognition. Their ability to handle high-dimensional data and effectively separate complex patterns makes them particularly valuable in these applications.

## 6. Naive Bayes

**Introduction:** Naïve Bayes is a probabilistic classification algorithm rooted in Bayes' Theorem. It operates under the assumption that features are conditionally independent given the class label, significantly reducing computational complexity. This simplification enhances efficiency, making Naïve Bayes particularly effective for large datasets and real-time applications.

**How It Works:** The algorithm determines the posterior probability of each class by combining its prior probability with the likelihood of the observed data given that class. The instance is then classified into the category with the highest posterior probability. Despite its straightforward nature, this approach proves remarkably effective across a wide range of real-world applications.

**Applications:** Naïve Bayes is a widely used probabilistic algorithm in machine learning, particularly effective for spam detection, sentiment analysis, and text classification. It plays a crucial role in categorizing content, such as distinguishing spam from legitimate emails, analyzing sentiment in reviews and social media posts, and classifying news articles into relevant topics with high efficiency and scalability.

## 7. Neural Networks

**Introduction:** Neural Networks, modelled after the intricate structure of the human brain, are powerful tools for tackling complex classification problems. They are composed of multiple layers of interconnected nodes (neurons), each designed to process data, recognize patterns, and refine their understanding through iterative learning.

**How It Works:** The input data flows through multiple layers of the network, where each layer performs a weighted summation of inputs, followed by the application of an activation function such as ReLU or sigmoid. During training, the network utilizes backpropagation to iteratively adjust weights, minimizing error and improving predictive accuracy. Deep Neural Networks (DNNs), consisting of numerous layers, excel at capturing complex, highly non-linear relationships, enabling them to recognize intricate patterns and features in data.

**Applications:** Neural networks are extensively utilized across various domains, including image recognition (such as facial recognition), speech processing, and natural language processing (NLP), where they power applications like chatbots, machine translation, and sentiment analysis. Their ability to learn complex patterns and make accurate predictions has made them indispensable in modern AI-driven technologies.

## 8. Gradient Boosting Methods (e.g., XGBoost, LightGBM, CatBoost)

**Introduction:** Gradient Boosting is a powerful ensemble learning technique that constructs models sequentially, with each iteration refining the errors of its predecessor to enhance overall performance. It excels in handling structured data and is highly competitive in predictive analytics, often outperforming traditional machine learning methods in accuracy and efficiency.

**How It Works:** The algorithm begins with a basic model and progressively refines it by incorporating additional models in an iterative process aimed at minimizing a specified loss function (e.g., log loss for classification). Each successive model is designed to correct the errors of its predecessor, ensuring that the overall predictive accuracy improves. The final prediction is derived by intelligently combining the outputs of all the models, resulting in a more robust and accurate outcome.

**Table 2.1: Classification Algorithms**

| Algorithm | Description | Applications |
|---|---|---|
| **Logistic Regression** | A statistical method that models the probability of a class based on input features. Used for binary and multinomial classification. | Medical diagnosis, credit scoring, fraud detection |
| **Decision Tree** | A tree-like model that splits data into branches based on feature values. Simple and interpretable. | Customer segmentation, medical diagnosis, risk assessment |
| **Random Forest** | An ensemble of multiple decision trees that improves accuracy and reduces overfitting. | Fraud detection, recommendation systems, stock market predictions |
| **Support Vector Machine (SVM)** | Finds an optimal hyperplane that separates classes with the maximum margin. Works well with high-dimensional data. | Image classification, text categorization, bioinformatics |
| **K-Nearest Neighbors (KNN)** | Classifies data based on the majority class among its k-nearest neighbors. A non-parametric approach. | Handwriting recognition, recommendation systems, anomaly detection |
| **Naïve Bayes** | A probabilistic classifier based on Bayes' theorem, assuming feature independence. | Spam detection, sentiment analysis, document classification |
| **Artificial Neural Networks (ANNs)** | Mimic human brain neurons to recognize complex patterns. Suitable for deep learning tasks. | Speech recognition, image classification, medical diagnosis |
| **Gradient Boosting (e.g., XGBoost, LightGBM, CatBoost)** | An ensemble learning method that builds trees sequentially, correcting previous errors. | Financial modeling, predictive analytics, anomaly detection |

**Applications:** Gradient Boosting methods are widely utilized in competitive machine learning platforms like Kaggle for high-impact predictive tasks, including customer churn analysis, click-through rate optimization, and sales forecasting. Their ability to iteratively refine predictions by minimizing errors makes them a powerful choice for handling complex, real-world datasets.The Table 2.1 brief classification algorithms, including their descriptions and applications:

## Perceptron and Backpropagation Neural Network

### Perceptron

The perceptron is one of the earliest and simplest machine learning algorithms for binary classification. Developed by Frank Rosenblatt in the late 1950s, it serves as the foundation for more advanced neural network architectures, as illustrated in Figure 2.3. This article explores how to implement binary classification using the Perceptron algorithm with Scikit-Learn, a widely used Python machine-learning library. As a basic linear classifier, the perceptron makes predictions by computing a weighted sum of input features. A threshold function then determines the output, assigning a value of 0 or 1 based on whether the weighted sum surpasses a predefined threshold. Despite its simplicity, the perceptron laid the groundwork for modern neural networks and remains an essential concept in machine learning.

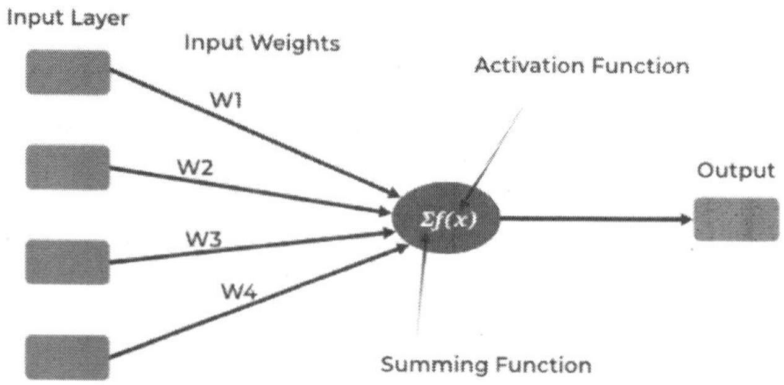


**Figure 2.3: Single Input Perceptron. [Source: geeksforgeeks]**

One of the fundamental assumptions underlying this algorithm is that the data must be linearly separable. In other words, there should exist a linear classifier capable of perfectly distinguishing between different classes without any misclassification during training, resulting in zero training error. Mathematically, for two sets A & B, linearly separable data can be defined such that,

$$x^T w + w_o \begin{cases} > 0 \; \forall \; x \; in \; set \; A \; (eg: class(+1)) \\ < 0 \; \forall \; x \; in \; set \; B \; (eg: class(-1)) \end{cases}$$

Definition of linearly separable data

where (w, wo) are some parameters that define the hyperplane for the linear classifier.

### *Algorithm Works*

We define the linear classifier with zero training error as,

$$f(x;w) = sign\left(x_i^T w\right) \forall\, i = 1, \dots, n$$

### *Linear Classifier*

Every algorithm operates by optimizing an objective functioneither maximizing or minimizing itwhile adhering to specific constraints. In the case of the Perceptron algorithm, it aims to minimize a defined objective function to accurately classify data points and assign the correct labels within the dataset.

The objective function (L) and constraints are defined as follows,

$$L = -\sum_{i=1}^{n} (y_i . f(x;w)) \mathbf{1}\{y_i \neq f(x;w)\}$$

s.t.

$$y_i . f(x;w) \begin{cases} > 0 \; if y_i = f(x;w) \\ < 0 \; if \; y_i \neq f(x;w) \end{cases}$$

If the predicted valuef(x;w) and the known labelyi share the same sign (either +1 or -1), then their dot product yif(x;w)will be greater than zero> 0. This indicates that the linear classifierf(x;w) has correctly predicted the label for the data pointxi.The algorithm aims to minimize an objective function that quantifies misclassification errors. Specifically, it sums the instances where the linear classifier fails to predict the correct output. Consequently, the objective function's value always falls within the range of 0 to some positive number. The function remains non-negative due to the inherent negative sign in its formulation. The algorithm terminates when the objective function reaches zero, signifying that no data points have been misclassified.

## Gradient Decent: Minimizing the objective function

Unlike other algorithms, the derivative of this objective function cannot be directly computed to determine its minimum. Consequently, we employ the gradient descent method to minimize L. Gradient descent operates on the principle that, even if the derivative of L cannot be solved analytically, it still provides valuable directional information specifically, the direction in which L increases with respect to ww. By iteratively updating w in the opposite direction of the gradient, we effectively navigate towards the function's minimum.

$$w_1 \leftarrow w - r\nabla L$$

$$\nabla L = \sum_{i \in N} y_i x_i$$

Thus, for sufficiently small positive 'r' value, we have L(w1) < L(w).

## Drawbacks of the Perceptron algorithm

One of the primary limitations of this algorithm is its fundamental assumption that the data must be linearly separable. If the data is not inherently linearly separable, the algorithm will fail to converge, causing the hyperplane to continuously adjust without ever reaching a stable solution.Moreover, this algorithm does not evaluate the quality of the hyperplane and simply converges to the first one it encounters. As a result, the potential to identify a more optimal hyperplaneone that could improve accuracy on new test datais overlooked. These limitations can be effectively addressed by employing more advanced classification algorithms, such as Support Vector Machines (SVM) and other sophisticated approaches.

## Components of a Perceptron

**Input Features (x):**Predictions are derived from the characteristics or attributes of the input data, commonly referred to as input featuresx. Each feature is represented by a numerical value, which serves as a quantitative measure of its properties. In binary classification, the two possible classes are typically encoded as numerical labels: 0, representing the negative class, and 1, representing the positive class. This numerical encoding facilitates efficient processing and analysis in machine learning models.

**Input Weights (w):** Each input carries an associated weight (w), which determines its influence on the prediction process. These weights are numerical values that are typically initialized as either zeros or small random numbers to facilitate learning and optimization.

**Weighted Sum (f(x)):** The weighted sum is computed as the dot product of the input features (x) and their corresponding weights (w). Mathematically, it is expressed as:

$$f(x) = w_1x_1 + w_2x_2 + \cdots + w_nx_n$$

**Activation Function (Step Function):**The activation function, commonly depicted as a step function, is applied to the weighted sum of inputs, denoted as ∑f(x). This function plays a crucial role in determining the perceptron's output. When the weighted sum exceeds or meets a predefined threshold, the step function activates, producing an output of 1, signifying the positive class. Conversely, if the weighted sum falls below the threshold, the output remains 0, representing the negative class. This binary decision mechanism forms the foundation of a perceptron's classification capability.

**Working of the Perceptron:**

**Initialization:** Initially, the weights (w) are initialized, usually with tiny random values or zeros.

**Prediction:** The Perceptron provides a forecast for a given input by computing the weighted total ($\sum f(x)$) of the input features and weights.

**Activation Function:** An activation function is used after the weighted sum ($\sum f(x)$) has been calculated. If $\sum f(x)$ is greater than or equal to a certain threshold, the perceptron outputs 1 (positive class); if not, it outputs 0 (negative class) because the activation function is a step function.

**Updating Weight:** Weights are adjusted whenever the perceptron makes a misclassification or an incorrect prediction. This update process aims to enhance the model's accuracy over time by minimizing future errors. Typically, the weight adjustment follows a specific rule designed to shift the weights in a direction that reduces prediction inaccuracy. The most commonly used approach is the perceptron learning rule, which updates the weights based on the difference between the expected and actual class labels, ensuring continuous refinement of the model's decision boundary.

**Repeat:** Each input data point in the training dataset undergoes an additional pass-through step 2 to 4. This iterative process continues until the model achieves convergence, meaning it has learned to classify the training data with a satisfactory level of accuracy. The number of iterations required for convergence depends on factors such as dataset complexity, model architecture, and learning rate.

## Backpropagation Neural Network

Backpropagation is a fundamental algorithm used to train artificial neural networks by minimizing the difference between predicted and actual outputs. It achieves this by iteratively adjusting the network's weights and biases to optimize performance. A neural network consists of interconnected computing units called neurons, which process information through weighted connections and activation functions. These activation functions determine the level of neuron activation, where higher values indicate stronger activation. The network's learnable parameters weights and biases enable it to approximate complex functions and make predictions. Backpropagation is particularly effective in training feedforward neural networks. It operates by propagating errors backward through the network, computing gradients using the chain rule from calculus, and updating weights accordingly. This optimization process follows an iterative approach, minimizing the cost function over multiple training epochs. Common optimization techniques, such as gradient descent and stochastic gradient descent (SGD), are employed to efficiently adjust the parameters. By systematically refining the network's parameters, backpropagation enables deep learning models to navigate complex data structures, improve accuracy, and enhance predictive capabilities. Figure 2.4 illustrates how the algorithm minimizes the cost function by efficiently traversing the neural network's layered structure.

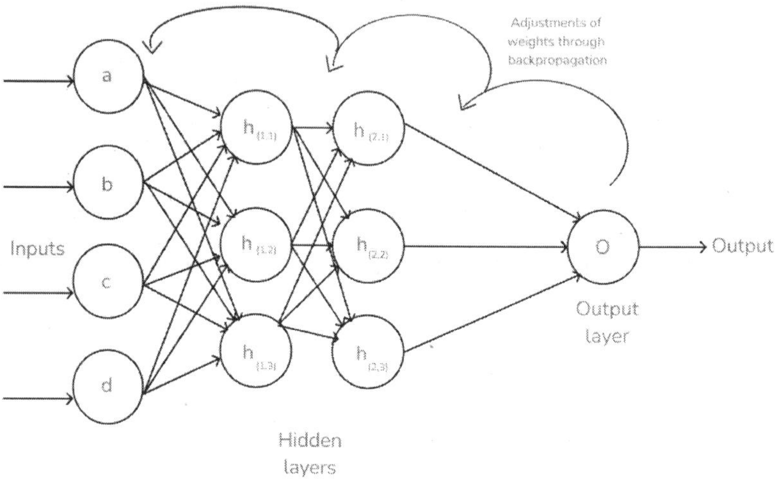


**Figure 2.4: A simple illustration of how the backpropagation works by adjustments of weights. [Source: geeksforgeeks]**

Backpropagation is a fundamental supervised learning algorithm designed for training neural networks. It optimizes model performance by systematically reducing errors through backward propagation, adjusting weights and biases based on gradient descent. By iteratively refining these parameters, backpropagation enhances the network's ability to make accurate predictions, ultimately improving learning efficiency and convergence.

## Working of Backpropagation Algorithm

### Backpropagation works in the following steps:

**Step 1: Forward Pass**

- Determine the network's output by transferring input data between the layers.
- Utilize activation functions, weights, and biases to compute intermediate and final outputs.

**Step 2: Compute Error**

- Calculate the error using a loss function (e.g., Mean Squared Error, Cross-Entropy).

$$E = \frac{1}{2} \sum (y - \hat{y})^2$$

Where $y$ is the actual output and $\hat{y}$ is the predicted output.

**Step 3: Backward Pass**

- Using the chain rule, calculate the gradients of the loss function with regard to each weight and bias and propagate the error backward through the network.
- Update weights and biases using

$$w_{\text{new}} = w_{\text{old}} - \eta \cdot \frac{\partial E}{\partial w}$$

Where $\eta$ is the learning rate.

**Step 4: Update Parameters**

For several iterations (epochs), repeat the forward and backward passes until the loss converges.

## Use Backpropagation in Neural Networks

Backpropagation is a fundamental algorithm for training neural networks, enabling them to learn efficiently by minimizing prediction errors. It operates by systematically calculating the influence of each weight in the network on the overall error, allowing for precise adjustments. By propagating error gradients backward from the output layer to the input layer, backpropagation refines the network's parameters, ensuring continuous performance enhancement. Through an iterative optimization process, it updates weights and biases to progressively reduce errors, ultimately improving prediction accuracy. This capability is especially critical in deep learning, where multiple interconnected layers require effective error management. By efficiently handling gradient computations, backpropagation empowers complex neural networks to converge on optimal solutions, solidifying its role as a cornerstone of modern machine learning.

## Example of Backpropagation

**Scenario:** Train a neural network to predict the XOR function.

***Forward Pass:***

- Inputs: $x_1=1$, $x_2=0$
- Target: $y=1$

**Backward Pass:**

- Compute error:

$$\delta_{\text{output}} = (o - y) \cdot \sigma'(z)$$

- Update weights for the output layer:

$$\Delta w = \eta \cdot \delta_{\text{output}} \cdot h$$

- Propagate the error to the hidden layer:

$$\delta_{\text{hidden}} = \delta_{\text{output}} \cdot w \cdot \sigma'(z)$$

### Calculate Deltas in Backpropagation Neural Networks

The delta ($\delta$) represents the gradient of the error with respect to the weighted input of a neuron. It quantifies the neuron's contribution to the overall error, serving as a crucial factor in weight adjustments during the learning process. By determining the direction and magnitude of necessary corrections, delta plays a fundamental role in optimizing the neural network's performance.

### Delta Calculation

1. **Output Layer Delta ($\delta_{\text{output}}$):**

$$\delta_{\text{output}} = (o - y) \cdot \sigma'(z)$$

Where:

- o: Predicted output
- y: Target output
- $\sigma'(z)$: Derivative of the activation function

2. **Hidden Layer Delta ($\delta_{\text{hidden}}$):**

$$\delta_{\text{hidden}} = \delta_{\text{output}} \cdot w_{\text{output}} \cdot \sigma'(z)$$

Figure 2.5 of the Error Reduction Plot can be found in the Word document's "Error Reduction Plot" section. It follows the section on Training Results and makes it evident how the error decreased over the course of the training process.

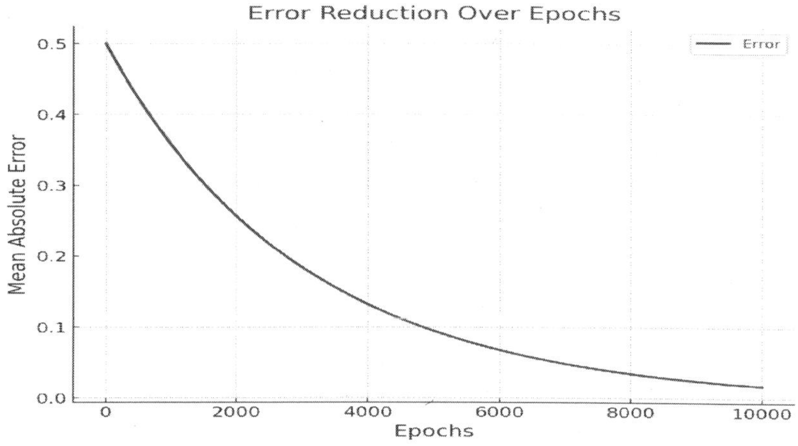


**Figure 2.5: Error Reduction Plot.**

The network has been successfully trained to approximate the XOR function. Here's the breakdown of the output:

### Training Output

Inputs: [0, 0] → Output: ~0

Inputs: [0, 1] → Output: ~1

Inputs: [1, 0] → Output: ~1

Inputs: [1, 1] → Output: ~0

### Error Reduction

The network's learning progress is demonstrated by the error plot above, which shows how the error drops as the number of epochs rises.

## k-nearest- neighbor Rule

The K-Nearest Neighbor (KNN) algorithm is a non-parametric, instance-based learning method widely used for both classification and regression tasks. It operates on the fundamental principle that data points with similar features tend to have similar outcomes. Unlike model-based algorithms, KNN is often termed a "lazy learner" because it does not construct a generalizable model during training. Instead, it stores the entire training dataset and defers computations until prediction time, where it determines the outcome based on the majority class (for classification) or the average of the nearest neighbors (for regression). This makes KNN highly intuitive yet computationally expensive for large datasets.

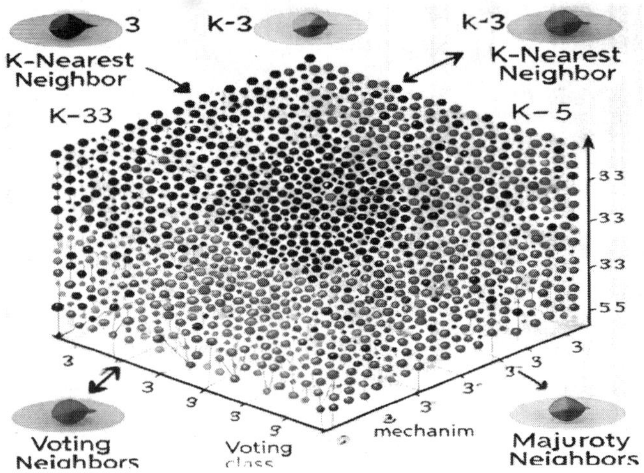


**Figure 2.6: K-Nearest Neighbor (KNN) Rule.**

The K-Nearest Neighbor (KNN) algorithm is visually represented in Figure 2.6, illustrating how a query point (depicted in green) is classified based on its nearest neighbors within a two-dimensional space. The classification is determined through a majority voting mechanism, where the identified neighboring points (highlighted for clarity) collectively influence the final category assignment.

***How It Works:***

### 1. Determine k:

Select the number (k) of closest neighbors to take into account when making predictions. The performance of the model can be greatly impacted by this hyperparameter.

### 2. Calculate Distances:

Determine the separation between a specific query point and every other point in the training dataset. Common distance metrics include:

$$: d = \sqrt{\sum_{i=1}^{n}(x_i - y_i)^2}$$

- **Euclidean Distance**:
- **Manhattan Distance**: $d = \sum_{i=1}^{n} |x_i - y_i|$
- **Minkowski Distance**: A generalization of Euclidean and Manhattan distances.

### 3. Find Nearest Neighbors:

Using the selected distance metric, determine which k training points are closest to the query point.

### 3. Make a Prediction:

**Classification**: Assign the class that is most frequent among the k nearest neighbors (majority voting).

**Regression**: Predict the average (or weighted average) value of the k nearest neighbors.

## Application:

The K-Nearest Neighbor (KNN) algorithm is a highly versatile machine learning technique with applications in both classification and regression tasks.In classification, KNN is extensively used for problems such as handwritten digit recognition (e.g., MNIST dataset), medical diagnosis, where it helps classify, diseases based on patient data, and email spam detection, analyzing features of email content to distinguish spam from legitimate messages.For regression, KNN is instrumental in predicting house prices by considering factors like size, location, and neighbourhood characteristics. It is also applied in stock market forecasting, leveraging historical trends to estimate future prices.Its simplicity, adaptability, and effectiveness in pattern recognition and predictive modeling make KNN a valuable tool across diverse domains, including healthcare, finance, real estate, and cybersecurity.

## Support Vector Machine

Support Vector Machine (SVM) is a powerful supervised learning algorithm extensively used for classification and regression tasks. Its primary objective is to identify the optimal hyperplane that best separates data points belonging to different classes. This hyperplane serves as a decision boundary, maximizing the margin between classes to enhance the model's generalization ability.SVM is particularly effective for high-dimensional datasets and excels in handling non-linearly separable data through a technique known as the kernel trick. By mapping input data into a higher-dimensional space, SVM transforms complex relationships into a linearly separable form, allowing for more accurate classification. The algorithm is also robust to noise and performs well even in the presence of outliers.A distinguishing feature of SVM is its reliance on support vectorsthe critical data points closest to the hyperplane. These points play a pivotal role in determining the position and orientation of the decision boundary, making SVM computationally efficient and less dependent on the overall dataset size.SVM supports multiple kernel functions, including linear, polynomial, and radial basis function (RBF) kernels, enabling it to tackle a wide range of complex, non-linear problems. Due to its versatility and high performance, SVM finds applications across diverse domains such as image recognition, text classification, bioinformatics, and financial forecasting.

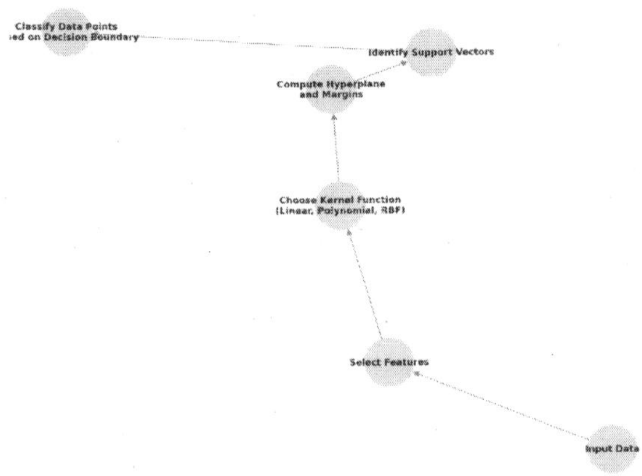


**Figure 2.7: Flowchart for the Support Vector Machine (SVM) Algorithm.**

Figure 2.7 shows a flowchart for the Support Vector Machine (SVM) algorithm that shows each step from input data to classification.

## How SVM Works:

### Hyperplane and Decision Boundary:

- A boundary that divides data points of various classes is called a hyperplane. For a dataset with
- The hyperplane is a $n-11$-dimensional plane with $n$-dimensional features.
- SVM attempts to identify the hyperplane with the maximum margin, or the maximum separation between the hyperplane and each class's closest data points (referred to as support vectors).

### Maximizing the Margin:

- The distance between the hyperplane and the closest data points of any class is known as the margin. Better generalization to unknown data is guaranteed by a larger margin.
- This optimization problem is resolved by SVM through the use of mathematical methods like quadratic programming.

### Support Vectors:

- The crucial data points that are closest to the hyperplane are these ones. The hyperplane's orientation and position are directly impacted by them.

### Kernel Trick:

- When data cannot be separated linearly, SVM projects the data into a higher-dimensional space wherein a hyperplane can divide the classes using a kernel function.

**Common kernel functions:**

- Linear Kernel: For linearly separable data.
- Polynomial Kernel: For more complex relationships.
- Radial Basis Function (RBF) or Gaussian Kernel: For non-linear separable data.

## Mathematics of SVM:

For linearly separable data, SVM finds the hyperplane w·x+b=0 by solving:

$$\text{Minimize: } \frac{1}{2}||w||^2$$

$$\text{Subject to: } y_i(w \cdot x_i + b) \geq 1 \quad \forall i$$

Here:

- w: Weight vector determining the hyperplane.
- $x_i$: Feature vector for the iii-th data point.
- b: Bias term.
- $y_i$: Class label (+1 or −1).

The use of kernel functions and slack variables is applied to non-linearly separable data.

## Applications of SVM:

- Text Classification: Sentiment analysis and the detection of spam emails.
- Image Recognition: Classification of handwritten numbers (e.g., MNIST dataset).
- Bioinformatics: Classification of gene expression or detection of cancerous cells.
- Face Detection: Distinguishing between face and non-face regions in images.

### *Example of Support Vector Machine (SVM):*

Scenario: Classifying Tumor Type (Malignant vs. Benign)

The objective of a hospital's tumor dataset, which includes characteristics like size, texture, and cell shape, is to categorize the tumors as either benign or malignant.

**Steps:**

Input Data:

- Features include tumor characteristics like size, texture, and cell shape.
- Labels: Malignant or Benign.

**Select Features:**

- For simplicity, select important features from the dataset, like cell shape and size.

**Kernel Selection:**

- Use the Linear Kernel if the dataset can be separated linearly.
- The RBF Kernel can be used to convert data into a higher-dimensional space if it is non-linearly separable.

**Compute Hyperplane and Margins:**

- SVM maximizes the margin between the closest data points of both classes while determining the best hyperplane to divide malignant and benign tumors.

***Identify Support Vectors:***

- The critical tumor data points that are closest to the hyperplane serve as support vectors, establishing the boundary.

**Classify New Tumor:**

- SVM determines a new tumor's position in relation to the hyperplane and classifies it as either benign or malignant based on certain size and cell shape values.

**Output:**

**Prediction:** It is categorized as malignant if the new tumor is located on the hyperplane's malignant side. It is categorized as benign otherwise.Figure 2.8 presents a visual representation of an SVM classification example. In the plot, red and blue points signify two distinct classes (e.g., malignant and benign tumors). The solid black line represents the decision boundary, while the dashed lines illustrate the margins that define the optimal separation between the classes. The critical support vectorsdata points that influence and define the decision boundaryare distinctly marked with circles.

The tumor data points are visualized in a two-dimensional space (e.g., size vs. shape), where a hyperplane distinctly separates malignant tumors (represented by red triangles) from benign ones (depicted as blue circles). This separation is reinforced by margin boundaries on either side of the hyperplane. The most influential data points, known as support vectors, lie near these margins and play a crucial role in defining the optimal classification boundary.

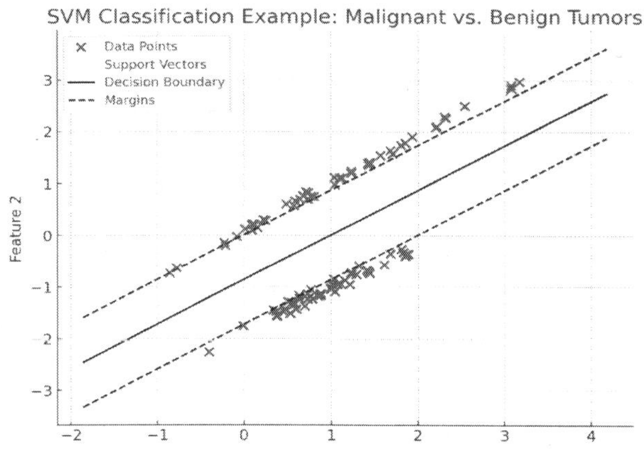


**Figure 2.8: SVM classification.**

## Multicategory Generalizations

Multicategory generalizations involve extending binary classification algorithms to address problems with more than two distinct classes. While many widely used classification models, such as Support Vector Machines (SVM) and Logistic Regression, are inherently designed for binary decision-making, real-world scenarios frequently require distinguishing among multiple categories. For instance, applications like handwritten digit recognition (0–9) or email classification into diverse topics necessitate techniques that can effectively manage and classify multiple classes within a dataset.

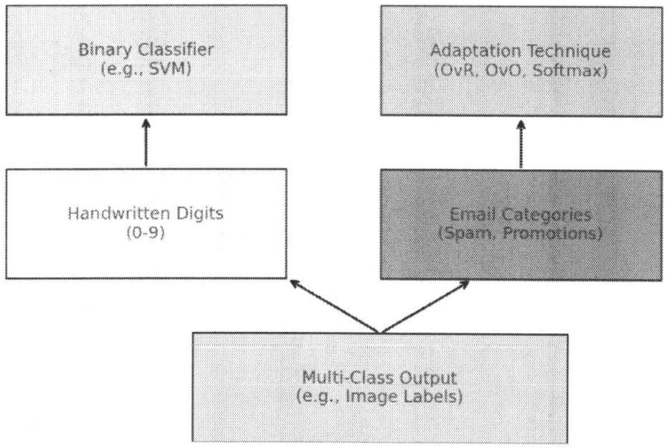


**Figure 2.9: Multicategory Generalization Process.**

Figure 2.9 presents a block diagram illustrating the multiclass generalization process. It demonstrates how a binary classifier, such as a Support Vector Machine (SVM), can be extended to handle multi-class classification challenges. This adaptation is achieved through strategies like One-vs-Rest (OvR) and One-vs-One (OvO), enabling effective categorization of complex datasets. Practical applications include handwritten digit recognition, email classification, and multi-class output generation, showcasing the versatility of these techniques in real-world scenarios.

To deal with these situations, particular techniques are used to expand binary classifiers to efficiently handle multiple categories.

## One-vs-One (OvO)

**How It Works:** The One-vs-One (OvO) strategy involves training a distinct binary classifier for each unique pair of classes within the dataset. GivenKclasses, this method necessitates the creation of (K(K-1)/2classifiers. For instance, in a dataset containing three classesA, B, and C—OvO would generate classifiers for the following class pairs: (A vs. B), (A vs. C), and (B vs. C). During the prediction phase, each classifier independently assigns its vote to one of the two classes it was trained to distinguish. The class that accumulates the highest number of votes across all classifiers is selected as the final prediction. Although this method demands significant computational resources, it is particularly effective for algorithms like Support Vector Machines (SVM), which handle binary classification efficiently and scale well with smaller datasets.

**Applications:** OvO (One-vs-One) is ideal for datasets with a moderate number of classes, especially when the underlying algorithm excels at handling smaller subsets of data. This approach is particularly advantageous in image classification tasks involving a reasonable number of categories, as it efficiently decomposes the problem into multiple binary classification tasks, improving performance and reducing computational complexity.

## 2. One-vs-Rest (OvR)

**How It Works:** The One-vs-Rest (OvR) approach involves training a separate binary classifier for each class, where each classifier distinguishes a specific class from all remaining classes combined. For a dataset with K classes, this results in the creation of Kclassifiers. During prediction, each classifier generates a confidence score (or probability) indicating the likelihood that a given instance belongs to its respective class. The class associated with the highest confidence score is chosen as the final prediction. Compared to the One-vs-One (OvO) strategy, OvR is computationally more efficient, as it requires significantly fewer classifiers while maintaining a straightforward implementation.

**Applications:** OvR is widely employed in text classification tasks, particularly for assigning articles to multiple topics. This approach is especially advantageous when working with large datasets containing numerous instances but a manageable number of classes, ensuring efficient and scalable classification.

## 3. Softmax Regression (Multinomial Logistic Regression)

**How It Works:** Softmax regression generalizes logistic regression for multi-class classification by leveraging the softmax function, which transforms raw scores into a probability distribution across all classes. Instead of breaking the problem into multiple binary classifications like One-vs-One (OvO) or One-vs-Rest (OvR), softmax regression directly optimizes a single objective function. The model assigns probabilities to each class, with the highest-probability class being selected as the final prediction, ensuring a more holistic and computationally efficient approach to multi-class classification.

**Applications:** Softmax regression is commonly employed in scenarios where the relationship between input features and class labels follows a linear pattern. It is particularly useful in applications such as multiclass sentiment analysis, fundamental image classification tasks, and structured data classification, where interpretability and computational efficiency are key considerations.

## 4. Decision Trees and Ensembles (e.g., Random Forests)

**How It Works:** Decision trees naturally handle multi-class classification by recursively splitting nodes to maximize class purity within each branch. Ensemble methods such as Random Forests enhance this capability by aggregating predictions from multiple decision trees, where each tree independently classifies the input, and the final decision is determined by majority voting. Unlike one-vs-one (OvO) or one-vs-rest (OvR) strategies, these approaches inherently manage multi-class scenarios without requiring explicit binary decomposition.

**Applications:** Decision trees and ensemble methods are extensively applied in real-world scenarios, such as assessing loan approval likelihood across multiple risk categories or efficiently categorizing products within an e-commerce platform to enhance user experience and recommendation accuracy.

## 5. Neural Networks

**How It Works:** Neural networks employ a multi-output layer with the softmax activation function to generate probability distributions across multiple classes. By leveraging multiple interconnected layers of neurons, these networks learn intricate patterns and complex relationships between input features and class labels, making them exceptionally powerful for solving non-linear problems. Additionally, neural networks excel at processing high-dimensional data, including images, audio, and text, enabling their widespread application in fields such as computer vision, speech recognition, and natural language processing.

**Applications:** Neural networks serve as the foundation for a wide range of modern applications, including handwritten digit recognition using datasets like MNIST, advanced object detection in images, and real-time language translation. Their ability to learn complex patterns and make intelligent predictions has revolutionized fields such as computer vision, natural language processing, and artificial intelligence.

## 6. Error-Correcting Output Codes (ECOC)

How It Works: ECOC (Error-Correcting Output Codes) assigns each class a unique binary representation and trains multiple binary classifiers, each responsible for predicting a specific bit of the code. During prediction, the algorithm deciphers the collective binary outputs to determine the most likely class. This approach enhances robustness by distributing class information across multiple classifiers, reducing the impact of errors from any single classifier and improving overall model resilience.

Applications: ECOC is widely utilized in machine learning competitions and advanced classification tasks that demand high robustness against misclassification. It plays a crucial role in critical applications such as medical diagnosis, where accurate predictions can impact patient outcomes, and fault detection systems, where early identification of errors is essential for preventing system failures.

## Regression Decision Trees

Regression Decision Trees are a powerful supervised learning algorithm designed for predicting continuous numerical outcomes. Unlike classification trees that categorize data into discrete classes, regression trees partition the feature space into distinct regions and assign each a representative numerical value typically the mean of the target variable within that region. Known for their intuitive structure and ease of interpretation, these trees effectively model complex, non-linear relationships, making them valuable tools in various predictive analytics tasks.

Figure 2.10 presents a visualization of a Regression Decision Tree. This tree iteratively splits the dataset based on a single feature (e.g., "Feature 1") at each decision node, aiming to minimize variance within each resulting subset. By progressively refining these partitions, the model enhances its predictive accuracy, ultimately assigning continuous target values to the leaf nodes.

## How They Work:

### Splitting the Data:

- Regression trees iteratively partition the dataset into progressively smaller subsets. At each step, the algorithm identifies the optimal feature and split point that minimize the variance within the target variable, ensuring that the resulting subsets exhibit the greatest possible homogeneity.
- The splitting criterion for regression models is typically determined using metrics such as Mean Squared Error (MSE), which measures the average squared difference between actual and predicted values. This approach ensures that splits minimize prediction error, leading to more accurate and reliable regression trees:

$$\text{MSE} = \frac{1}{N}\sum_{i=1}^{N}(y_i - \bar{y})^2$$

Here, $y_i$ is the actual value, and $\bar{y}$ is the predicted value.

### Leaf Nodes:

- When a predefined stopping criterion is reachedsuch as exceeding the maximum tree depth or falling below the minimum required samples per node—the algorithm ceases further splitting. At this point, the resulting leaf nodes serve as the final predictors, representing the outcome for instances within their respective regions. Typically, the predicted value for each leaf node is determined by computing the mean of the target variable for all instances contained in that subset.

### Prediction:

- For a given input, the decision tree navigates from the root node to a specific leaf node by making sequential decisions based on the input's feature values. The value assigned to the reached leaf node serves as the predicted output.

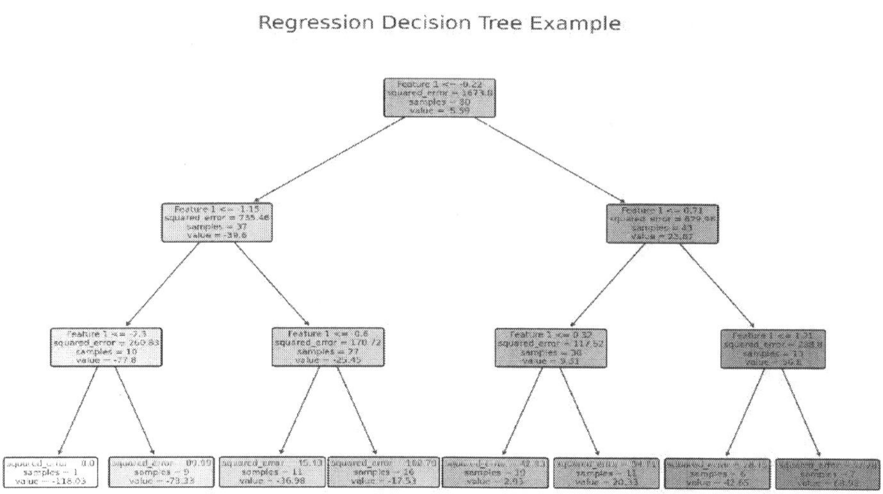


**Figure 2.10: Regression Decision Tree.**

## Advantages of Regression Decision Trees

Regression decision trees are highly interpretable and user-friendly, offering a clear and intuitive visualization of the decision-making process. This transparency makes it easy to understand how predictions are derived at each step. Unlike linear models, decision trees seamlessly capture complex, non-linear relationships between features and the target variable without requiring intricate transformations.A key strength of decision trees is their inherent ability to perform feature selection, as they automatically identify and prioritize the most influential features at each split. Their versatility allows them to handle both numerical and categorical data effortlessly, making them well-suited for diverse datasets. Moreover, they are resilient to missing values and outliers, as their splitting mechanism partitions data into distinct regions, reducing sensitivity to anomalies.In terms of computational efficiency, decision trees are particularly effective for smaller datasets, delivering quick and reliable predictions. They also serve as a foundational building block for advanced ensemble techniques such as Random Forests and Gradient Boosting, which enhance predictive accuracy, robustness, and generalization.

## Applications of Regression Decision Trees

Regression decision trees are extensively utilized across diverse industries due to their versatility and predictive accuracy. In real estate, they serve as powerful tools for estimating property values by analyzing key factors such as location, size, amenities, and market trends. Within the energy sector, they play a crucial role in forecasting electricity consumption by assessing weather patterns, historical usage data, and demand fluctuations. In healthcare, professionals rely on them to predict patient recovery times and the likelihood of hospital readmissions, leveraging insights from medical histories, treatment plans, and other relevant clinical variables.

Decision trees are widely utilized in various fields, including sales forecasting, where they analyze historical data to predict future revenue trends, and environmental modeling, where they estimate pollutant levels and temperature fluctuations. Their adaptability, clarity, and ability to handle complex datasets make them an invaluable tool for decision-makers in data-driven industries.

## Classification and Regression Tree-random Forest

The Classification and Regression Tree (CART) algorithm is a powerful decision tree-based technique designed for both classification and regression tasks. It operates by recursively partitioning the dataset into smaller, more homogeneous subsets based on feature values, aiming to minimize prediction error or maximize purity. Each split is strategically chosen to optimize a specific criterionsuch as Gini Impurity for classification or Mean Squared Error (MSE) for regression ensuring the most informative division at each step. However, while CART efficiently captures patterns in the data, standalone decision trees are prone to overfitting and can exhibit high variance, making them sensitive to slight variations in the training data.

Figure 2.11 presents a visual representation of the Random Forest method, demonstrating how multiple decision trees collaboratively contribute to the final output. Additionally, a table is provided to summarize its key features and essential aspects.

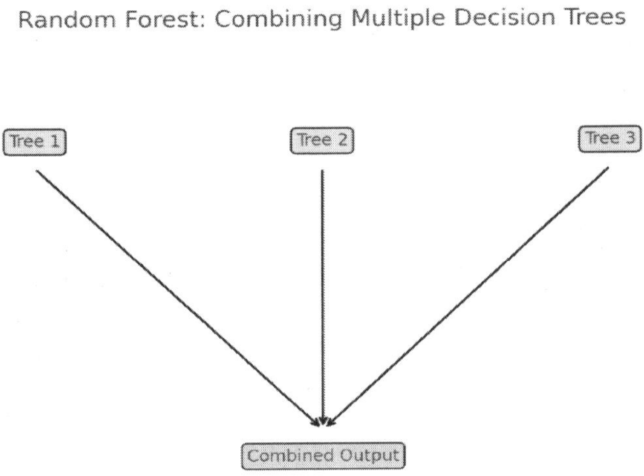


**Figure 2.11: Random Forest Method.**

## Random Forest: An Ensemble of CART

Random Forest enhances the CART algorithm by constructing an ensemble of decision trees, significantly improving accuracy, robustness, and generalization. It achieves this by aggregating the predictions of multiple decision treesusing majority voting for classification tasks and averaging for regression problems. Additionally, Random Forest introduces randomness through two key mechanisms:

- Bootstrap Aggregation (Bagging): Each tree is trained on a randomly selected subset of the dataset, drawn with replacement, ensuring diversity and reducing overfitting in the ensemble model.
- Feature Randomness: At each split, a randomly selected subset of features is evaluated to identify the most optimal splitting criterion, ensuring diversity and reducing the risk of overfitting.

Random Forest is more resistant to data noise and less likely to overfit thanks to these randomizations.

### *How Random Forest Works?*

Random Forest operates by generating multiple bootstrap samples from the original training dataset. Bootstrap sampling involves randomly selecting data points with replacement, allowing some instances to appear multiple times in a sample while others may be left out. Each bootstrap sample serves as the training set for an individual decision tree, promoting diversity among the trees.To further introduce variability, at each node split, a random subset of features is considered rather than using the entire feature set. This randomness in feature selection ensures that the trees in the forest are decorrelated, enhancing the ensemble's robustness and mitigating the risk of overfitting.Once the ensemble of decision trees is constructed, predictions from all trees are aggregated to generate the final output. For classification tasks, each tree casts a vote for a class, and the majority vote determines the final prediction. For regression tasks, the model averages the predictions from all trees to produce the final output.This aggregation mechanism enhances model stability and predictive accuracy by reducing individual errors and biases. By leveraging both data and feature randomness, Random Forest achieves strong generalization capabilities, making it a powerful and reliable machine learning algorithm.

## Advantages of Random Forest:

- Robustness: Random Forest lowers the chance of overfitting by combining several trees as opposed to just one decision tree.
- Handling Non-Linearity: The intricate and non-linear connections between features and target variables are captured by it.
- Feature Importance: When it comes to feature selection, Random Forest offers valuable insights into feature significance.
- Versatility: It can handle both numerical and categorical data and performs well on both classification and regression tasks.

## Classification and Regression Tree (CART) and Random Forest

### Introduction to CART:

The Classification and Regression Tree (CART) algorithm is a powerful decision tree-based technique designed for both classification and regression tasks. It operates by recursively partitioning the dataset into smaller, more homogeneous subsets based on feature values, aiming to minimize error or maximize purity. At each node, CART selects the optimal split by evaluating a specific criterion such as Gini Impurity for classification or Mean Squared Error (MSE) for regression ensuring the most effective division of data. However, while CART can generate highly interpretable models, individual decision trees are prone to overfitting and can exhibit instability, making them sensitive to small variations in the training data.

### Random Forest: An Ensemble of CART

Random Forest enhances the Classification and Regression Trees (CART) algorithm by constructing an ensemble of multiple decision trees to boost accuracy, robustness, and generalization. By aggregating predictions from numerous independently trained trees, it mitigates overfitting and enhances model stability. For classification tasks, it determines the final outcome through majority voting, while for regression, it computes the average prediction across all trees, ensuring more reliable and precise results. Random Forest introduces randomness in two ways:

- Bootstrap Aggregation (Bagging): A randomly selected subset of the data with replacement is used to train each tree.
- Feature Randomness: To choose the optimal split, a random subset of features is taken into account at each split.
- Random Forest is more resistant to data noise and less likely to overfit thanks to these randomizations.

## What a Random Forest Works:

Data Sampling: Create a number of bootstrap samples using the training set.

Tree Construction: Choose a random subset of features at each split to create a decision tree for every sample.

### Prediction Aggregation:

- Classification: To determine the final class, use a majority vote across all trees.
- Regression: Average all trees' predictions.

### Advantages of Random Forest:

- Robustness: Random Forest lowers the chance of overfitting by combining several trees as opposed to just one decision tree.
- Handling Non-Linearity: It records intricate, non-linear connections between target variables and features.
- Feature Importance: Random Forest aids in feature selection through providing insights into feature significance.
- Versatility: Both classification and regression tasks are effectively handled by it, and it can handle both numerical and categorical data.

### Disadvantages of Random Forest:

- Computational Cost: The computational cost of training multiple trees can be high, particularly for large datasets.
- Interpretability: Random Forest's ensemble nature makes it more difficult to explain predictions, even though individual decision trees can be interpreted.
- Memory Usage: Multiple tree storage can use a lot of memory.

### Applications of Random Forest:

- Healthcare: Leveraging predictive analytics to forecast disease progression, anticipate patient readmission rates, and optimize drug efficacy for personalized treatment plans.

- Finance: Enhancing financial security through advanced credit scoring, real-time fraud detection, and comprehensive risk assessment strategies.
- E-commerce: Driving customer engagement with AI-powered recommendation engines, precise customer segmentation, and data-driven sales forecasting for business growth.
- Environment: Utilizing AI and big data to predict weather anomalies, monitor deforestation trends, and estimate agricultural yields for sustainable resource management.

## Summary

This chapter explores fundamental and advanced algorithms for classification and regression tasks, starting with Perceptron and Backpropagation Neural Networks—key models for binary and multi-layer neural classification, respectively. The k-Nearest Neighbor (KNN) algorithm, an instance-based learning approach, leverages proximity-based decision-making for both classification and regression. Next, Support Vector Machines (SVM) are examined, extending from binary classification to multi-class generalizations using techniques like One-vs-One (OvO) and One-vs-Rest (OvR). The chapter further delves into Regression Decision Trees, which partition data into distinct regions for continuous target prediction, and Classification and Regression Trees (CART), known for their intuitive, rule-based decision structures. Finally, the chapter introduces Random Forest, a powerful ensemble learning method that integrates multiple decision trees to enhance predictive accuracy and robustness across both classification and regression tasks.

## Exercise Questions

- Explain the working principle of the Perceptron algorithm and its limitations.
- How does the Backpropagation algorithm optimize weights in a neural network?
- Describe the k-Nearest Neighbor rule and provide an example of its application in regression tasks.
- What are the key differences between One-vs-One (OvO) and One-vs-Rest (OvR) strategies in multicategory generalization?
- Explain how Support Vector Machines (SVM) handle non-linear classification problems.
- Illustrate the process of constructing a Regression Decision Tree with a simple dataset.
- What is the role of bootstrapping and feature randomness in Random Forest, and why are they important?

- Compare and contrast the advantages of Regression Decision Trees and Random Forest.
- Discuss a real-world application where Random Forest outperforms a single decision tree.
- Describe the concept of splitting criteria (e.g., Gini Impurity and Mean Squared Error) used in CART and their relevance in tree construction.

CHAPTER - 3

# Component Analysis and Clustering Techniques

In the era of big data, extracting meaningful patterns and reducing dimensionality are crucial for efficient data analysis. Component analysis and clustering techniques are fundamental methods in unsupervised learning that help in understanding complex datasets. These techniques are widely used in various fields, including finance, healthcare, marketing, and image processing, to reveal hidden structures and improve decision-making. Component analysis focuses on transforming high-dimensional data into a lower-dimensional space while preserving essential information. The most commonly used method is Principal Component Analysis (PCA), which identifies the directions (principal components) along which data variation is maximized. PCA and related methods help in noise reduction, visualization, and feature selection, making them valuable tools in machine learning and statistical analysis.

On the other hand, clustering techniques aim to group similar data points based on their inherent properties without predefined labels. Popular clustering methods include K-Means, Hierarchical Clustering, and DBSCAN (Density-Based Spatial Clustering of Applications with Noise). These techniques help in customer segmentation, anomaly detection, and pattern recognition by grouping data points that exhibit similar characteristics. Both component analysis and clustering play complementary roles in data analysis. While component analysis reduces redundancy and simplifies datasets, clustering techniques utilize the transformed data to form meaningful groups. For example, in image recognition, PCA can first be applied to reduce dimensionality before clustering techniques classify images into distinct categories.

The effectiveness of these techniques depends on the nature of the dataset and the selection of appropriate algorithms. Various modifications and advancements, such as kernel PCA and spectral clustering, have been developed to handle nonlinear and complex datasets. The choice of method depends on factors like data distribution, noise levels, and computational efficiency.Overall, component analysis and clustering techniques form the backbone of modern data science, enabling businesses and researchers to uncover hidden patterns, improve predictive modeling, and enhance decision-making processes. Their applications continue to expand across domains, making them essential tools for handling large and complex datasets.

## Principal Component Analysis (PCA)

Principal Component Analysis (PCA) is a powerful dimensionality reduction technique used in statistics and machine learning. It is primarily employed to simplify complex datasets while preserving as much relevant information as possible. By transforming correlated variables into a smaller set of uncorrelated variables called principal components, PCA helps in visualizing high-dimensional data and improving computational efficiency in various applications, such as image processing, pattern recognition, and finance.The fundamental idea behind PCA is to identify the directions (principal components) along which the variance of the data is maximized. These principal components are linear combinations of the original features and are orthogonal to each other, ensuring that they capture the most significant variations in the dataset. The first principal component accounts for the highest variance, while each subsequent component captures the remaining variance in decreasing order.

Mathematically, PCA is achieved through eigenvalue decomposition or Singular Value Decomposition (SVD) of the covariance matrix of the dataset. The eigenvectors represent the principal components, and the corresponding eigenvalues indicate the amount of variance captured by each component. By selecting only the top few principal components, PCA reduces the dimensionality of the data while retaining its essential characteristics.One of the key advantages of PCA is its ability to eliminate redundancy and noise in data by removing less significant components. This is particularly useful in machine learning applications, where reducing the number of features can help in avoiding overfitting and improving model performance. However, PCA assumes that the data is linearly correlated and may not be effective for datasets with non-linear relationships.

PCA is widely used in various fields, including image compression, genetics, and finance. In image processing, it helps in reducing the number of pixels while maintaining the key features of an image. In genetics, PCA is used to analyze gene expression data and identify patterns among different genetic samples. Similarly, in finance, it assists in portfolio optimization by identifying major factors influencing asset returns.Despite its usefulness, PCA has some limitations, such as the difficulty in interpreting transformed features and its sensitivity to the scaling of data. Since PCA depends on variance, it is important to standardize the dataset before applying it, especially when features have different units. Nevertheless, PCA remains one of the most widely used techniques for exploratory data analysis and dimensionality reduction in the field of data science.

Principal component analysis (PCA) computes two major components: the first principal component (PC1) and the second principal component (PC2).

### *First principal component*

The first principal component (PC1) represents the direction in space that captures the maximum variance within the dataset. It serves as the optimal axis that best preserves the structural integrity of the projected data points. The greater the variance encapsulated by PC1, the more information it retains from the original dataset. Importantly, no subsequent principal component can exhibit a higher variance than PC1, as each successive component captures the highest remaining variance while maintaining orthogonality to the previous components.

### *Second principal component*

The second principal component (PC2) is calculated using the same approach as the first principal component (PC1). However, PC2 captures the next highest variance in the dataset while remaining uncorrelated with PC1. This means that PC2 must be orthogonal—or mathematically perpendicularto PC1. In other words, the correlation between PC1 and PC2 is zero, ensuring that they represent distinct, independent directions of variance in the data. Typically, a scatterplot is used to visualize the relationship between PC1 and PC2 when principal component analysis (PCA) is applied to a dataset, as illustrated in Figure 3.1. In this plot, the PC1 and PC2 axes will be perpendicular to each other, reflecting their uncorrelated nature.

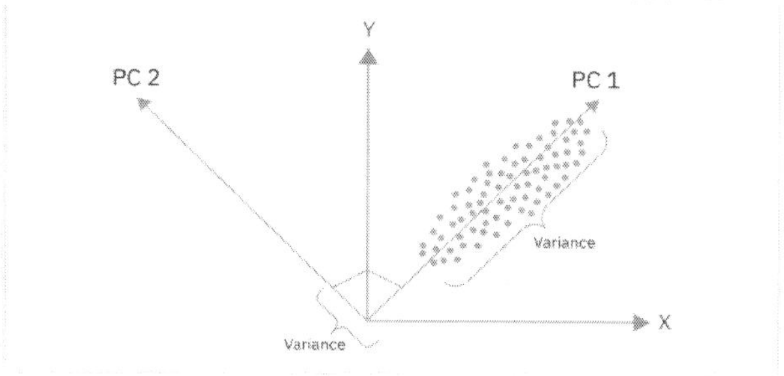


**Figure 3.1: Principal Component Analysis.**

*Source (https://www.ibm.com/topics/principal-component-analysis)*

Principal Component Analysis (PCA) is a powerful dimensionality reduction technique that transforms a high-dimensional dataset into a lower-dimensional representation while preserving as much variance as possible. It identifies a set of orthogonal axes, known as principal components, that successively capture the maximum variance in the data. These principal components are linear combinations of the original variables and are ranked in descending order of significance. The total variance retained by all principal components collectively equals the total variance present in the original dataset. The first principal component captures the highest variance in the data, while the second principal component captures the maximum variance orthogonal to the first, and this process continues iteratively for subsequent components.Principal Component Analysis (PCA) serves multiple purposes, including data visualization, feature selection, and data compression, making it a valuable tool in data analysis.data visualization in PCA enables the transformation of high-dimensional data into two or three dimensions, facilitating intuitive graphical representation and interpretation.Feature SelectionBy identifying the most significant variables in a dataset, PCA helps in selecting features that contribute the most to data variance, improving model efficiency and interpretability.Data Compression in PCA reduces the dimensionality of datasets while preserving essential information, allowing for efficient storage and faster computations without significant information loss.PCA operates on the fundamental assumption that variance within a dataset encapsulates its most crucial informationfeatures with higher variation are considered to carry more meaningful insights. Ultimately, PCA is a powerful technique for simplifying complex datasets, improving interpretability, and enhancing computational efficiency in data-driven applications.

## *Step-by-Step Explanation of PCA*

### Step 1: Standardization

The purpose of this step is to standardize the range of continuous initial variables, ensuring that each contributes equally to the analysis. Standardization is particularly crucial before performing Principal Component Analysis (PCA) because PCA is highly sensitive to variations in the scales of the initial variables. If the variables have significantly different ranges, those with larger ranges will disproportionately influence the analysis, overshadowing those with smaller ranges. For instance, a variable ranging from 0 to 100 would dominate a variable ranging from 0 to 1, leading to biased results. By transforming the data to a common scale, standardization mitigates this issue, allowing for a more balanced and accurate analysis.

Mathematically, this process involves standardizing each value of every variable by first subtracting the mean and then dividing the result by the standard deviation. This transformation ensures that the data is centered around zero with a unit variance, making it more suitable for comparative analysis and statistical modeling.

$$z = \frac{value - mean}{standard\ deviation}$$

Following the completion of standardization, every variable will be converted to the same scale.

### *Step 2: Covariance Matrix Computation*

The purpose of this step is to analyze how the variables in the input dataset deviate from the mean relative to one another, thereby identifying potential relationships among them. In some cases, variables exhibit high correlation, leading to redundancy in the dataset. To detect such correlations, we compute the covariance matrix. This matrix, which is a p×p symmetric matrix (where p represents the number of dimensions), contains the covariances for all possible pairs of the original variables. For instance, in a 3-dimensional dataset with variables x, *y*andz, the covariance matrix takes the form of a 3×3 matrix, where each entry represents the covariance between a pair of variables.:

$$\begin{bmatrix} \text{Cov}(x,x) & \text{Cov}(x,y) & \text{Cov}(x,z) \\ \text{Cov}(y,x) & \text{Cov}(y,y) & \text{Cov}(y,z) \\ \text{Cov}(z,x) & \text{Cov}(z,y) & \text{Cov}(z,z) \end{bmatrix}$$

Since the covariance of a variable with itself represents its varianceCov(a, a) =Var(a), the main diagonal of the covariance matrix (extending from the top left to the bottom right) contains the variances of the individual variables. Additionally, because covariance is a symmetric measureCov(a, b) =Cov(b, a), the covariance matrix is symmetric. This symmetry ensures that the entries above and below the main diagonal are identical, meaning the upper and lower triangular portions of the matrix are mirror images of each other.

### *Step 3: Compute the Eigenvectors and Eigenvalues*

Eigenvectors and eigenvalues are fundamental concepts in linear algebra that must be derived from the covariance matrix to identify the principal components of a dataset. A key aspect to understand about eigenvectors and eigenvalues is that they always appear in pairs—each eigenvector is associated with a corresponding eigenvalue. Furthermore, the number of these pairs is equal to the dimensionality of the dataset. For instance, in a three-dimensional dataset with three variables, there will be exactly three eigenvectors, each paired with its respective eigenvalue.

Eigenvectors and eigenvalues are the driving forces behind the magic of Principal Component Analysis (PCA). The eigenvectors of the covariance matrix define the directions of the axes along which the data exhibits the greatest variancethese directions are what we call Principal Components. Eigenvalucs, on the other hand, represent the magnitude of variance carried by each corresponding eigenvector. By ranking the eigenvectors in descending order of their eigenvalues, we prioritize the Principal Components from most to least significant, ensuring that the most informative directions are considered first.

## Principal Component Analysis Example:

Consider a two-dimensional dataset with two variables,xandy. The eigenvectors and eigenvalues of its covariance matrix are given as follows:

$$v_1 = \begin{bmatrix} 0.6778736 \\ 0.7351785 \end{bmatrix}, \quad \lambda_1 = 1.284028$$

$$v_2 = \begin{bmatrix} -0.7351785 \\ 0.6778736 \end{bmatrix}, \quad \lambda_2 = 0.04908323$$

If we rank the eigenvalues in descending order, we obtain $\lambda_1 > \lambda_2$. This implies that the eigenvector corresponding to the first principal component (PC1) is $v_1$, while the eigenvector associated with the second principal component (PC2) is $v_2$. Once the principal components are determined, we can compute the percentage of variance (or information) explained by each component by dividing its respective eigenvalue by the sum of all eigenvalues. Applying this method to the given example, we find that PC1 and PC2 account for approximately 96% and 4% of the total variance in the data, respectively.

## Create a Feature Vector

As observed in the previous step, computing the eigenvectors and ranking them in descending order based on their corresponding eigenvalues enables us to identify the principal components in order of significance. In this step, we decide whether to retain all these components or discard those with lower significance (i.e., those associated with smaller eigenvalues). The remaining selected eigenvectors form a matrix known as the Feature Vector. Essentially, the feature vector is a matrix where the columns consist of the eigenvectors corresponding to the retained principal components. This step is crucial for dimensionality reduction, as choosing to keep only p eigenvectors out of n reduces the final dataset to just p dimensions, thus simplifying the data while preserving its most important characteristics.

## Principal Component Analysis Example:

Continuing with the example from the previous step, we can either form a feature vector with both of the eigenvectors $v_1$ and $v_2$:

$$\begin{bmatrix} 0.6778736 & -0.7351785 \\ 0.7351785 & 0.6778736 \end{bmatrix}$$

Or discard the eigenvector $v_2$, which is the one of lesser significance, and form a feature vector with $v_1$ only:

$$\begin{bmatrix} 0.6778736 \\ 0.7351785 \end{bmatrix}$$

Eliminating the eigenvector$v_2$reduces the dimensionality by one, inevitably leading to some information loss in the final dataset. However, since$v_2$ accounts for only

4% of the total information, this loss is minimal, leaving 96% of the data's variance preserved by$v_1$. As demonstrated in the example, the decision to retain or discard components depends on the specific objectives of your analysis. If your goal is simply to transform the data into uncorrelated principal components without reducing dimensionality, excluding less significant components is unnecessary.

## Recast the Data along the Principal Components Axes

In the previous steps, aside from standardization, no modifications are made to the data itself; rather, the principal components are selected, and the feature vector is constructed. However, the input dataset remains expressed in terms of the original axes (i.e., the initial variables). In this final step, the goal is to transform the data from its original coordinate system to the new axes defined by the principal components. This transformation is achieved by multiplying the transpose of the original dataset by the transpose of the feature vector, which is composed of the eigenvectors of the covariance matrix. This process is the essence of Principal Component Analysis (PCA), as it reorients the data along its principal components, maximizing variance along these new dimensions.

$$FinalDataSet - FeatureVector^T \times StandardizedOriginalDataSet^T$$

## Interpreting PCA Results

A Principal Component Analysis (PCA) plot is a scatter plot that visualizes data by projecting it onto a new coordinate system defined by the first two principal components. The first principal component ($PC_1$) serves as the x-axis, while the second principal component ($PC_2$) is the y-axis. Each point in the plot represents an observation, positioned according to its values for $PC_1$ and $PC_2$.This visualization helps reveal patterns, clusters, and relationships between observations in a reduced-dimensional space. The arrows in the plot (also known as loadings) indicate how strongly each original variable contributes to the principal components. The length and direction of these arrows highlight the influence of specific variables on the newly transformed data. A variable with a high loading on a particular principal component is highly correlated with it, providing insights into which features drive variations in the dataset.The number of principal components retained after applying PCA determines how much of the original data's variability is preserved. The first principal component captures the largest variance, with each subsequent component explaining progressively less. Retaining too few components may result in losing important data patterns, whereas keeping too many can make interpretation more complex.To determine the optimal number of components, you can use a scree plot, which visualizes the variance explained by each component, or examine the cumulative explained variance to assess how much of the total information is retained.

## Use Principal Component Analysis

There are numerous dimensionality reduction techniques available, each with distinct strengths and applications. Some notable methods include Linear Discriminant Analysis (LDA) for maximizing class separability, Random Forest-based feature selection for evaluating feature importance, Uniform Manifold Approximation and Projection (UMAP) for preserving global and local data structures, and t-Distributed Stochastic Neighbor Embedding (t-SNE) for effectively visualizing high-dimensional data in lower dimensions. Consider the following factors to decide if PCA is the right approach for your analysis:

**Linearity:** PCA is a linear dimensionality reduction technique, making it ideal for datasets where variables exhibit linear relationships. In contrast, methods like t-SNE and UMAP are non-linear, allowing them to capture intricate, non-linear patterns and complex structures within the data. As a result, PCA is more effective when the underlying data distribution follows a linear structure, whereas t-SNE and UMAP excel in preserving local and global structures in datasets with non-linear dependencies.

**Computation:** PCA leverages matrix operations for efficient computation, making it well-suited for handling large datasets. In contrast, techniques like t-SNE and UMAP, while effective for nonlinear dimensionality reduction, are computationally expensive and may not scale well to large datasets.

**Information Preservation:** PCA is designed to retain the maximum variance in the dataset, making it particularly effective for identifying the most significant variables. In contrast, t-SNE and UMAP prioritize preserving the local structure and relationships within the data, making them more suitable for revealing intricate patterns and clusters. As a result, PCA is ideal for feature selection and dimensionality reduction in analytical tasks, while non-linear techniques like t-SNE and UMAP excel at visualizing complex datasets in lower-dimensional spaces.

**Feature Extraction:** Principal Component Analysis (PCA) is a powerful feature extraction technique that transforms the original variables into a new set of uncorrelated variables, known as principal components, which are linear combinations of the original features. Unlike non-linear dimensionality reduction methods such as UMAP and t-SNE, which primarily focus on preserving local structure without generating new variables, PCA retains the ability to rank and identify the most significant contributors to data variance. While PCA is useful for feature selection and interpretation, non-linear techniques like UMAP and t-SNE excel at visualizing complex, high-dimensional data in lower-dimensional spaces by capturing intricate patterns and relationships that PCA might overlook.

## Linear Discriminant Analysis

Linear Discriminant Analysis (LDA) is a fundamental technique in supervised machine learning, primarily used for solving multi-class classification problems. It achieves this by reducing data dimensionality while preserving as much class-discriminative information as possible. By identifying optimal linear combinations of features, LDA effectively separates multiple classes, making it a valuable tool in data science for optimizing machine learning models.Also known as Normal Discriminant Analysis (NDA) or Discriminant Function Analysis (DFA), LDA operates within a generative model framework. This means it estimates the probability distribution of each class and applies Bayes' theorem to classify new data points. Bayes' theorem enables LDA to compute conditional probabilities—determining the likelihood that an input data instance belongs to a specific class based on observed features. This probabilistic approach makes LDA particularly effective for structured classification problems.LDA works by projecting high-dimensional data onto a lower-dimensional space, ensuring that class separation is maximized. By transforming multi-dimensional input data into a single dimension (or a lower-dimensional subspace), LDA simplifies classification while preserving critical discriminative information. This characteristic makes LDA an essential dimensionality reduction technique, especially useful when dealing with complex datasets.One of LDA's advantages over logistic regression is its ability to handle multi-class classification problems rather than being limited to binary classification. As a result, it is often integrated into advanced machine learning pipelines to enhance classification performance. LDA is commonly used alongside other machine learning algorithms, such as decision trees, random forests, and support vector machines (SVMs), to improve classification accuracy and computational efficiency.For a deeper understanding of Bayesian statistics and its impact on supervised learning, particularly in probabilistic classification, refer to Naïve Bayes classifiers, which employ a similar Bayesian framework for classification tasks.

## Fisher's Linear Discriminant

Linear Discriminant Analysis (LDA) in Machine Learning is a generalized extension of Fisher's Linear Discriminant (FLD). Initially, Ronald A. Fisher, in his research, introduced a discriminant function to distinguish between two plant species: Iris Setosa and Iris Versicolor. The core principle of FLD involves projecting data points onto a linear axis in a manner that maximizes inter-class variance (between-class scatter) while simultaneously minimizing intra-class variance (within-class scatter). This optimization enhances the separability of different classes by ensuring that data points are well-distributed along a single linear dimension. While this concept may seem abstract, it is visually intuitive, as illustrated in Figure 3.2.Before delving into the mathematical derivation, it is essential to familiarize ourselves with some key terms and expressions that form the foundation of FLD.

- Let's suppose we have d-dimensional data points x1.... xn with 2 classes Ci=1,2 each having $N_1$& $N_2$ samples.
- Consider W as a unit vector onto which we will project the data points. Since we are only concerned with the direction, we choose a unit vector for this purpose.
- Number of samples: $N = N_1 + N_2$

- If x(n) are the samples on the feature space then WTx(n) denotes the data points after projection.
- Means of classes before projection: $m_i$
- Means of classes after projection: $M_i = W^T m_i$

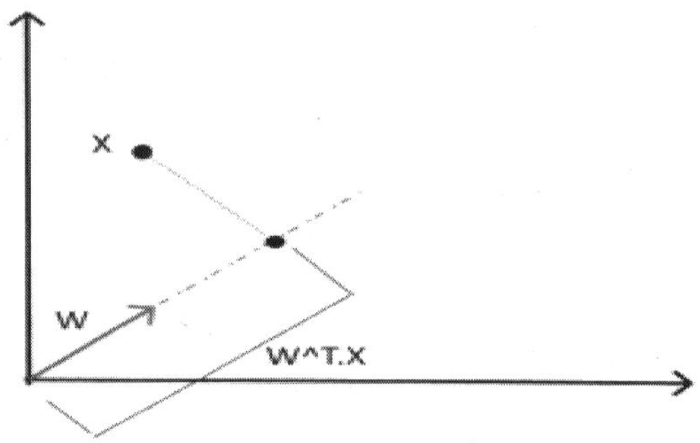


**Figure 3.2:Datapoint X before and after projection.**

**Source (Analytics Vidhya)**

**Scatter matrix:** The covariance matrix is estimated using this method. It is a semi-definite matrix with a m x m value.

Given by: sample variance * no. of samples.

Note: The only difference between scatter and variance is the scale on which they measure it. Therefore, we could use both terms interchangeably. Thus, avoid becoming confused.

## Two Types of Scatter Matrices

Here let's will be dealing with two types of scatter matrices in Figure 3.3.

Between class scatter = $S_b$ = measures the distance between class means

Within class scatter = $S_w$ = measures the spread around means of each class.

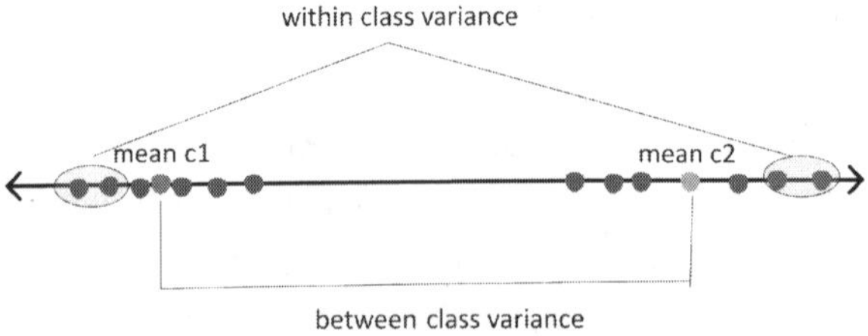


**Figure 3.3: Two Types of Scatter Matrices.**

**Source (Analytics Vidhya)**

## As per Fisher's LDA:

$$\arg\max J(W) = \frac{(M_1 - M_2)^2}{S_{12} + S_{22}}$$

The numerator represents the between-class scatter, while the denominator corresponds to the within-class scatter. To maximize the function, we aim to increase the between-class scatter while minimizing the within-class scatter—a straightforward mathematical principle.To proceed with optimization, we first need to express the given equation in terms of W.

## Numerator

$$\begin{aligned}(M_1 - M_2)^2 &= (W^T m_1 - W^T m_2)(W^T m_1 - W^T m_2)^T \\ &= W^T (m_1 - m_2)(m_1 - m_2)^T W \\ &= W^T S_b W\end{aligned}$$

$S_b$=between class scatter

Denominator

For denominator we have $1S^2 + 2S^2$.

**Class scatter before projection:**

$$S_i = \sum_{x(n) \in C_i} (x(n) - m_i)(x(n) - m_i)^T$$

**Scatter for projected samples:**

$$S_i^2 = \sum_{x(n) \in C_i} (W^T x(n) - M_i)(W^T x(n) - M_i)^T$$

$$M_i = W^T m_i$$

**With little re-arrangement we will get:**

$$S_i^2 = W^T \left( \sum_{x(n) \in C_i} (x(n) - m_i)(x(n) - m_i)^T \right) W$$

$$S_i^2 = W^T S_i W$$

**So,**

$$S_1^2 + S_2^2 = W^T(S_1 + S_2)W = W^T S_w W$$

$S_w$=within class scatter

The denominator and numerator should now be expressed in terms of W.

$$J(W) = \frac{W^T S_b W}{W^T S_w W}$$

The previously mentioned function becomes a generalized eigenvalue-eigenvector problem when it is differentiated with respect to W and equated with 0.

$$S_b W = \nu S_w W$$

$S_w$ being a full-rank matrix, inverse is feasible

$$S_w^{-1} S_b W = \nu W$$

Where v = eigen value

W = eigen vector

## LDA for classification

Until now, we have only reduced the dimensionality of the data points; however, this transformation alone does not yet ensure discrimination between classes. To achieve discrimination, we can utilize the projected data to construct a classifier by applying Bayes' theorem. Consider that the data points, X=$x_1$, $x_2$,$x_p$, follow a multivariate Gaussian distribution. LetK represent the total number of classes, andY be the response variable indicating class membership. Furthermore, let πk denote the prior probability, which represents the likelihood that a randomly chosen observation belongs to thekthclass. Additionally, the conditional probability P(X=x|Y=k) represents the posterior probability, which describes the probability of observingX = x given that it belongs to class k

Let fk(X) = $P_r$ (X = x | Y = k) is our probability density function of X for an observation x that belongs to Kth class. fk(X) is large if there is a high probability of an observation in Kth class has X=x.

**Bayes' theorem**

$$\Pr(Y = k \mid X = x) = \frac{p_{ik} f_k(x)}{\sum_{i=1}^{K} p_{ik} f_k(x)}$$

We must now determine the prior πk and density function fk(X) in order to compute the posterior probability. Pik is easily calculable. We only need to calculate the percentage of training observations that fall into the Kth class if we have a random sample of Ys drawn from the population. However, calculating fk(X) can be a little challenging.

Let's consider that the probability density function of x follows a multivariate Gaussian distribution, characterized by class-specific means mk and a shared covariance matrix Σ. Mathematically, the multivariate Gaussian density function is expressed as:

$$f(x|pi_k) = \frac{1}{(2\pi)^{\frac{p}{2}}|\Sigma|^{\frac{1}{2}}} \exp\left(-\frac{1}{2}(x - m_k)^T|\Sigma|^{-1}(x - m_k)\right)$$

|sigma| = determinant of covariance matrix (same for all classes)

mk = class means

Now, by plugging the density function in the above equation, taking the logarithm and doing some algebra, we will find the Linear score function

$$\delta_k(x) = x^T\Sigma^{-1}m_k - \frac{1}{2}m_k{}^T\Sigma^{-1}m_k + \log pi_k$$

A sample unit is assigned to the class with the highest Linear Score function. In the equation above, the Linear Discriminant Function is directly dependent on x in a linear manner, which is why this technique is called **Linear Discriminant Analysis (LDA)** in Machine Learning.

## Addressing LDA shortcomings

When applying Linear Discriminant Analysis (LDA) for classification, you may encounter the limitation of linearity. LDA seeks to identify a linear transformation that maximizes class separability. However, if the classes are not linearly separable, finding an optimal lower-dimensional projection becomes infeasible. This issue is particularly evident when classes share the same mean, as the key discriminatory information resides not in the mean but in the data's scatter, leading to a between-class scatter matrix(SbS)of zero.To overcome this challenge, Kernel functions offer a powerful solution. Commonly used in methods such as Support Vector Machines (SVM) and Support Vector Regression (SVR), kernel functions facilitate non-linear transformations by mapping input data into a higher-dimensional feature space. This mapping enables the computation of inner products directly in the transformed space, allowing LDA to capture complex, non-linear class structures and enhance classification performance.

**Small Sample problem:** This issue occurs when the dimensionality of the samples (D) exceeds the number of samples (N), a common challenge in

Linear Discriminant Analysis (LDA) within machine learning. In such cases, the covariance matrix becomes singular, making it non-invertible. To overcome this limitation, regularization techniques were introduced. Instead of directly using the covariance matrix (Σ), a modified approach is applied to ensure stability and improve generalization:

$$\tilde{\Sigma} = \alpha\Sigma + (1 - \alpha)I$$

Here, α is a tuning parameter that takes a value between 0 and 1. The identity matrix, **I**, is introduced to adjust the covariance matrix by adding a small bias to its diagonal elements. This regularization technique helps enhance numerical stability and prevent overfitting. Moreover, the regularization parameter must be carefully optimized to achieve optimal model performance.

In discriminant analysis within machine learning, Scikit-Learn's Linear Discriminant Analysis (LDA) integrates a shrinkage parameter to mitigate issues related to under-sampling. This parameter plays a crucial role in enhancing the classifier's generalization performance. When set to 'auto', it intelligently determines the optimal shrinkage value. However, it is important to note that this functionality is only available when the solver parameter is set to 'lsqr' or 'eigen'. Users also have the flexibility to manually adjust this parameter within the range of 0 to 1, allowing fine-tuned control over regularization.Beyond shrinkage, other techniques can also address under-sampling challenges. For instance, combining Principal Component Analysis (PCA) with LDA is a common approach. In this method, PCA is first applied to reduce the dimensionality of the dataset, followed by the standard LDA classification process, thereby improving both computational efficiency and discriminative performance.

## PCA versus LDA versus Factor Analysis

Principal Component Analysis (PCA) is a powerful dimensionality reduction technique, similar to Linear Discriminant Analysis (LDA). However, unlike LDA, which is specifically designed for supervised learning tasks, PCA is versatile and applicable to both supervised and unsupervised learning. In the context of unsupervised learning, PCA reduces dimensionality without relying on class labels or predefined categories, making it particularly useful for exploratory data analysis and pattern recognition.PCA also shares conceptual similarities with factor analysis, as both techniques aim to reduce the number of variables in a dataset while minimizing information loss. However, their objectives differ. PCA transforms the original variables into a smaller set of linearly independent principal components that capture the most variance in the data. In contrast, factor analysis focuses on uncovering latent variables—unobserved factors that explain the underlying structure of the data distribution. While PCA emphasizes variance maximization, factor analysis seeks to model correlations and identify hidden constructs influencing the observed variables.

### *PCA versus K-means clustering*

PCA (Principal Component Analysis) and k-means clustering are both unsupervised machine learning techniques used in data analysis, but they serve distinct purposes and operate using different methodologies.PCA is primarily a dimensionality reduction technique that transforms high-dimensional data into a lower-dimensional subspace while preserving as much variance as possible. It does so by generating new variables, known as principal components, which are linear combinations of the original variables. This method is widely used in exploratory data analysis, feature extraction, and preprocessing to improve the performance of predictive models by reducing computational complexity and mitigating the curse of dimensionality.

On the other hand, k-means clustering is a clustering algorithm that partitions data points into distinct groups based on their similarities. It operates by assigning each data point to the nearest cluster centroid, iteratively refining cluster assignments to minimize intra-cluster variance. K-means is frequently applied in various real-world scenarios, including image segmentation, customer segmentation, pattern recognition, and anomaly detection.The choice between PCA and k-means depends on the specific dataset and the objectives of the analysis. If the goal is to reduce the number of features while retaining essential information, PCA is the preferred approach. However, if the objective is to identify natural groupings within the data, k-means clustering is the more suitable technique. In some cases, these methods can be used togetherPCA can be applied first to reduce dimensionality before performing k-means clustering on the transformed dataset for better clustering performance.

## *Independent Component Analysis*

Independent Component Analysis (ICA) is a widely used approach for blind source separation, applied across various domains. Despite its broad utility, ICA is often employed as a "black box" technique, with limited understanding of its underlying mechanisms. To bridge this gap, this paper provides a comprehensive resource for researchers interested in ICA by elucidating its fundamental principles and operational framework.The tutorial begins with an introduction to the definition and core concepts of ICA, followed by a step-by-step exploration of numerical examples. These examples illustrate the preprocessing stages, as well as the mixing and unmixing procedures involved in ICA. Additionally, various ICA algorithms, their practical applications, and the challenges associated with their implementation are discussed in detail.As a statistical and computational technique, ICA plays a crucial role in machine learning by decomposing multivariate signals into their independent, non-Gaussian components. The central premise of ICA is that observed data consists of a linear mixture of statistically independent and non-Gaussian source signals. The primary objective of ICA is to determine a linear transformation that extracts these independent components, thereby enabling meaningful signal separation and analysis.

- Noise significantly impacts recorded signals and cannot be entirely eliminated from measurements. For example, in a street recording of a person's voice, background sounds such as footsteps, people walking, and ambient noise inevitably interfere. This makes it challenging to achieve a clean, isolated measurement.
- This occurs because source signals are inevitably contaminated by noise, while additional independent signals from other sourcessuch as the sounds of passing carsfurther contribute to the overall auditory complexity.
- The measurements can be described as a comprehensive aggregation of multiple independent sources, each contributing unique data points to ensure accuracy and reliability.
- Blind Source Separation (BSS) is the process of isolating individual source signals from a mixture without prior knowledge of their specific characteristics. The term "blind" signifies that separation can be achieved even when minimal information about the original signals is available.

The cocktail party problem, a classic challenge in signal processing, involves isolating and separating the speech signals of multiple individuals speaking simultaneously in a noisy environment. Among the most widely used techniques to address this issue is Independent Component Analysis (ICA), a powerful method for source separation. Despite the presence of overlapping environmental noises, the goal is to accurately identify and extract the desired speech signal from a single audio source.

- ICA is a powerful technique with a wide range of applications, including data compression, image processing, and signal analysis, offering versatile solutions across various fields.
- These basis functions are carefully chosen to be non-Gaussian and statistically independent. Once detected, these basis functions can be utilized to decompose the observed data into its underlying independent components, enabling a clearer and more effective separation of the data's intrinsic structure.
- ICA is often integrated with other machine learning techniques, such as classification and clustering, to enhance performance. For example, ICA can be employed to extract meaningful features that are then used in tasks like clustering and classification, or it can serve as a preprocessing step to refine data before these operations are performed.
- One of the limitations of ICA is its assumption that the underlying sources are linearly mixed and non-Gaussian. Additionally, if the data is not properly pre-processed, ICA can encounter convergence issues and become computationally expensive.
- Despite these limitations, ICA remains a powerful and widely-used technique in signal processing and machine learning.

## Statistical Independence Concept

The probability theory states that if two random variables, X and Y, are statistically independent, the joint probability distribution of the pair is simply the product of their individual probability distributions. This implies that the outcome of one variable has no effect on the probability distribution of the other variable, meaning that knowing the value of one does not alter the likelihood of the other's outcome.

$$P(X and Y) = P(X) * P(Y)$$

or $P(X \cap Y) = P(X) * P(Y)$

## Assumptions in ICA

- The first assumption posits that the source signals (or original signals) are statistically independent from one another.
- The second assumption posits that each source signal follows a non-Gaussian distribution.

## Mathematical Representation of Independent Component Analysis

The observed random vector representing the observed data with m components= $X = (x_1, \ldots, x_m)^T$

The hidden components are represented by the random vector,. $S = (s_1, \ldots, s_n)^T$

Where n is the number of hidden sources.

## Linear Static Transformation

The observed dataX is transformed into hidden components Sthrough a linear static transformation, represented by the matrixW.

Here, W = transformation matrix.

The objective is to modify the observed datax such that the resulting hidden components become statistically independent from one another. The independence is measured by some function= $F(s_1, \ldots, s_n)$

The objective is to determine the optimal transformation matrixWthat maximizes the statistical independence of the hidden components.

## Clustering Algorithms

In the real world, not all datasets have a predefined target variable, making them unsuitable for analysis using supervised learning algorithms. For such data, unsupervised learning algorithms are more appropriate. One of the most commonly used techniques within unsupervised learning is cluster analysis. Cluster analysis involves grouping similar data points based on their inherent characteristics.

This process, known as clustering, is a core aspect of unsupervised learning, which focuses on extracting insights from unlabelled datameaning there is no target variable to guide the analysis, unlike in supervised learning.The objective of clustering is to form groups of similar data points from a diverse dataset. This is achieved by evaluating the similarity between data points using distance metrics such as Euclidean distance, Cosine similarity, or Manhattan distance, and then grouping those with the highest similarity scores together. The result is the creation of homogeneous clusters within a heterogeneous dataset, helping to reveal patterns or structures that might otherwise remain hidden. For Example, In the graph given below, we can clearly see that there are 3 circular clusters forming on the basis of distance Figure 3.4.

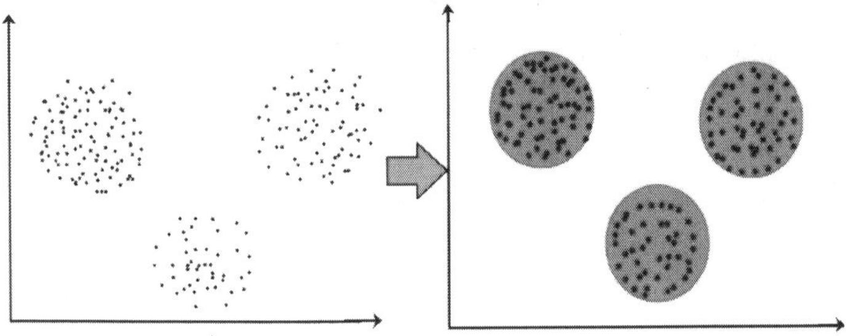

**Figure 3.4: Circular clusters forming on the basis of distance.**

**Source(geeksforgeeks)**

It is no longer a requirement for clusters to be circular in shape; instead, they can take on arbitrary forms. Several algorithms are designed to effectively detect clusters with complex, non-circular shapes.

## k-Mean clustering

K-means clustering is a popular unsupervised learning algorithm used to partition unlabelled data into distinct groups or clusters. As one of the most widely adopted clustering techniques in machine learning, K-means operates without predefined labels, meaning it doesn't rely on data with established classification structures. Unlike supervised learning, where labeled data is used, K-means categorizes data based solely on inherent similarities.While there are various clustering methods, including exclusive, overlapping, hierarchical, and probabilistic approaches, K-means is an example of an exclusive or "hard" clustering method. This means that each data point belongs to only one cluster, ensuring distinct groupings. K-means is commonly applied in data science for tasks like market segmentation, document clustering, image segmentation, and image compression, due to its simplicity, efficiency, and effectiveness.The K-means algorithm is centroid-based and operates iteratively. It aims to partition data into clusters by minimizing the variance within each group, with the centroid representing the center of each cluster. The centroid is typically calculated as the mean or median of all points within the cluster, depending on the nature of the data. This approach makes K-means a robust and efficient tool for cluster analysis.

## k-means clustering work

K-means clustering is an iterative algorithm designed to minimize the sum of squared distances between data points and their respective cluster centroids. This method categorizes data points into distinct clusters by calculating the distance—typically using Euclidean distance—from each point to the cluster centers. The algorithm seeks to minimize the overall distance between data points and their assigned centroids. Data points that are closest to a particular centroid are grouped together within the same cluster. A higher value of k, the number of clusters, results in smaller, more detailed clusters, whereas a lower k leads to larger clusters with broader generalizations and less granularity.

### *Initialize k*

The traditional k-means clustering algorithm involves several key steps. The initial step is to select k centroids, where k represents the number of clusters predefined for the dataset. This selection process can be carried out using either random initialization or more advanced centroid sampling techniques.

### *Assign Centroids*

The next step involves a two-phase iterative process driven by the expectation maximization (EM) machine learning algorithm. In the expectation phase, each data point is assigned to the closest centroid based on distance, typically using the Euclidean distance metric. During the maximization phase, the algorithm recalculates the centroid of each cluster by computing the mean of all points within that cluster, then updates the centroid's position. This cycle of assignment and recalculation continues until the centroids converge, or the maximum number of iterations is reached. K-means clustering is simple yet highly sensitive to initial conditions and outliers. Therefore, it is crucial to carefully optimize both the initialization of centroids and the selection of the number of clusters (k) to ensure meaningful results. Various strategies, including the use of evaluation metrics and refined initial centroid sampling methods, can be employed to assess and enhance the performance of the clustering algorithm.

## Cluster Evaluation Metrics

Quality clusters contain at least two properties:

- Every data point in a cluster ought to be comparable.
- Clusters should have a unique identity.

These properties are attained by minimizing the intracluster distance while simultaneously maximizing the intercluster distance between all data points in a dataset. In other words, a better clustering result is achieved when each cluster is more compact and well-separated from other clusters. The objective of the k-means clustering algorithm is to minimize the sum of squared errors (SSE). By calculating the SSE, which is the squared Euclidean distance of each data point to its nearest centroid, we can assess the quality of the cluster assignments and measure the total variation within each cluster. Cluster evaluation metrics play a crucial role in assessing the clustering quality, providing different perspectives to analyze the results. These metrics assist in determining the optimal number of clusters and the best initialization of centroids. Below is some common evaluation metrics used to measure both intracluster and intercluster distances in clustering.

### *Inertia*

The K-means clustering algorithm seeks to determine centroids, or cluster centers, that minimize inertia, a key evaluation metric that quantifies the effectiveness of clustering based on distance measurements. Inertia is computed by calculating the squared distance between each data point and its respective centroid, then summing these squared distances for all points within a cluster. This total, or inertial value, represents the intracluster distance. A lower inertia value is preferable, as it indicates that the data points within the cluster are closer together, signifying greater compactness and similarity.

### *Dunn Index*

The second property is assessed using the Dunn index, which quantifies the relationship between the minimum intercluster distance and the maximum intracluster distance. A higher intercluster distance suggests better cluster quality, as it indicates that the clusters are as distinct from one another as possible, enhancing their separation and individuality.

## Optimizing k-means performance

Optimization plays a crucial role in achieving the best clustering results when using the k-means algorithm. Due to its random initialization step, k-means is nondeterministic, meaning that running the algorithm multiple times on the same dataset may yield different cluster assignments. To ensure optimal performance, selecting appropriate initial centroids and determining the optimal number of clusters are essential, as these factors significantly enhance both the accuracy and efficiency of the algorithm.

### *Initializing the cluster centroids*

Each cluster in the k-means algorithm is defined by a centroid, which serves as the central representative data point of that cluster. The algorithm groups similar data points into clusters by minimizing the distance between each point and its respective centroid or mean value. The main objective of k-means is to reduce the total distance between the data points and their assigned centroids. This process is iterative, and the choice of initial cluster partitions can significantly influence the final clustering results. Random initialization introduces the risk of inconsistency, potentially leading to suboptimal outcomes. To address this, various centroid initialization methods have been developed to enhance the algorithm's reliability. A study by NUS Computing explores and compares different initialization techniques, including the widely used k-means+ method, as an alternative to random initialization.

### *K-means +*

K-means+ is an enhanced version of the standard k-means algorithm that optimizes the selection of initial cluster centroids. Developed by researchers Arthur and Vasilevskiy, K-means+ improves the overall quality of final cluster assignments by addressing the initialization step. The initialization process begins by selecting a single centroid from the dataset. For each subsequent centroid, the algorithm calculates the distance from each data point to its nearest cluster center. The next centroid is chosen based on the probability that a point's distance from its nearest centroid is proportional to that distance. This iterative process continues until the desired number of cluster centers has been selected.

## Choosing the optimal number of clusters

The k-means algorithm typically continues to iterate until the optimal number of clusters is determined. The process concludes when the centroids converge, or the maximum number of iterations is reached.

### *Elbow Method*

One effective method for determining the optimal number of clusters is the elbow method. This graphical technique helps identify the ideal number of clusters in a k-means clustering algorithm. It works by calculating the Euclidean distance between each data point and its corresponding cluster center, then selecting the number of clusters at the point where the "within-cluster sum of squares" (WCSS) starts to level off. WCSS represents the total variance within each cluster, which is plotted against the number of clusters.To apply the elbow method, the first step is to compute the WCSS for various values of k (the number of clusters). These WCSS values are then plotted on the y-axis, while the number of clusters is plotted on the x-axis. As the number of clusters increases, the plot should show a consistent trend. The "elbow" point, where the rate of decrease in WCSS slows significantly, indicates a range for the optimal number of clusters. However, when determining the number of clusters, computational costs must also be considered. A higher number of clusters generally requires more processing power, especially when dealing with large datasets. It is important to note that the elbow method may not be the best choice for datasets with high dimensionality or irregular shapes, where more advanced techniques might be needed. Another method for choosing the optimum number of clusters is the silhouette analysis in Figure 3.5.

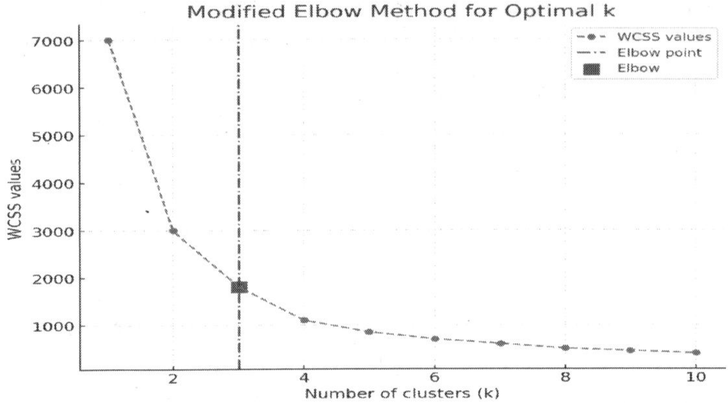


**Figure 3.5:Elbow Method for determining the optimal number of clusters (k).**

## Applications in machine learning

The K-means clustering algorithm is widely utilized across diverse domains and industries due to its versatility and efficiency. It is typically applied to machine learning data that is low-dimensional, numeric, and easily divisible. Researchers have successfully integrated K-means clustering with advanced deep learning techniques, such as Convolutional Neural Networks (CNNs) and Recurrent Neural Networks (RNNs), to significantly improve the performance of various machine learning tasks, including computer vision, natural language processing (NLP), and numerous other fields. Here is a list of common k-means clustering applications:

**Customer Segmentation:** The practice of segmenting a company's customer base into distinct groups based on shared characteristics, reflecting similarities in their preferences or behaviors. This strategy enables companies to tailor targeted advertising campaigns to specific clusters, optimizing engagement and effectiveness.

**Document Classification:** A systematic approach for assigning different classes or categories to documents, commonly employed by organizations to manage and moderate content. Explore the Watson Discovery documentation for guidance on creating an efficient document classifier.

**Image Segmentation:** This research explores a computer vision technique that segments a digital image into distinct clusters of pixels, focusing on how k-means clustering models are leveraged to identify and delineate boundaries within medical images.

**Recommendation Engines:** Recommendation engines are widely employed across various applications on the web. E-commerce businesses often leverage advanced techniques such as Principal Component Analysis (PCA) and k-means clustering to develop highly effective product recommendation systems.

## Fuzzy C-Means Clustering (FCM) Algorithm

Fuzzy logic principles offer a powerful approach to clustering multidimensional data by assigning each data point a membership value for each cluster center, ranging from 0 to 100 percent. This is in contrast to traditional hard-threshold clustering, where each data point is strictly assigned to one distinct cluster. The fuzzy clustering algorithm works by calculating the degree of membership of each data point to each cluster center based on the distance between the point and the center. The closer a data point is to a cluster center, the higher its membership value for that cluster. Importantly, the sum of the membership values for each data point across all clusters must always equal one. This unsupervised clustering technique allows for the creation of a fuzzy partition of the data, providing more nuanced classification. The algorithm's behavior is influenced by a parameter, m, which controls the degree of fuzziness in the solution. Larger values of m result in greater overlap between clusters, with elements increasingly belonging to multiple clusters. Consequently, the optimization outcomes vary with different values of m, leading to different clustering partitions. Given below is a gif that shows the effect of the selection of m obtained from the fuzzy c-means in Figure 3.6.

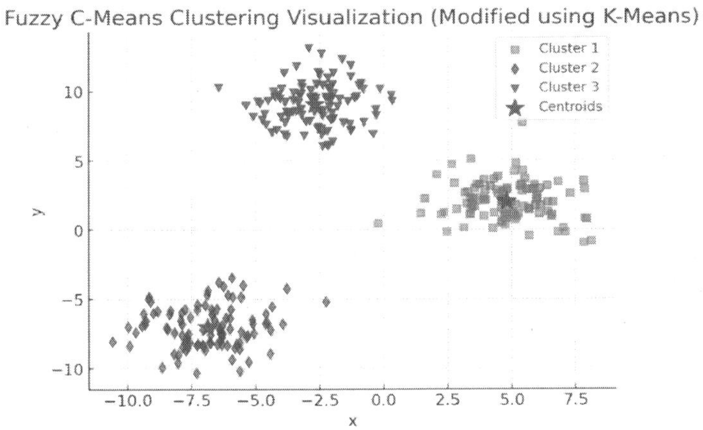


**Figure 3.6: Shows the effect of the selection of m obtained from the fuzzy c-means.**

Source(https://medium.com/geekculture/fuzzy-c-means-clustering-fcm-algorithm-in-machine-learning-c2e51e586fff)

Hard clustering and soft clustering are two distinct methods of partitioning data points into clusters. Hard clustering, also referred to as crisp clustering, assigns each data point to a single cluster based on specific criteria, such as its proximity to the cluster centroid. This method results in non-overlapping clusters, where each point belongs exclusively to one cluster. K-Means is an example of hard clustering in Figure 3.7.

Soft clustering, also referred to as fuzzy clustering or probabilistic clustering, assigns each data point a degree of membership or probability value, reflecting the likelihood of that point belonging to each cluster. Unlike hard clustering, which forces data points into a single cluster, soft clustering allows for the representation of data points that may belong to multiple clusters simultaneously. Notable examples of soft clustering techniques include Fuzzy C-Means and Gaussian Mixture Models (GMMs).

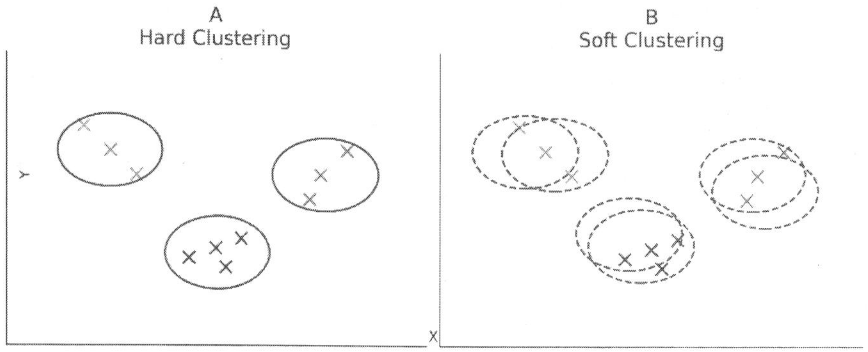


**Figure 3.7: fig (a) Hard clustering fig. (b) soft clustering. Source (ResearchGate)**

Let's compare these two powerful algorithms to gain a clearer understanding of how the fuzzy c-means algorithm fits within the broader context.

**Attribution to a cluster:** In fuzzy clustering, each data point is assigned a probability of belonging to each cluster, in contrast to the traditional k-means approach where a point is strictly assigned to a single cluster. Specifically, in Fuzzy-C Means clustering, each data point carries a degree of membership to a cluster, meaning it doesn't simply "belong" to a cluster but instead has a varying level of association. This level of association is determined by the inverse of the distance from the point to the center of the cluster, with closer points having a stronger affiliation and farther points having a weaker connection.

**Speed:**,Fuzzy C-Means tends to run slower than K-Means because it performs more complex calculations. While K-Means only requires a simple distance calculation to assign each data point to the nearest cluster, Fuzzy C-Means evaluates each point against every cluster and incorporates more operations, including the computation of inverse-distance weighting for each evaluation. This additional complexity results in increased processing time.

**Personal Opinion:** FCM (Fuzzy C-Means) / Soft-K-Means is more effective than Hard-K-Means when handling elongated clusters, particularly in cases where points that are consistent in other dimensions tend to spread along one or two specific dimensions. This flexibility allows FCM/Soft-K-Means to better capture the inherent structure of such clusters.

## Fuzzy C Means

Now that we have a clear understanding of the distinction between hard and soft clustering, let's delve into how the Fuzzy C-Means algorithm operates.

## How to Run the FCM Algorithm

**Initialization:** Randomly select and initialize cluster centroids from the dataset, while specifying a fuzziness parameter (m) to regulate the extent of fuzziness in the clustering process.

**Membership Update:** Calculate the degree of membership for each data point to every cluster by evaluating its proximity to the cluster centroids, utilizing an appropriate distance metric(ex: Euclidean distance).

**Centroid Update:** Revise the centroid values and recompute the cluster centroids according to the updated membership assignments.

**Convergence Check:** Repeat steps 2 and 3 continuously until either the specified number of iterations is completed or the membership values and centroids converge to stable, unchanging values.

## Maths Behind Fuzzy C Means

In a traditional k-means algorithm, we mathematically solve it via the following steps:

- Initialize the cluster centers at random using the k-value.
- Using a distance metric, determine the distance to each centroid. For instance, Manhattan distance and Euclidean distance.
- After assigning the clusters to every data point, create k-clusters.
- Next, update each cluster's centroid by calculating the mean of the data points that belong to that cluster.
- Update until the centroids don't change or a pre-defined number of iterations are over.

But in Fuzzy C-Means, the algorithm differs.

Here:

- n = number of data point
- c = number of clusters
- x = 'i' data point
- v = centroid of 'j' cluster

w = membership value of data point of i to cluster j

m = fuzziness parameter (m>1)

Update the membership values using the formula:

$$w_{ij} = \frac{1}{\sum_{k=1}^{c} \left( \frac{\|x_i - v_j\|}{\|x_i - v_k\|} \right)^{\frac{2}{m-1}}}$$

Update cluster centroid values using a weighted average of the data points:

$$\mathbf{v}_j = \frac{\sum_{i=1}^{n} w_{ij}^{m} \cdot \mathbf{x}_i}{\sum_{i=1}^{n} w_{ij}^{m}}$$

Iteratively update the membership values and cluster centers until the changes in both become negligible, or a specified number of iterations is reached. For each data point, assign it to the cluster or clusters corresponding to its highest membership value.

## Fuzzy C Means Different from K-Means

There are various differences in both these clustering algorithms in Table 3.1. A few of them are:

**Table 3.1: Show the Fuzzy C Means Different from K-Means.**

| Fuzzy C Means | K-Means |
|---|---|
| Each data point is assigned a degree of membership to each cluster, indicating the probability or likelihood of the point belonging to each cluster. | Each data point is exclusively assigned to one and only one cluster, based on the closest centroid, typically determined using Euclidean distance. |
| It does not impose any constraints on the shape or variance of clusters. It can handle clusters of different shapes and sizes, making it more flexible. | It assumes that clusters are spherical and have equal variance. Thus, it may not perform well with clusters of non-spherical shapes or varying sizes. |
| It is less sensitive to noise and outliers as it allows for soft, probabilistic cluster assignments. | It is sensitive to noise and outliers in the data |

## Expectation-Maximization (EM) Algorithm

The Expectation-Maximization (EM) algorithm is undoubtedly one of the most influential and widely utilized algorithms in the field of machine learning. When I first encountered the EM algorithm, I found it surprisingly challenging to find a tutorial that not only provides an intuitive understanding of its purpose but also offers a thorough theoretical analysis of why it works. This, of course, is no easy feat. On the surface, the algorithm appears deceptively simple, consisting of just two steps. However, beneath this simplicity lies a complex mathematical foundation that makes it difficult to fully grasp.

- The latent variable model is utilized to estimate the Maximum Likelihood Estimation (MLE) and Maximum a Posteriori (MAP) parameters for latent variables.
- It is employed to predict parameter values in situations where data is missing or unobservable, continuously refining these predictions until the values converge to an optimal solution.

The EM (Expectation-Maximization) algorithm integrates several unsupervised machines learning techniques, including the k-means clustering algorithm. As an iterative approach, it operates in two distinct phases. In the first phase, known as the Expectation (E-step), it estimates the missing or latent variables. In the second phase, called the Maximization (M-step), the algorithm optimizes the model parameters to better fit the data, thereby improving the model's explanatory power. The second mode is known as the maximization-step or M-step in Figure 3.8.

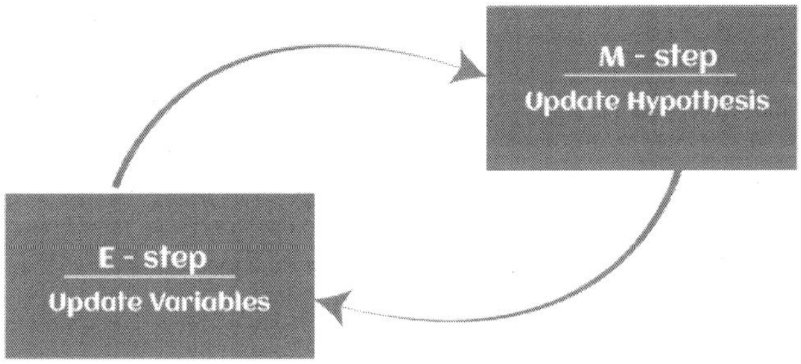


**Figure 3.8: show the process of E-step and M-step variable. Source (https://www.specialsale.store)**

**Expectation step (E - step):** It involves the estimation or prediction of all missing values in the dataset, ensuring that once this process is complete, no missing values remain.

**Maximization step (M - step):** This step entails utilizing estimated data during the E-step and subsequently updating the model parameters accordingly.

Repeat E-step and M-step until the convergence of the values occurs.

The main objective of the EM algorithm is to leverage the observed data from the dataset to infer the missing values of the latent variables, and then utilize these inferred values to iteratively update the parameter estimates during the M-step.

## Convergence in the EM algorithm

Convergence in probability refers to a specific situation where two or more random variables exhibit minimal differences in their probabilities. In simpler terms, it occurs when the values of the given variables closely align or converge with one another.

### *Steps in EM Algorithm*

The EM algorithm is completed mainly in 4 steps, which include Initialization Step, Expectation Step, Maximization Step, and convergence Step in Figure 3.9. These steps are explained as follows:

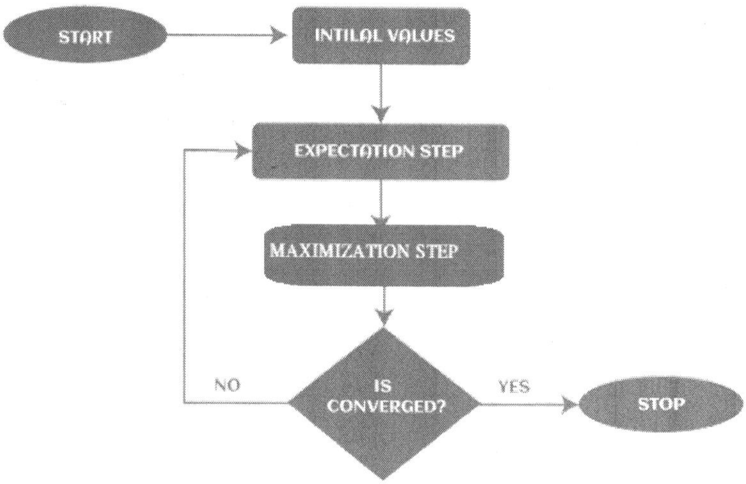


**Figure 3.9:Steps in EM Algorithm.**

*Source (https://www.specialsale.store)*

**1st Step:** Initializing the parameter values is the first step. Additionally, incomplete observed data is supplied to the system under the presumption that the data comes from a particular model.

**2nd Step:** This step, called Expectation or E-Step, uses the observed data to estimate or guess the values of the missing or incomplete data. Additionally, the variables are mainly updated by E-step.

**3rd Step:**This step, called Maximization or M-step, is where we update the parameter values using all of the data from the second step. Additionally, M-step mainly modifies the hypothesis.

**4th step:**The final step is to determine whether or not the values of the latent variables are convergent. Close the process if it returns "yes"; if not, continue from step 2 until convergence is achieved.

## Gaussian Mixture Models (GMM)

The Gaussian Mixture Model (GMM) is a probabilistic model commonly used for clustering and density estimation tasks. It assumes that the data is generated from a mixture of several Gaussian distributions, each corresponding to a distinct cluster. Unlike hard clustering methods, GMM assigns probabilities to data points, allowing them to belong to multiple clusters simultaneously, offering a more nuanced approach to categorization. GMM is extensively applied in machine learning and pattern recognition, particularly when the underlying data exhibits multiple modes or distributions.At its core, the Gaussian Mixture Model operates on the assumption that complex, multi-modal data distributions can be approximated by combining simpler Gaussian distributions. Each of these Gaussian components represents a separate cluster within the data. The model assigns parameters to each componentsuch as the mean, variance, and weightthat characterize the cluster. The mean represents the central tendency of the data points in the cluster, while the variance measures the spread or dispersion of the points around the mean. A smaller variance indicates that the data points are tightly grouped around the mean, while a larger variance suggests a broader, more dispersed cluster.

The weight of each Gaussian component is particularly significant in a GMM. It represents the proportion of the dataset that belongs to that particular Gaussian component, reflecting the cluster's prominence in the overall mixture. Higher weights indicate that a larger portion of the data is associated with that specific component, highlighting its importance within the model.This triad of parametersmean; variance, and weightprovides GMM with remarkable flexibility, allowing it to model a wide range of data distributions, whether the clusters are tightly packed, widely spread, or overlapping. One of the key strengths of GMM lies in its ability to compute the probability of each data point belonging to a particular cluster, a process known as 'soft clustering.' In contrast to hard clustering methods like K-Means, which assign each data point to only one cluster, GMM offers a probabilistic approach, where a data point can have varying degrees of membership in multiple clusters.

In many real-world scenarios, datasets can be effectively modeled by Gaussian distributions (both univariate and multivariate). Therefore, it is both intuitive and natural to assume that the clusters within the data come from different Gaussian distributions, and GMM seeks to model the dataset as a mixture of several such distributions. This is the fundamental principle behind the Gaussian Mixture Model, which combines the simplicity of Gaussian distributions with the complexity of multi-modal data.

The probability density function (PDF) of a Gaussian distribution in one dimension is expressed as.

$$G(X \mid \mu, \sigma) = \frac{1}{\sigma\sqrt{2\pi}} e^{-\frac{(x-\mu)^2}{2\sigma^2}}$$

where μ and $\mu^2$ are respectively the mean and variance of the distribution. For Multivariate (let us say d-variate) Gaussian Distribution, the probability density function is given by:

$$G(X \mid \mu, \Sigma) = \frac{1}{\sqrt{(2\pi)^d|\Sigma|}} \exp\left(-\frac{1}{2}(X-\mu)^T\Sigma^{-1}(X-\mu)\right)$$

Here, μ represents a d-dimensional vector that indicates the mean of the distribution, while Σ is the d × d covariance matrix that captures the distribution's variance and relationships between its components.

## Initial Derivations

First, let's suppose let want to know what is the probability that a data point $x_n$ comes from Gaussian k. It can express this as:

$$P(z_{nk} = 1|X_n)$$

Given a data point xx, we aim to determine the probability that it originated from Gaussian distribution k. In this context, z is a latent variable that can take only two values: it is 1 if x was generated by Gaussian k, and 0 otherwise. While we do not directly observe the z variable in practice, understanding its probability distribution is crucial for estimating the parameters of the Gaussian mixture, as we will explore in more detail later.

Likewise, we can state the following:

$$\pi_k = p(z_k = 1)$$

This implies that the probability of observing a data point originating from Gaussian component k is directly proportional to the mixing coefficient associated with that Gaussian. This is intuitive, as a larger Gaussian would naturally lead to a higher expected probability. Now, let z represent the set of all possible latent variables:

$$\mathbf{z} = \{z_1, \ldots, z_K\}$$

Please be informed in advance that each z occurs independently of the others and can only take the value of one whenk corresponds to the cluster from which the point originates. Therefore:

$$p(\mathbf{z}) = p(z_1 = 1)^{z_1} p(z_2 = 1)^{z_2} \ldots p(z_K = 1)^{z_K} = \prod_{k=1}^{K} \pi_k^{z_k}$$

It turns out that it is, in fact, the Gaussian function itself! Following the same reasoning, let us definep(z), which can then be expressed as:

$$p(\mathbf{x}_n|\mathbf{z}) = \prod_{k=1}^{K} \mathcal{N}(\mathbf{x}_n|\mu_k, \mathbf{\Sigma}_k)^{z_k}$$

Our initial goal was to determine the probability of z given our observation x. As it turns out, the equations we've just derived, in conjunction with Bayes' rule, will enable us to calculate this probability. Leveraging the product rule of probabilities, we can deduce that.,

$$p(\mathbf{x}_n, \mathbf{z}) = p(\mathbf{x}_n|\mathbf{z})p(\mathbf{z})$$

Well, it appears that we are moving forward at this point. We have just discovered the operands on the right. Some of you might be expecting that in order to obtain the probability we ultimately require, we will apply the Bayes rule. But first, rather than p $(x_n, z)$, we will need $p(x_n)$. So, how do we eliminate Z in this situation? You guessed correctly. Being marginalized! All we have to do is add up the terms on z, so.

$$p(\mathbf{x}_n) = \sum_{k=1}^{K} p(\mathbf{x}_n|\mathbf{z})p(\mathbf{z}) = \sum_{k=1}^{K} \pi_k \mathcal{N}(\mathbf{x}_n|\mu_k, \Sigma_k)$$

This is the equation that defines a Gaussian Mixture, and you can clearly see that it depends on all parameters that let mentioned previously. To determine the optimal values for these we need to determine the maximum likelihood of the model. We can find the likelihood as the joint probability of all observations xn, defined by:

$$p(\mathbf{X}) = \prod_{n=1}^{N} p(\mathbf{x}_n) = \prod_{n=1}^{N} \sum_{k=1}^{K} \pi_k \mathcal{N}(\mathbf{x}_n|\mu_k, \Sigma_k)$$

The log should be applied to both sides of the equation, just as it was for the original Gaussian density function:

$$\ln p(\mathbf{X}) = \sum_{n=1}^{N} \ln \sum_{k=1}^{K} \pi_k \mathcal{N}(\mathbf{x}_n|\mu_k, \Sigma_k)$$

It only needs to differentiate this equation with respect to the parameters to determine the ideal parameters for the Gaussian mixture, right? It is evident that the second summation is being impacted by a logarithm. It will be very difficult to calculate the derivative of this expression and then solve for the parameters. But first, keep in mind that we were meant to determine the likelihood of z given x. Let's already have everything set up to define this probability's appearance.

From Bayes rule, it knows that

$$p(z_k = 1|\mathbf{x}_n) = \frac{p(\mathbf{x}_n|z_k = 1)p(z_k = 1)}{\sum_{j=1}^{K} p(\mathbf{x}_n|z_j = 1)p(z_j = 1)}$$

It discovered from our previous derivations that:

$$p(z_k = 1) = \pi_k, \qquad p(\mathbf{x}_n|z_k = 1) = \mathcal{N}(\mathbf{x}_n|\mu_k, \mathbf{\Sigma}_k)$$

So, let's now replace these in the previous equation:

$$p(z_k = 1|\mathbf{x}_n) = \frac{\pi_k \mathcal{N}(\mathbf{x}_n|\mu_k, \Sigma_k)}{\sum_{j=1}^{K} \pi_j \mathcal{N}(\mathbf{x}_n|\mu_j, \Sigma_j)} = \gamma(z_{nk})$$

## Auto-Associative Neural Networks

Auto-associative neural networks are a specialized type of neural network where the input and output vectors are identical. These networks are designed to simulate and explore associative processes, effectively mapping input data back to itself. The association in this architecture is achieved through a set of simple processing elements, known as units, which are interconnected by weighted connections. This structure allows the network to recall or reconstruct the input from partial or noisy information, making it particularly useful for tasks like pattern recognition and memory recall.

### Architecture

The AN architecture consists of a five-layer perceptron feed-forward network, which can be divided into two distinct neural networks, each with three layers, connected in series, similar to an autoencoder structure. The network begins with an input layer, followed by a hidden layer and a bottleneck layer, which serves as a crucial component shared between both networks. This bottleneck layer plays a vital role in data compression and topology, while also enabling powerful feature extraction. After the bottleneck layer, the network proceeds with a second non-linear hidden layer, followed by the output layer of the second network, as illustrated in Figure 3.10.

The first network compresses the information from an n-dimensional vector into smaller-dimensional vectors, retaining key characteristic variables that effectively represent the entire process. The second network operates in reverse, utilizing this compressed data to reconstruct the original n-dimensional vector with its redundant measures.

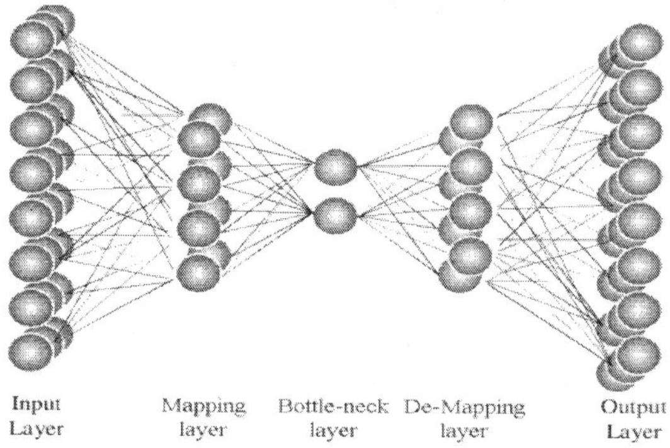


**Figure 3.10:Auto-Associative NN Architecture.**

Source(https://www.cs.rit.edu/~lr/courses/nn/student/Autoassoc.PDF)

### *Input layer*

The input layer is the first layer of the network, tasked with receiving incoming data. Each neuron in this layer corresponds to a specific variable or characteristic from the input dataset. The choice of activation function for this layer depends on the type of data being processed. For instance, a linear activation function is typically employed when dealing with numerical data.

### *Mapping layer*

This layer is the second level of the network and plays a crucial role in transforming the input data into a latent representation within a new dimension. Each neuron in this layer is connected to every neuron in the input layer, and it generates a distinct output that represents a linear combination of the received inputs. Additionally, the activation function applied in this layer is typically nonlinear, such as the sigmoid or ReLU function, which helps introduce complexity and nonlinearity into the model's learning process.

### *Bottleneck layer*

The third layer of the network plays a critical role in reducing the dimensionality of the representation. With fewer neurons than both the input and mapping layers, it functions as a bottleneck that compels the network to learn a more compact and efficient representation of the data. Typically, a linear activation function is employed in this layer, irrespective of the data being processed.

### *Decoding layer*

After traversing the bottleneck layer, the learned representation is passed to the decoding layer, which is essentially a reverse counterpart of the mapping layer. The primary function of the decoding layer is to reconstruct the original input from the latent representation. Consequently, the activation function in this layer must mirror that of the mapping layer to maintain consistency. The process begins with the input layer receiving the raw data, followed by the mapping layer, which learns a latent representation. The bottleneck layer then reduces the dimensionality of this representation, and finally, the decoding layer reconstructs the original input from the compressed latent space.

### *Training*

$$\frac{1}{n}\sum_{i=1}^{n}(y_i - \tilde{y}_i)^2$$

Anomaly detection in predictive maintenance using auto-associative neural networks (AANNs) begins by training the network on a dataset that represents the "normal" or typical behavior of the system. During this training phase, the network learns to compress the input data into a lower-dimensional representation that retains the essential characteristics of the original data. This compact representation is stored in the network's hidden layer, which is then utilized to reconstruct the original input. However, when presented with unusual or anomalous patterns in the input data, the network's learned representation fails to capture the unique features of these outliers. As a result, the reconstructed output for anomalous data will deviate substantially from the original. This discrepancy, or reconstruction error, can be quantified using metrics such as Mean Squared Error (MSE), providing a measure of the degree of anomaly in the data.:

MSE=

Or Euclidean distance:

$$d(x,y) = \sqrt{\sum_{i=1}^{n} |y_i - x_i|^2}$$

Figure 3.11 shows the distances between the original input data and the encoded data after the model has been trained. These distances can then be used for deployment.

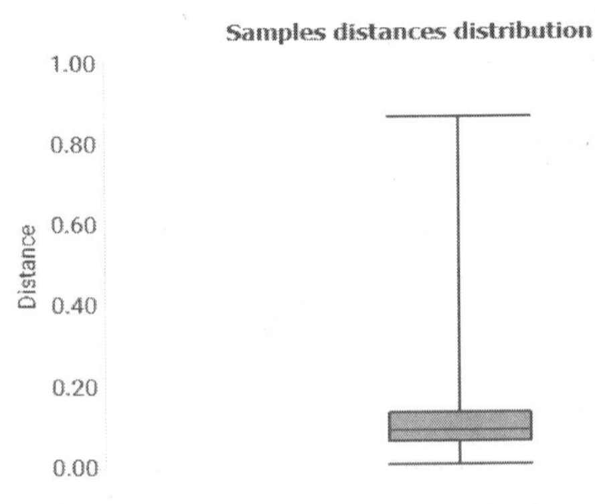


**Figure 3.11: Sample Distance Distribution.** *(Source: neural designer)*

A threshold for acceptable error is established based on normal data. Any new data that generates a reconstruction error surpassing this threshold will be flagged as abnormal.

## *Deployment*

The deployment stage entails feeding new data into the trained model, transforming it into a new representation. The model then evaluates the distances between the encoded input data and the original data to assess whether the new data falls within an acceptable range, as illustrated in Figure 3.12.

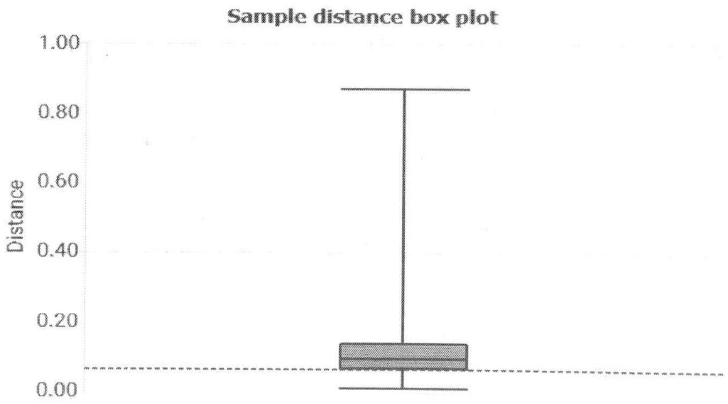


**Figure 3.12: Sample Distance Box Plot.** Source (neuraldesigner)

If the distance surpasses the defined threshold, the input data is classified as anomalous, warranting further investigation. Additionally, the deployment process includes continuous monitoring of the model's performance to ensure its ongoing accuracy. Necessary updates and adjustments are made as needed to maintain precise predictions on new data.

## Summary

Component analysis and clustering algorithms are essential in data science for dimensionality reduction and pattern recognition. Principal Component Analysis (PCA) identifies the orthogonal directions of maximum variance in the data, effectively reducing dimensionality while preserving key information. Linear Discriminant Analysis (LDA) enhances class separability by maximizing the ratio of inter-class to intra-class variance, making it a critical tool for supervised classification tasks. Independent Component Analysis (ICA) focuses on separating statistically independent sources, proving especially useful in signal processing. In clustering, K-means is a simple yet effective algorithm that divides data into predefined clusters by minimizing intra-cluster variance. Fuzzy K-means extends this by assigning degrees of membership to data points, allowing for overlap between clusters. The Expectation-Maximization (EM) algorithm iteratively refines parameter estimates for probabilistic models, often used in conjunction with Gaussian Mixture Models (GMMs) to cluster data into Gaussian-distributed subgroups. These probabilistic methods excel in capturing the complexity of data, though they may require careful initialization to avoid converging to local optima. Autoencoders, a type of auto-associative neural network, merge dimensionality reduction and clustering by learning compact representations of data while retaining essential features. Together, these techniques empower researchers to reveal the structure within high-dimensional datasets, improving interpretability and facilitating informed decision-making across various applications, including image processing, bioinformatics, and more. Mastery of these methods is crucial for addressing complex, real-world problems.

## Exercise Questions

- What is the primary objective of PCA?
- How does PCA reduce dimensionality in a dataset?
- What criterion is used to select principal components in PCA?
- How does LDA differ from PCA in terms of objective?
- What is the role of the scatter matrix in LDA?
- Can LDA be used for dimensionality reduction in an unsupervised setting? Why or why not?
- What is the goal of ICA?
- How does ICA differ from PCA in terms of the assumptions about data structure?
- In the K-means clustering algorithm, how is the "centroid" of a cluster calculated?
- What are some common limitations of K-means clustering?
- How does fuzzy K-means clustering differ from standard K-means clustering?
- What role does the EM algorithm play in fitting GMM?

CHAPTER - 4

# Supervised and Unsupervised Learning With Neural Networks

Artificial Intelligence (AI) and Machine Learning (ML) have emerged as transformative fields in the realm of computer science, enabling computers to mimic human-like intelligence. At the core of machine learning lie two main types of learning: supervised and unsupervised learning. These techniques are the foundation for the functioning of neural networks, which are computational models inspired by the human brain. By learning patterns from data, neural networks make it possible for machines to perform tasks such as classification, prediction, and even complex decision-making. Supervised learning is a type of machine learning where the model is trained on labeled data. This means that for each input in the training set, the corresponding output is provided. The goal is for the neural network to learn the mapping between inputs and outputs, so that it can make accurate predictions on new, unseen data. In supervised learning, the process typically involves two main stages: training and testing. During the training phase, the neural network adjusts its weights based on the errors it makes, and in the testing phase, it evaluates its performance on previously unseen data. Common applications of supervised learning include image recognition, speech recognition, and financial forecasting.

In contrast, unsupervised learning deals with unlabelled data, meaning the output is not provided along with the input. Instead, the neural network must identify patterns, structures, or relationships in the data without explicit guidance. Unsupervised learning techniques include clustering, where the model groups data points based on similarities, and dimensionality reduction, where the model simplifies data by identifying the most important features. This type of learning is particularly useful for data exploration, anomaly detection, and market basket analysis, among other tasks. Unsupervised learning allows the model to learn from the inherent structure of the data itself, making it suitable for large and complex datasets where labelling is impractical. Neural networks, particularly deep learning models, have been at the forefront of both supervised and unsupervised learning due to their ability to automatically extract relevant features from raw data. In supervised learning, deep neural networks (DNNs) can handle large amounts of labeled data, processing them through multiple layers of nodes to identify intricate patterns. In unsupervised learning, techniques like autoencoders and generative adversarial networks (GANs) leverage neural networks to extract meaningful representations and generate new data based on learned distributions.

While supervised learning is highly effective in scenarios where labeled data is abundant, unsupervised learning shines when data is vast, and labelling is time-consuming or impossible. The use of neural networks in unsupervised learning, for instance, can lead to the discovery of hidden patterns that might not be immediately apparent to human analysts. This characteristic makes unsupervised learning an important tool for industries such as healthcare, marketing, and cybersecurity, where uncovering underlying trends in data is crucial.The distinction between supervised and unsupervised learning lies not only in the presence or absence of labels but also in their overall approach to problem-solving. Supervised learning focuses on making predictions based on prior knowledge provided through labeled data, whereas unsupervised learning emphasizes uncovering the structure or distribution inherent in the data without predefined outputs. This distinction leads to different applications and methodologies in neural networks, depending on whether the task requires prediction, classification, or pattern discovery.

As neural networks continue to evolve, the line between supervised and unsupervised learning is becoming increasingly blurred. Semi-supervised learning, a hybrid approach, seeks to combine the strengths of both techniques by leveraging a small amount of labeled data alongside a large amount of unlabeled data. This hybrid approach helps to improve the performance of models when labeled data is scarce or expensive to obtain, offering a balance between the precision of supervised learning and the flexibility of unsupervised learning. The integration of neural networks with supervised and unsupervised learning has revolutionized the way machines interpret and interact with data. Whether it's predicting outcomes from labeled data or uncovering hidden structures in unlabeled datasets, neural networks provide the foundation for solving complex problems across various fields. As research in this domain continues to progress, the development of more sophisticated models and algorithms will only expand the potential applications of both supervised and unsupervised learning techniques, shaping the future of AI.

## Supervised learning

Supervised machine learning relies on labeled input and output data during the model's training phase. In this phase, data scientists typically label the training data in advance, preparing it for use in both training and testing the model. Once the model has successfully learned the relationships between input and output, it can be applied to classify new, unseen data and predict future outcomes. The term "supervised" refers to the need for human oversight during this process, as at least part of the learning requires human intervention in labeling the data. Since the majority of available data is raw and unlabeled, human involvement is essential to accurately label it for supervised learning, a process that can be time-consuming and resource-intensive, as large volumes of labeled data are often needed.Supervised machine learning is frequently used for tasks such as classifying new data into predefined categories or predicting future trends. Models developed with these techniques can recognize patterns and objects, learning the specific features that define them. Predictive models, for example, can be trained using supervised learning to forecast changes in various sectors, such as predicting shifts in housing prices or customer purchase behavior. By understanding the relationships between input and output data, these models can offer reliable predictions even for data they have never encountered before.

***Supervised machine learning is often used for:***

- Classifying different file types such as images, documents, or written words.
- Forecasting future trends and outcomes through learning patterns in training data.

## Unsupervised Learning

Unsupervised machine learning involves training models on raw, unlabeled data to uncover hidden patterns, trends, or structures within the dataset. This approach is often employed to identify underlying relationships or group similar data points into clusters, making it particularly valuable in the initial exploratory phase of data analysis. Unlike supervised machine learning, which relies on labeled data, unsupervised learning takes a more autonomous, hands-off approach. While human intervention is required to set certain hyperparameters, such as the number of clusters, the model can process large volumes of data efficiently without continuous human oversight. Consequently, unsupervised learning is ideal for discovering new insights and revealing previously unseen trends in data. However, due to its minimal human supervision, ensuring the explainability of unsupervised models becomes crucial. Given that most available data is raw and unlabelled, unsupervised learning serves as a powerful tool for extracting valuable insights by organizing data based on common features or detecting underlying patterns, in contrast to supervised learning, which can be more resource-intensive due to the need for labeled data.

**Unsupervised machine learning is mainly used to:**

- Cluster datasets based on feature similarities or segment data into meaningful groups.
- Analyze relationships between various data points, such as generating

automated music recommendations.

- Conduct preliminary data analysis to uncover trends and insights.

## Supervised vs unsupervised learning compared

The key distinction between supervised and unsupervised learning lies in the type of training data used. Supervised learning depends on labeled input-output pairs, where the model learns the relationship between them to predict outcomes for unseen data. During training, the model is refined to achieve accurate predictions based on this labeled data. However, obtaining labeled data can be resource-intensive and time-consuming. In contrast, unsupervised learning operates on unlabelled, raw data. It identifies hidden patterns or relationships within the data, making it ideal for uncovering trends or structures that may not be immediately obvious, as seen in Table 4.1.Ultimately, the two approaches differ not only in the type of data they use but also in their training methods and final applications. Supervised learning is typically applied for predictive tasks, such as forecasting house price fluctuations or analyzing sentiment in text messages, while unsupervised learning is often employed to explore and understand the inherent structure of data. Each approach has its specific strengths based on the type of problem being addressed.

Models are also employed to classify unseen data based on previously learned patterns. In contrast, unsupervised machine learning techniques are primarily used to uncover patterns and trends within unlabelled data. This can involve clustering data based on similarities or differences, or identifying hidden structures within datasets. Unsupervised machine learning is particularly useful in applications such as segmenting customer data for marketing campaigns, as well as detecting anomalies and outliers in various data-driven scenarios. The main differences of supervised vs unsupervised learning include:

**The need for labelled data in supervised machine learning.**

- The problem the model is designed to addresssupervised machine learning is typically employed for classification tasks or making predictions, whereas unsupervised learning is primarily used to uncover patterns and relationships within datasets.
- Resource demands in supervised machine learningtends to be more resource-intensive due to the necessity of labeled data for training the model.
- Challenges in explainability with unsupervised learningcan present greater difficulties in achieving sufficient levels of explainability, as it generally involves less human supervision and guidance during the learning process.

**Table 4.1: Difference between Supervised and unsupervised learning.**

| Feature | Supervised Learning | Unsupervised Learning |
|---|---|---|
| Definition | A type of machine learning where the model is trained on labeled data. | A type of machine learning where the model is trained on unlabeled data. |
| Data Labeling | Requires labeled data (input-output pairs). | Works with unlabeled data (no predefined output). |
| Objective | To map input to output based on given labels. | To find patterns, structures, or relationships in data. |
| Common Algorithms | Linear Regression, Logistic Regression, Decision Trees, Random Forest, Support Vector Machines (SVM), Neural Networks. | Clustering (K-Means, Hierarchical), Principal Component Analysis (PCA), Association Rules, Autoencoders. |
| Examples | - Spam detection (Email classified as spam or not spam).<br>- Fraud detection (Identifying fraudulent transactions).<br>- Image classification (Cats vs. Dogs). | - Customer segmentation (Grouping customers based on behavior).<br>- Anomaly detection (Identifying unusual patterns).<br>- Market basket analysis (Finding associations between items). |
| Model Training | The model learns from past labeled data and predicts future outcomes. | The model discovers hidden patterns and relationships within the data. |
| Type of Learning | Task-driven learning (Guided learning). | Data-driven learning (Self-discovery of patterns). |
| Output Type | Predicts known categories (classification) or values (regression). | Identifies groups or patterns in the data without predefined labels. |
| Complexity | Relatively easier to interpret and implement. | More complex and requires deeper data analysis. |

## Supervised vs unsupervised learning examples

A key distinction between supervised and unsupervised learning lies in the specific problems that each model is designed to address. While both types of machine learning models learn from training data, their strengths are better suited to different applications. Supervised learning focuses on learning the relationship between input and output through labeled training data, making it ideal for tasks such as classifying new data based on learned patterns or predicting specific outcomes. In contrast, unsupervised learning excels at uncovering hidden patterns and relationships within unlabelled, raw data. This makes it particularly valuable for exploratory data analysis, segmenting or clustering datasets, and developing models that reveal how data features interact with one another, such as in automated recommendation systems.

***Examples of supervised machine learning include:***

- Classification, identifying input data as part of a learned group.
- Regression, predicting outcomes from continuously changing data.

***Examples of unsupervised machine learning include:***

- Clustering, grouping together data points with similar data.
- Association, understanding how certain data features connect with other features.

***Examples of supervised learning classification***

A classification problem in machine learning refers to the task of using a model to categorize data into predefined groups or object classes. In this process, the model assigns a class label to each data point based on patterns it learns from training on labeled data. During training, the model is provided with both input data and corresponding output labels, allowing it to identify the features that are most relevant for distinguishing between different classes. Since the model relies on labeled data to learn these associations, classification is considered a supervised learning task. Examples of how classification models are used include:

- Spam detection as part of an email firewall.
- Identifying and classifying objects in an image file type.
- Speech recognition and facial recognition software.
- Automated classification of documents and writing.
- Analysing the sentiment of written language and messages.

There are various kinds of classification problems, and they typically vary based on how many class labels are applied to the data in a real-world setting. The main classification problems include:

## Binary classification

Binary classification refers to a type of model that assigns data into one of two distinct categories or class labels. A common application of binary classification is in spam email detection, where a model is trained to classify incoming emails as either "junk" or "safe." This classification is based on patterns the model has learned to recognize, distinguishing spam from legitimate messages. Binary classification tasks are typically carried out by algorithms like logistic regression, decision trees, and support vector machines:

## Multiple Class Classification

Multiclass classification refers to models that involve more than just the two class labels seen in binary classification. Instead of limiting the possibilities to a binary outcome, multiclass classification encompasses a broad spectrum of potential class labels that can be assigned to the data or object. For instance, in facial recognition software, a model may compare an image against an extensive set of possible class labels, each representing a different individual, in order to accurately identify the person in the image. Multiple class classification is commonly performed by algorithms such as:

- Random Forest
- k-Nearest Neighbors
- Naive Bayes

## Multiple label classification

Multi-label classification refers to a scenario where a single object or data point can be assigned multiple class labels by a machine learning model. In this approach, the model typically generates several outputs, each corresponding to a different label. For example, in image classification, an image may contain multiple objects, and the model can be trained to identify, classify, and label a variety of subjects within a single image. This enables the model to capture the complexity of real-world data, where multiple categories can coexist in a single instance. Multiple label classification is commonly performed by algorithms such as:

- Multiple label Gradient Boosting
- Multiple label Random Forests
- Using different classification algorithms for each class label

## Examples of Supervised Learning Regression

Supervised machine learning models are also widely employed in predictive analytics. Regression, in particular, is often used to enable these models to predict continuous outcomes. Through training on a labeled dataset, the model learns to recognize patterns and relationships between the input data and the corresponding expected outputs. Once the model has identified these relationships, it can accurately process and make predictions on new, unseen data. Regression is therefore used in predictive machine learning models, which could be used to:

- Forecast stock or trading outcomes and market fluctuations, a key role of machine learning in finance.
- Predict the success of marketing campaigns so organisations can assign and refine resources.
- Forecast changes in market value in sectors like retail or the housing market.
- Predict changes in health trends in a demographic or area.

***Common algorithms used in supervised learning regression include:***

## Simple Linear Regression

Simple Linear Regression is a widely-used statistical method for predicting a target variable based on a single input variable. It assumes a linear relationship between the input and the target output. After training a model to capture this relationship, it can be applied to make predictions on new, unseen data. For example, it can be used to estimate a person's salary based on factors such as age and gender.

## Decision Tree Regression

As the name implies, Decision Tree models adopt a tree-like structure, where the model progressively branches out at each decision point. These models are widely used in supervised machine learning for both regression and classification tasks. The dataset is recursively split into smaller, more manageable subsets, helping to identify relationships and correlations between independent variables. The final tree structure can then be utilized to make predictions, providing insights into how new data will likely behave based on the learned patterns.

## Examples of unsupervised learning clustering

Clustering is the process of organizing data points into distinct groups based on their similarities (or differences). By doing so, raw, unlabeled data can be analyzed and categorized according to patterns within the dataset. The number of clusters is typically defined by hyperparameters set by the data scientist. As a key application of unsupervised learning, clustering helps identify underlying trends and groupings in unstructured data. Additionally, it can reveal outliers or anomalous data points that deviate from the established patterns, making it a valuable tool for anomaly detection and gaining deeper insights into the data. Clustering as an approach can be used to:

- Segment audience or customer data into distinct groups within marketing environments to enable targeted strategies.

- Conduct initial exploratory analysis on raw datasets to uncover patterns and understand the clustering of data points.
- Identify outliers and anomalies that deviate from established clusters, ensuring data integrity and accuracy.

***Common approaches to unsupervised learning clustering include:***

## K-means clustering

K-means clustering is a widely used technique for partitioning data into distinct groups. The variable K represents the number of clusters, which is determined by the data scientist. Each cluster is defined based on the proximity of data points to its centroid, the central point of the cluster. A higher K value results in finer, more detailed clusters, while a lower K value produces broader, less specific groupings. This method can be employed to identify both exclusive and overlapping clusters. In exclusive clustering, each data point is assigned to a single cluster, whereas in overlapping clustering, a data point can belong to multiple clusters simultaneously.

## Gaussian Mixture Models

Gaussian Mixture Models (GMM) represent a probabilistic clustering technique where data points are assigned to clusters based on the likelihood of their belonging to a specific group. Unlike K-means clustering, which relies on the distance from a cluster's center to determine membership, GMM uses probability distributions to evaluate the degree of association between data points and each cluster, providing a more nuanced and flexible clustering approach.

## Examples of unsupervised learning association rules

Association refers to the process of uncovering the relationships between different variables, helping to understand how the features of one data point connect with those of others. This involves mapping and interpreting the connections between various data points to reveal patterns and correlations. A prime example of this is in automated recommendation systems on e-commerce platforms or news websites. By utilizing unsupervised algorithms, these systems can analyze user or customer behavior to make personalized product or content suggestions based on the preferences of similar users.

The Apriori algorithm is a widely used method for generating association rules, operating by identifying patterns and trends within a database based on frequency. This technique is particularly effective in scenarios such as analyzing retail product purchases or user interactions with film streaming services. Unsupervised machine learning association rules can be leveraged to uncover hidden relationships and insights from data without the need for labeled outcomes:

- Make product and service recommendations to clients based on their purchasing patterns.
- Based on user behavior or interests, suggest media such as TV shows, movies, or songs.
- Recognize consumer preferences and interests to guide marketing initiatives or e-commerce.

## Neural Network Architectures and Generative Models

Neural network architectures and generative models empower machines to learn from vast datasets and generate actionable insights. These architectures have a broad array of applications across numerous fields, including image classification, object detection, speech recognition, natural language processing, recommendation systems, autonomous driving, and drug discovery. Similarly, generative models are versatile tools with widespread use in areas such as image generation, text synthesis, anomaly detection, data augmentation, medical image analysis, virtual reality, gaming, and data compression. They facilitate the creation of realistic images, coherent and contextually relevant text, anomaly identification, enhanced training datasets, improved medical diagnostics, immersive virtual environments, and efficient data compression. Let's delve deeper into how neural network architectures and generative models operate and revolutionize these domains.

## Neural Network Architectures

Neural network architectures serve as the foundational components of deep learning models. These structures are made up of interconnected units known as neurons, which are systematically arranged in multiple layers. Each neuron receives input data, performs complex mathematical computations, and generates corresponding output signals, facilitating the network's ability to learn and make predictions.

## Main Components of Neural Network Architecture

Neural network architectures are composed of various interconnected components that collaborate to process, analyze, and learn from data. The key components of a neural network architecture include:

**Input Layer:** The input layer is the first layer of the neural network, tasked with receiving and processing the input data. Each neuron in this layer corresponds to a specific feature or attribute of the input, serving as the foundation for subsequent layers to analyze and learn from the data.

**Hidden Layers:** Hidden layers are intermediate layers situated between the input and output layers in a neural network. They carry out complex computations and progressively transform the input data by applying weighted connections. The architecture of these layers, including the number of hidden layers and the neurons within each layer, can vary based on the complexity of the task and the volume of data being processed. This flexibility allows the model to learn intricate patterns and make accurate predictions.

**Neurons (Nodes):** Neurons, often referred to as nodes, serve as the fundamental computing units within a neural network. Each neuron receives input either from the preceding layer or directly from the input layer. It then processes this input by applying weights and biases, performs a computation, and generates an output value through an activation function. This output is subsequently passed on to the next layer, enabling the network to learn and make predictions.

**Weights and Biases:** Weights and biases are key parameters that govern the connections between neurons in a neural network. The weights define the strength and significance of these connections, influencing how information flows between neurons, while the biases introduce a constant value that helps regulate the activation of neurons. These parameters are fine-tuned during the training process to enhance the network's ability to learn and optimize its performance.

**Activation Functions:** Activation functions are specialized mathematical formulas that introduce non-linearities into neural networks, enabling them to model and learn complex patterns. Some of the most commonly used activation functions include the sigmoid function, the rectified linear unit (ReLU), and the hyperbolic tangent (tanh) function. Each neuron applies its respective activation function to the weighted sum of its inputs to generate an output. These functions exhibit distinct behaviors and unique characteristics, contributing to the network's ability to process and transform input data in ways that make it more suitable for capturing the nuances of real-world information. By helping neurons make informed decisions and identify intricate relationships within the data, activation functions empower neural networks to excel at tasks such as pattern recognition and generating accurate predictions.

**Output Layer:** The output layer is the final component of a neural network, responsible for generating the network's predictions or outputs after processing the input data through the network's previous layers. The structure of the output layer is determined by the specific nature of the task at hand. For binary classification tasks, where the objective is to distinguish between two categories (e.g., yes/no, true/false), the output layer typically contains a single neuron. In contrast, for multi-class classification tasks, where the goal is to categorize data into multiple classes (e.g., identifying different objects in an image), the output layer is composed of multiple neurons, each corresponding to one of the possible categories.

**Loss Function:** The loss function quantifies the discrepancy between a network's predicted output and the actual target, serving as a critical measure of its performance during training. It acts as a feedback mechanism that guides the adjustment of the network's weights and biases. For tasks involving numerical predictions—such as estimating house prices based on various features—the mean squared error (MSE) loss function is commonly used. MSE computes the average of the squared differences between the network's predicted values and the true values, providing a clear indication of prediction accuracy. In contrast, for classification tasks, where the objective is to categorize input data into specific classes, the cross-entropy loss function is typically employed. Cross-entropy evaluates the divergence between the predicted probabilities assigned to each class and the actual class labels, helping the network gauge its classification accuracy. These components collectively facilitate the processing of input data, the propagation of information through the network, and the generation of the desired output. Throughout the training process, optimization algorithms adjust the weights and biases to minimize the loss function, thereby enhancing the network's performance and accuracy.

## Types of Neural Network Architectures

**Feedforward Neural Networks (FNNs):** A Feedforward Neural Network (FNN) is the most basic and foundational type of neural network, where data flows in a single direction, from the input layer to the output layer, without any feedback loops. FNNs are widely employed in a variety of tasks, including classification, regression, and pattern recognition, due to their simplicity and effectiveness in handling supervised learning problems.

**Convolutional Neural Networks (CNNs):** Convolutional Neural Networks (CNNs) excel at processing grid-like data, such as images and videos, by leveraging convolutional layers that effectively capture spatial relationships within the data. These layers identify essential features like edges, textures, and shapes, allowing the network to extract both local patterns and hierarchical representations. This capability is particularly beneficial for tasks such as image classification, object detection, and image segmentation, where understanding spatial context and feature relationships is crucial for accurate analysis and decision-making.

**Recurrent Neural Networks (RNNs):** Recurrent Neural Networks (RNNs) are specifically designed to handle sequential data, where the order of inputs is crucial. By leveraging recurrent connections, RNNs enable the persistence of information over time, making them ideal for tasks that require context and temporal understanding, such as speech recognition, language translation, and text generation.

**Long Short-Term Memory (LSTM) Networks:** LSTMs (Long Short-Term Memory networks) are a specialized type of Recurrent Neural Network (RNN) designed to overcome the vanishing gradient problem. This issue occurs when the gradients used to adjust the network's weights and biases become exceedingly small, hindering the network's ability to learn from information that is far back in the sequence. LSTMs address this challenge by incorporating memory cells and gating mechanisms, which enable the network to retain and access crucial information over long time spans. These features allow LSTMs to effectively capture long-term dependencies in sequential data, making them highly effective for tasks that require learning from past contexts.

## Generative Models

A generative model is a type of deep learning model designed to identify hidden patterns within training data, capture its underlying characteristics, and generate new, synthetic data samples that closely resemble the original data. These models function by learning the joint probability distribution between the input data and their corresponding labels or target variables. Labels, in this context, refer to the desired outputs the model aims to predict, while the joint probability distribution encapsulates the statistical relationship between the inputs and their associated labels. Upon training, a generative model becomes proficient in understanding the underlying distribution of both the input data and its labels. This learned distribution acts as a probabilistic representation of the training data, which the model then uses to sample and generate new, realistic data instances.

## Main Components of Generative Models

***The main components of generative models are:***

**Latent Space:** The latent space is an abstract, low-dimensional representation in which a generative model encodes the fundamental features and characteristics of the training data. It effectively captures the underlying structure and variations within the data distribution. For instance, consider a dataset of customer preferences for various product attributes. The latent space could identify and encapsulate the key drivers of these preferences, such as price sensitivity, brand loyalty, or specific feature inclinations, revealing hidden patterns that influence consumer behavior.

**Encoder:** The encoder network transforms the input data into a latent space representation. It compresses and encodes the input into a meaningful, compact form that enables the decoder to either reconstruct the original input or generate new, similar samples. For instance, the encoder might take customer demographic information and purchasing behavior as input, learning to represent these features as latent variables that capture the key factors influencing customer preferences.

**Decoder:** The decoder network, often referred to as the generator, is responsible for reconstructing input data from its latent space representation or generating entirely new data samples. It learns to map the latent variables back into meaningful data points that mirror the distribution of the training data. To illustrate this, consider the example of customer preferences: the decoder could generate personalized product recommendations tailored to individual customers by interpreting their latent preferences, producing novel product options that align with their specific needs and desires.

**Training Data:** Generative models rely on a training dataset that accurately represents the target data distribution. This dataset serves as the foundation for teaching the model to capture and replicate the underlying patterns, relationships, and statistical characteristics of the data. The quality, variety, and comprehensiveness of the training data are pivotal to the model's success in generating realistic and meaningful samples. In the context of customer data, the training dataset might encompass historical customer information, such as demographics, purchase behavior, and product preferences. By learning from this data, the generative model can create new customer profiles, simulate potential customer behaviors, and offer valuable insights into customer trends.

**Loss Function:** The loss function measures the difference between the generated output and the target output, acting as a critical guide during the training process. It provides a quantitative assessment of how accurately the generative model is capturing the underlying distribution of the training data. The choice of loss function depends on the specific architecture of the generative model and the characteristics of the data being generated. For instance, in a recommendation system, the loss function could evaluate the alignment between generated product recommendations and actual customer purchasing behavior, aiming to minimize the gap between recommended products and the items customers ultimately purchase.

**Sampling Mechanism:** Generative models facilitate the generation of new data samples by sampling from the learned distribution. This sampling process involves drawing random samples from the latent space and decoding them into meaningful data points. The mechanism can be fine-tuned to either generate specific types of samples or explore the full diversity within the learned distribution. For instance, this sampling technique could be employed to generate simulated customer profiles or create hypothetical purchasing scenarios, all based on the distribution of customer preferences learned by the model.

**Evaluation Metrics:** Evaluating the performance of generative models is crucial for assessing the quality, diversity, and authenticity of the generated samples. A range of evaluation metrics, including likelihood-based measures, visual inspection, and domain-specific criteria, are employed to rigorously analyze the fidelity, diversity, and coherence of the generated data, ensuring that the models produce realistic and varied outputs aligned with the intended goals.

## Types of Generative Models

There are several types of generative models, but there are two prominent ones that you should be aware of:

**Generative Adversarial Networks (GANs):** Generative Adversarial Networks (GANs) consist of two neural networks: the generator and the discriminator, which engage in a competitive and collaborative training process. The generator network learns to create synthetic samples, while the discriminator's role is to distinguish between real and synthetic data. The generator's goal is to produce samples that are so realistic that the discriminator is unable to tell them apart from real data. Over multiple iterations of this adversarial training, GANs progressively improve their ability to generate highly realistic samples that closely resemble the training data.

For example, imagine you work at a fashion e-commerce company aiming to generate realistic images of clothing items for showcasing new designs. By training a GAN on a dataset of existing product images, the generator can create synthetic images of clothing that appear almost identical to real product photos. This allows the generation of virtual representations of new designs, eliminating the need for costly photoshoots and offering a more efficient way to showcase fresh products.

**Variational Autoencoders (VAEs):** Variational Autoencoders (VAEs) fuse the capabilities of autoencodersneural networks optimized for dimensionality reduction and data reconstruction—with the core concepts of variational inference. They consist of two primary components: an encoder network that maps input data to a lower-dimensional latent space, and a decoder network that reconstructs the original data from this latent representation. By enabling sampling from the latent space, VAEs facilitate the generation of new, synthetic data samples. This is achieved by sampling latent variables and decoding them, which allows for the creation of entirely new data points that follow the underlying distribution of the original dataset.

## Convolution Neural Network

Convolutional neural networks (CNNs) utilize three-dimensional data to perform image classification and object recognition tasks. As a specialized subset of machine learning, neural networks form the foundation of deep learning algorithms. They consist of multiple layers of nodes: an input layer, one or more hidden layers, and an output layer. Each node within the network is connected to others and has an associated weight and threshold. When the output of a node surpasses its threshold, it activates and transmits data to the next layer; otherwise, it does not propagate any data further. Although this discussion centers around feedforward networks, it's important to note that various types of neural networks exist, each tailored to specific applications and data types. For instance, recurrent neural networks (RNNs) are commonly employed for tasks like natural language processing and speech recognition, while convolutional neural networks (CNNs) excel in classification and computer vision applications. Prior to the advent of CNNs, object recognition in images relied on manual, labor-intensive feature extraction methods. In contrast, CNNs provide a more efficient, scalable approach by leveraging linear algebra concepts, particularly matrix multiplication, to detect patterns within images. However, this advanced computational power comes with its own challenges, as training these models often demands high-performance graphical processing units (GPUs).

## CNN Architectures

Convolutional Neural Network consists of multiple layers like the input layer, Convolutional layer, Pooling layer, and fully connected layers in Figure 4.1

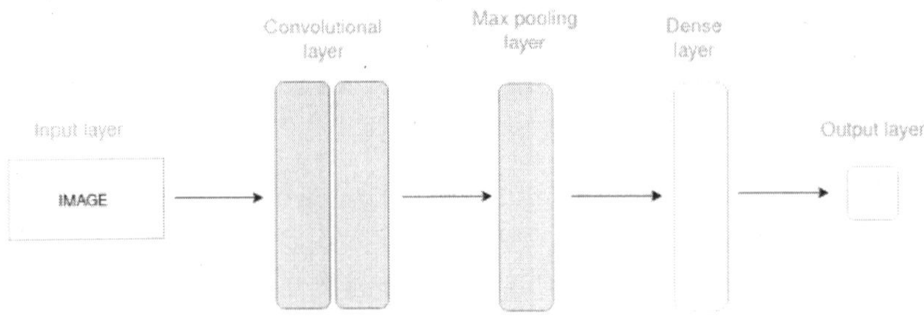


**Figure 4.1: Represent the Architecture of CNN.**

***(Source: geeksforgeeks)***

## LeNet

LeNet, created by Yann LeCun and his team, was one of the pioneering convolutional neural networks (CNNs), originally designed for handwritten digit recognition tasks like those found in the MNIST dataset. Its architecture featured alternating convolutional and pooling layers, followed by fully connected layers, with Sigmoid or Tanh activation functions. LeNet was instrumental in introducing core CNN concepts such as local receptive fields, parameter sharing, and subsampling, laying the groundwork for the development of modern deep learning techniques and applications.

## AlexNet

AlexNet, developed by Alex Krizhevsky, Ilya Sutskever, and Geoffrey Hinton, revolutionized the field of computer vision by winning the 2012 ImageNet competition. Building on the foundation laid by LeNet, AlexNet introduced deeper architectures and innovative techniques, including the use of ReLU activation functions to accelerate training and dropout for improved regularization. By leveraging GPUs to manage the heavy computational demands of its five convolutional layers and three fully connected layers, AlexNet achieved groundbreaking accuracy, marking a pivotal moment in the evolution of deep learning.

## VGG

VGG, introduced by Karen Simonyan and Andrew Zisserman, prioritized simplicity and depth in its design, utilizing small 3x3 convolutional filters to build networks ranging from 16 to 19 layers. This innovative architecture highlighted the power of deep networks, achieving groundbreaking performance on the ImageNet benchmark. Despite its high computational cost, VGG's consistent structure and the use of smaller convolutional filters set a new standard, influencing the design of many subsequent deep learning architecture.

**Table 4.2: Comparison of 5 different types of CNN architecture.**

| CNN Architecture | Main Features | Advantages | Use Cases |
|---|---|---|---|
| LeNet-5 | Early CNN model, designed for digit recognition. 7 layers (2 convolutional, 3 fully connected). | Simple, efficient for smaller datasets. | Handwritten digit classification (MNIST). |
| AlexNet | Deeper architecture (8 layers), uses ReLU activation, dropout, and data augmentation. | Significantly improved image classification performance. | ImageNet classification, object recognition. |
| VGGNet | Uses small 3x3 filters in a deep architecture (16 or 19 layers). | Simpler design, highly consistent performance. | Object recognition, scene parsing. |
| ResNet (Residual Network) | Introduced residual connections (skip connections) to ease training of deep networks. | Can train very deep networks (over 1000 layers). | Image classification, object detection. |
| Inception (GoogLeNet) | Uses inception modules with filters of different sizes, handles different spatial resolutions. | Efficient in terms of computational cost and memory usage. | Object classification, detection, and segmentation. |

### ResNet

ResNet, developed by Kaiming He and his team, addressed the challenge of training exceptionally deep neural networks by introducing residual connections. These connections allowed layers to learn residual functions rather than directly mapping inputs to outputs, significantly alleviating the vanishing gradient problem. As a result, ResNet enabled the training of networks with over 1,000 layers, setting new performance benchmarks on ImageNet. Its pioneering architecture not only revolutionized deep learning but also became a foundational model for the development of modern deep network architectures.

### Inception Network

The Inception Network, pioneered by Christian Szegedy and the Google Brain team, revolutionized computational efficiency by integrating multiple filter sizes (1x1, 3x3, 5x5) within its inception modules. This innovative approach also employed 1x1 convolutions for dimensionality reduction, enhancing both speed and resource efficiency, while incorporating auxiliary classifiers to improve gradient flow during training. Through successive advancements, including Inception-v3 and Inception-ResNet, the network not only achieved remarkable accuracy on ImageNet but also expertly balanced performance with resource utilization, setting a new standard in deep learning architecture.

These architectures represent milestones in CNN development, each addressing specific challenges and pushing the boundaries of deep learning capabilities in Table 4.2.

## Layers in CNN

The superior performance of convolutional neural networks with inputs of images, speech, or audio sets them apart from other neural networks. They have three main types of layers, which are:

- Convolutional layer
- Pooling layer
- Fully-connected (FC) layer

The convolutional layer serves as the foundational building block of a convolutional neural network (CNN). Although it is often followed by additional convolutional or pooling layers, the fully connected layer marks the network's final stage. As the data passes through each successive layer, the complexity of the network increases, allowing it to capture progressively larger and more intricate features of the image. Early layers detect basic features, such as colors and edges, while deeper layers recognize more complex patterns, shapes, and structures. Ultimately, the network synthesizes this hierarchical feature extraction to accurately identify the object in the image.

## Layers in CNN

The convolutional layer serves as the fundamental building block of a Convolutional Neural Network (CNN), where most of the computational operations take place. This layer requires several key components: input data, a filter (or kernel), and a feature map. Let's consider the input as a color image, represented by a 3D matrix of pixels. In this case, the input has three dimensions—height, width, and depth—which correspond to the RGB channels of the image. A feature detector, also known as a kernel or filter, scans across the receptive fields of the image, identifying the presence of specific features. This scanning process is referred to as convolution.

The feature detector is a two-dimensional (2-D) array of weights that encodes specific characteristics of an image. While the size of the filter can vary, a common configuration is a 3x3 matrix, which also defines the dimensions of the receptive field. This filter is applied to a localized region of the image, and a dot product is computed between the filter weights and the corresponding input pixels. The result of this calculation is then stored in an output array. After each operation, the filter shifts by a specified stride, and the process is repeated across the entire image. The collective results of these dot products, derived from the interactions between the filter and the image, produce a feature map (also known as an activation map or convolved feature).

The weights in the feature detector remain constant as it traverses the image, a concept referred to as parameter sharing. While certain parameters, such as weight values, are updated during training via backpropagation and gradient descent, there are three critical hyperparameters that influence the output volume size. These hyperparameters must be determined prior to the start of the neural network's training process. These include:

1. The **number of filters** directly influences the depth of the output. For instance, using three separate filters would generate three unique feature maps, resulting in an output depth of three.

2. **Stride** refers to the distance or number of pixels that the kernel shifts across the input matrix. Although stride values greater than one are uncommon, increasing the stride results in a smaller output size.

3. **Zero-padding** is commonly applied when the filter size does not perfectly align with the input image. This technique sets all elements outside the bounds of the input matrix to zero, resulting in an output that is either larger or of the same size as the original. There are three primary types of padding used in convolutional operations:

- **Valid padding:** No padding is another name for this. If the dimensions are not aligned in this instance, the final convolution is removed.
- **Same padding:** The output layer will be the same size as the input layer thanks to this padding.

- **Full padding:** This kind of padding enlarges the output by appending zeros to the input's border.

After each convolution operation, a CNN applies a Rectified Linear Unit (ReLU) transformation to the feature map, introducing nonlinearity to the model in Figure 4.2.

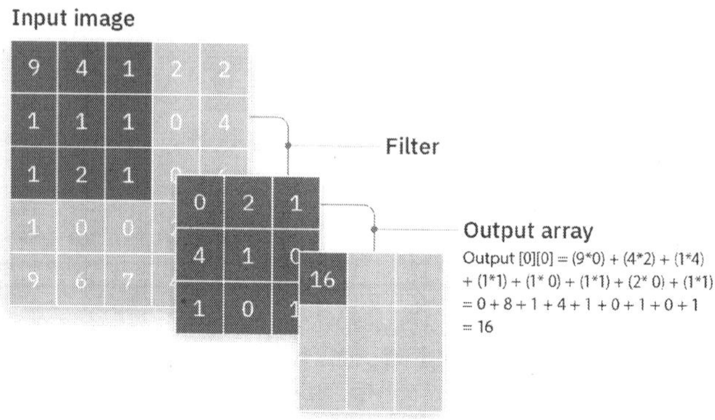


**Figure 4.2: Convolution Operation in a Neural Network.**

***(Source: https://www.ibm.com/topics/convolutional-neural-networks)***

## Additional Convolutional layer

The convolutional layer can follow the initial convolution layer, enabling the structure of the Convolutional Neural Network (CNN) to become hierarchical. In this arrangement, the later layers are able to process the pixels within the receptive fields of the earlier layers. For instance, consider the task of identifying whether an image contains a bicycle. A bicycle can be seen as a composition of individual components—such as the frame, handlebars, wheels, and pedals. In the neural network, each of these components corresponds to a lower-level feature, while the combination of these parts forms a higher-level feature. This creates a feature hierarchy within the CNN. Ultimately, the convolutional layers transform the image into numerical values, which the neural network then uses to interpret and extract meaningful patterns for recognition.

## Pooling layer

Pooling layers, also referred to as downsampling, perform dimensionality reduction by decreasing the number of parameters in the input data. Much like the convolutional layer, the pooling operation moves a filter across the entire input. However, unlike the convolutional layer, this filter does not have learnable weights. Instead, it applies an aggregation function—such as max or average poolingover the values within the receptive field, effectively reducing the size of the input and populating the output array with the aggregated values. There are two main types of pooling:

**Max pooling:** As the filter moves across the input, it identifies the pixel with the highest value and passes it to the output array. Notably, this method is more commonly used than average pooling due to its ability to retain the most prominent features in the data.

**Average Pooling:** As the filter slides across the input, it computes the average value within the receptive field and passes the result to the output array.

Although the pooling layer loses a lot of information, it offers the CNN several advantages. They lessen the chance of overfitting, increase efficiency, and simplify things.

**Activation function:** A ReLU (Rectified Linear Unit) activation function is applied following each convolution operation. This function enables the network to capture non-linear relationships between image features, enhancing its ability to recognize diverse patterns. Additionally, ReLU helps alleviate the vanishing gradient problem, ensuring more effective training and improved performance.

## Fully-Connected Layer

The name "fully-connected layer" precisely reflects its structure and function. Unlike partially connected layers, where the pixel values of the input image are not directly linked to the output layer, every node in the output layer of a fully-connected layer is directly connected to a node in the previous layer. This layer is responsible for classification, utilizing the features extracted by the preceding layers and their various filters. While convolutional and pooling layers typically use ReLU activation functions, fully-connected layers commonly employ a softmax activation function to classify inputs effectively, producing probabilities ranging from 0 to 1.

## Practical Applications of CNNs

Convolutional Neural Networks (CNNs) have transformed the field of computer vision, driving groundbreaking progress across a wide range of real-world applications. Below are several key examples showcasing their practical implementation.

**Image Classification:**Convolutional Neural Networks (CNNs) are widely employed for image classification, where they categorize images into predefined labels or groups. A common application of this technology is the automatic organization of photos on social media platforms, enabling efficient sorting and tagging of user-uploaded images.

**Object Detection:** Convolutional Neural Networks (CNNs) possess the ability to detect and pinpoint multiple objects within an image. This functionality is essential in various retail applications, particularly in shelf scanning, where it plays a critical role in identifying out-of-stock items.

**Facial Recognition:**This is also one of the primary industries where CNNs are applied. For example, this technology can be integrated into security systems to streamline access control by leveraging facial recognition for enhanced accuracy and efficiency.

## Recurrent Neural Network

A Recurrent Neural Network (RNN) is a type of deep learning architecture specifically designed to process sequential or time-series data. It is trained to build machine learning (ML) models capable of making predictions or drawing conclusions based on the patterns observed in sequential inputs. For example, an RNN can be employed to predict daily flood levels by analyzing historical data such as past flood measurements, tide information, and meteorological conditions. Beyond this, RNNs are versatile and can tackle a variety of complex temporal and ordinal problems, including language translation, natural language processing (NLP), sentiment analysis, speech recognition, and even image captioning.

### RNNs work

Recurrent Neural Networks (RNNs), much like traditional neural networks such as feedforward and convolutional neural networks (CNNs), learn from training data. However, RNNs are distinguished by their unique ability to retain "memory" of prior inputs, which influences both current inputs and outputs. Unlike traditional deep learning models, which treat inputs and outputs as independent of one another, RNNs rely on previous elements within a sequence to determine the current output. While future events could enhance the accuracy of predictions, unidirectional RNNs can only consider past inputs, excluding the impact of future data.

To illustrate the workings of RNNs, let's take the idiom "feeling under the weather," commonly used to describe someone who is ill. The phrase needs to follow a specific order to make sense. Thus, RNNs must account for the sequence and position of each word in the phrase to make accurate predictions. Each word in "feeling under the weather" is part of a sequence, where the order plays a crucial role. The RNN tracks the context by maintaining a hidden state at each time step, creating a feedback loop that passes the hidden state forward from one time step to the next. This hidden state serves as a form of memory, storing information about previous inputs. At each time step, the RNN processes the current input (e.g., a word in a sentence) alongside the hidden state from the previous step, enabling it to "remember" earlier data points and use that information to influence the current output.

Recurrent neural networks (RNNs) possess a key feature that sets them apart from feedforward networks: they share parameters across each layer of the network. Unlike feedforward networks, where each node has its own unique set of weights, RNNs maintain the same weight parameters across all nodes within each layer. Despite this parameter sharing, RNN weights are still fine-tuned through the backpropagation and gradient descent processes, ensuring the model learns effectively, including in reinforcement learning tasks. RNNs leverage forward propagation and backpropagation through time (BPTT) to calculate gradients or derivatives, a method tailored to sequence data. While the underlying principles of BPTT mirror traditional backpropagation—training the model by calculating errors from the output layer back to the input layer—BPTT uniquely sums errors at each time step. In contrast, feedforward networks do not need to sum errors since they lack parameter sharing across layers (as illustrated in Figure 4.3).

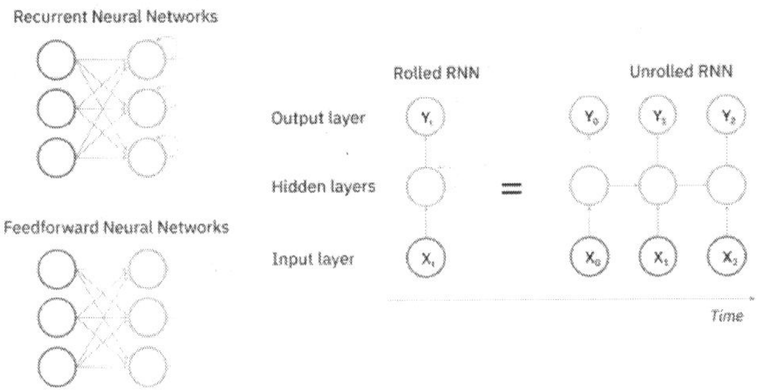


**Figure 4.3: Feed backward versus recurrent neural network.**

*(Source: https://www.ibm.com/topics/recurrent-neural-networks)*

## Common Activation Functions

An activation function is a mathematical operation applied to the output of each layer of neurons within a neural network, introducing nonlinearity that enables the model to learn and represent more complex patterns in the data. Without activation functions, a neural network, including Recurrent Neural Networks (RNNs), would only perform linear transformations on the input, rendering it incapable of solving nonlinear problems. Nonlinearity is essential for learning intricate patterns, especially in tasks like natural language processing (NLP), time-series forecasting, and sequential data prediction. The activation function also regulates the output magnitude of each neuron, ensuring that the values stay within a specified range (e.g., between 0 and 1, or -1 and 1). This normalization helps prevent the values from growing too large or shrinking too small during both forward and backward passes, improving stability. In RNNs, activation functions are applied at each time step to the hidden states, guiding how the network updates its internal memory based on the current input and the past hidden states. Common activation functions, such as the Sigmoid function, are often used to interpret outputs as probabilities or to control gates that determine how much information is retained or forgotten. However, the Sigmoid function is prone to the vanishing gradient problem, which can hinder learning in deeper networks, making it less suitable for such architectures.

The Tanh (Hyperbolic Tangent) function is commonly utilized because it produces output values that are centered around zero, facilitating improved gradient flow and enhancing the model's ability to learn long-term dependencies more effectively.

The ReLU (Rectified Linear Unit) activation function can lead to issues with exploding gradients due to its unbounded nature. However, variations like Leaky ReLU and Parametric ReLU have been developed to address and mitigate these challenges. For a more in-depth understanding of Recurrent Neural Networks (RNNs), refer to our detailed exploration of RNNs in Figure 4.4.

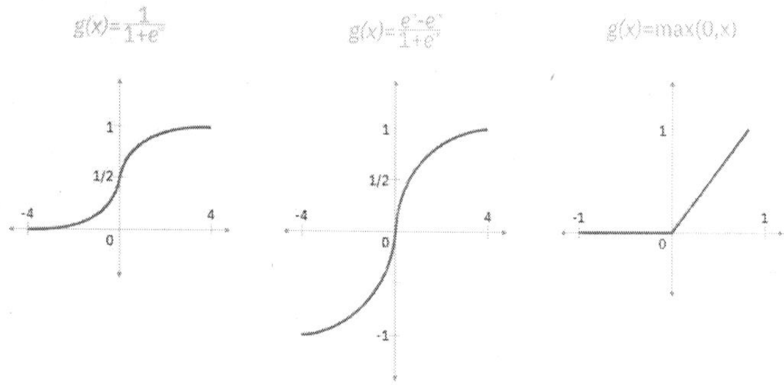

**Figure 4.4: Represent the waveform of sigmoid, Tanh, and ReLu.**

(Source: https://www.ibm.com/topics/recurrent-neural-networks)

## Types of RNNs

Feedforward networks establish a one-to-one mapping between inputs and outputs. While we've previously visualized recurrent neural networks (RNNs) in a similar manner in earlier diagrams, RNNs do not adhere to this constraint. Unlike feedforward networks, RNNs allow for varying lengths in both inputs and outputs. This flexibility makes them suitable for diverse applications, such as music generation, sentiment classification, and machine translation, as illustrated in Figure 4.5. Among the most widely used RNN architectures are several specialized variants, each designed for specific use cases:

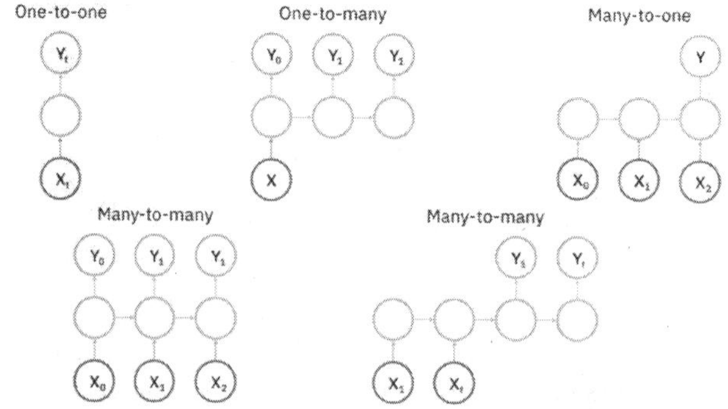


**Figure 4.5: Different types of RNN.**

(Source: https://www.ibm.com/topics/recurrent-neural-networks)

The architecture of a Recurrent Neural Network (RNN) can vary significantly based on the specific problem being addressed. It can range from simple models with a single input and output to more complex ones with multiple inputs and outputs, along with various intermediate configurations. Below are some common RNN architectures that can help you gain a deeper understanding of these variations.

**One To One:**,This is the only pair present. Conventional neural networks use a one-to-one architecture.

**One To Many:** In a one-to-many network, a single input could produce a large number of outputs. For instance, music production uses far too many networks.

**Many To One:** The inputs from different time steps are combined into a single output in this case. These networks, in which a string of words determines the class label, are used in sentiment analysis and emotion identification.

**Many to Many:** Numerous options are available to many. There are three outputs from two inputs. Machine translation systems that translate from English to French or the other way around use many-to-many networks.

## *Standard RNNs*

The simplest form of a Recurrent Neural Network (RNN), where the output at each time step relies on both the current input and the hidden state from the previous time step, is prone to issues like vanishing gradients. This makes it challenging for the network to effectively learn long-term dependencies. However, RNNs excel in tasks with short-term dependencies, such as predicting the next word in a sentence (for short, straightforward sentences) or forecasting the next value in a simple time series. They are particularly well-suited for tasks involving real-time sequential data processing, like analyzing sensor data to detect anomalies in short time intervals, where inputs are processed one by one, and predictions must be made instantaneously based on the most recent data.

## *Bidirectional recurrent neural networks (BRNNs)*

While unidirectional RNNs can only utilize past inputs to predict the current state, bidirectional RNNs (BRNNs) leverage both past and future data, enhancing prediction accuracy. For instance, in the phrase "feeling under the weather," a BRNN-based model can more accurately predict that the second word is "under" by considering the context provided by the final word, "weather." This dual-directional processing enables the model to make more informed and precise predictions.

## *Long short-term memory (LSTM)*

Long Short-Term Memory (LSTM) networks, a widely used architecture in Recurrent Neural Networks (RNNs), were introduced by Sepp Hochreiter and Juergen Schmidhuber as a solution to the vanishing gradient problem. LSTMs were specifically designed to address challenges in modeling long-term dependencies in sequential data. In traditional RNNs, when the information from a distant past state influences the current prediction, the model may struggle to maintain accuracy. For instance, consider the sentence: "Alice is allergic to nuts. She can't eat peanut butter." The context of Alice's nut allergy informs the prediction that she cannot eat foods containing nuts. However, if this information were buried several sentences earlier, an RNN might fail to link the distant context with the current prediction. LSTM networks overcome this limitation by incorporating "cells" in their hidden layers, which are governed by three types of gates: the input gate, the output gate, and the forget gate. These gates regulate the flow of information, enabling the network to retain essential context and make accurate predictions. For example, if gender pronouns like "she" are mentioned repeatedly in previous sentences, the LSTM can adjust the cell state to filter out irrelevant information, maintaining focus on the important contextual cues for prediction.

### *Gated Recurrent Units (GRUs)*

A Gated Recurrent Unit (GRU) is similar to a Long Short-Term Memory (LSTM) network in that it also addresses the short-term memory problem inherent in traditional Recurrent Neural Networks (RNNs). However, instead of utilizing a "cell state" to manage information flow, GRUs rely on hidden states. Additionally, GRUs use two gatesthe reset gate and the update gate— compared to the three gates found in LSTMs. These gates serve a similar function as those in LSTMs, regulating the amount and type of information to be retained. Due to its more streamlined architecture, a GRU is computationally more efficient, requiring fewer parameters than an LSTM. As a result, GRUs are faster to train and often better suited for applications that are resource-constrained or require real-time performance.

### *Encoder-decoder RNNs*

These models are widely employed in sequence-to-sequence tasks, such as machine translation. The encoder transforms the input sequence into a fixed-length vector, known as the context, which encapsulates the essential information. The decoder then utilizes this context to generate the corresponding output sequence. However, the reliance on a fixed-length context vector can create a bottleneck, particularly when dealing with long input sequences, as it may struggle to capture all the necessary details.

## RNN Architecture

One kind of neural network that has hidden states and accepts previous outputs as inputs is called an RNN. They usually go like this: Here's a breakdown of its key components:

**Input Layer:** In this layer, the first element of the sequence data is received. For instance, it may receive the first word as a vector representation in a sentence.

**Hidden Layer:** A collection of connected neurons makes up the hidden layer, which is the core of the RNN. The information from the state of the previous hidden layer is processed by each neuron in addition to the current input. This "state" enables the network to comprehend the current element in context by capturing its memory of previous inputs.

**Activation Function:** This function allows the network to learn intricate patterns by introducing non-linearity. It changes the input from both the previous hidden layer state and the current input layer before sending it on.

**Output Layer:** Using the information that has been processed, the output layer creates the network's prediction. The following word in the sequence could be predicted by a language model.

**Recurrent Connection:** A defining characteristic of Recurrent Neural Networks (RNNs) is the recurrent connection within the hidden layer. This connection enables the network to transfer the hidden state information—essentially the network's memory—into the next time step. It's akin to a relay race, where the baton, representing crucial information about previous inputs, is passed forward to maintain continuity and context throughout the sequence.

## Applications of RNN

Speech-to-text technology converts spoken language into written text, facilitating seamless interaction between humans and machines. It plays a crucial role in accessibility tools, such as real-time transcription for individuals with hearing impairments, and is a key feature in virtual assistants like Siri, Alexa, and Google Assistant, enabling users to control devices with voice commands. This technology has widespread applications across various sectors, including customer service, where it helps call centers analyze conversations, and healthcare, where doctors use it for dictation and note-taking. In education, speech-to-text boosts productivity by transcribing lectures and providing captions for online courses. As advancements in natural language processing and machine learning continue, the technology's accuracy and adaptability to diverse accents and languages are improving. Furthermore, it is essential in the media and entertainment industries, enabling the creation of subtitles for videos and podcasts, which enhances accessibility for a broader audience. Speech-to-text has also become a vital component of hands-free communication systems in smart homes and vehicles, offering both convenience and safety. With breakthroughs in neural networks and edge computing, speech-to-text solutions are becoming faster, more accurate, and capable of offline operation, making them an increasingly ubiquitous and valuable tool in everyday life.

## Image Classification

Image classification is the process of training machines to recognize and categorize objects or patterns within visual data, and its applications are vast and transformative. In healthcare, it plays a crucial role in diagnosing diseases by analyzing medical images such as X-rays and MRIs, enabling early detection and better treatment outcomes. Autonomous vehicles depend on image classification to interpret their surroundings, recognizing road signs, pedestrians, and obstacles, which ensures safe and efficient navigation. In retail and e-commerce, the technology automates product identification and inventory management, optimizing operations and enhancing the customer experience. Additionally, in security, facial recognition and anomaly detection systems use image classification to improve surveillance and strengthen access control measures. Beyond these sectors, image classification supports agriculture through the use of drones and satellites to monitor crop health, and aids social media platforms in content moderation and categorization. As advancements in deep learning and convolutional neural networks (CNNs) continue, classification accuracy has improved dramatically, even in complex or noisy environments. This progress has unlocked innovative applications in areas such as augmented reality, wildlife monitoring, and environmental conservation.

## Time Series Prediction

Time series prediction analyses sequential data to forecast trends and patterns, making it indispensable across various industries. In finance, it is leveraged to predict stock prices, detect fraudulent activities, and optimize investment strategies. Energy companies utilize it to forecast electricity demand, ensuring balanced grid operations and efficient resource management. In healthcare, time series models track patient data, such as heart rate or glucose levels, facilitating early detection of anomalies and providing predictive health insights. Weather forecasting relies heavily on time series prediction to accurately predict storms, rainfall, and temperature fluctuations. In supply chain and logistics, this technology enhances demand forecasting, optimizing inventory management and resource allocation. Manufacturing industries harness it for predictive maintenance, reducing downtime and minimizing costs. With advancements in algorithms like recurrent neural networks (RNNs) and long short-term memory (LSTM) networks, time series prediction has become more sophisticated, allowing real-time applications in personalized marketing, ride-sharing services, and urban planning. These tools are increasingly integral to informed decision-making processes across industries.

## Natural Language Processing (NLP)

Recurrent Neural Networks (RNNs) have made profound advancements in Natural Language Processing (NLP), revolutionizing tasks such as language modeling, machine translation, and sentiment analysis. In language modeling, RNNs excel in predicting the next word in a sequence by effectively capturing contextual information from preceding words, leading to more accurate predictions. Furthermore, specialized RNN variants like Long Short-Term Memory (LSTM) networks and Gated Recurrent Units (GRU) have demonstrated remarkable effectiveness in complex tasks. For example, in machine translation,

RNNs facilitate the translation of sentences across languages by understanding the intricate dependencies between words. Similarly, in sentiment analysis, RNNs assess the sentiment of text by comprehensively considering the order and context of words, enhancing the model's ability to interpret meaning more accurately.

## Time Series Analysis and Forecasting

Recurrent Neural Networks (RNNs) are highly effective in time series analysis, a domain that focuses on data collected sequentially over time. Their ability to model temporal dependencies makes them particularly adept at forecasting future values based on past data. This capability is invaluable in applications such as stock market prediction, weather forecasting, and demand forecasting. In stock market prediction, RNNs analyze historical stock price movements, identifying patterns and trends to forecast future market behavior. Similarly, in weather forecasting, RNNs process historical climate data to predict future weather conditions. In demand forecasting, RNNs leverage past sales data to predict future demand patterns, aiding businesses in optimizing inventory management and resource allocation.

## Speech and Audio Processing

Recurrent Neural Networks (RNNs) have made remarkable advancements in speech and audio processing tasks. In speech recognition, RNNs excel at processing sequential audio data, transforming spoken words into accurate written text. By capturing the temporal dependencies inherent in speech signals, RNNs have significantly improved the accuracy of converting spoken language into text, facilitating the development of applications like voice assistants. Additionally, when paired with techniques such as Mel-frequency cepstral coefficients (MFCC), RNNs enhance speaker identification by effectively analyzing distinctive vocal patterns and variations, enabling the precise identification of individuals based on their unique voice characteristics.

## Image and Video Analysis

Recurrent Neural Networks (RNNs), particularly Convolutional Recurrent Neural Networks (CRNNs), have significantly contributed to the progress of image and video analysis tasks in deep learning. In image captioning, which involves generating descriptive captions for images, RNNs analyze the visual content and produce coherent textual descriptions. For video analysis, RNNs are leveraged for tasks such as object tracking, action recognition, and video summarization. By accounting for the temporal evolution of visual features, RNNs offer a deeper understanding of dynamic content in videos. When combined with Convolutional Neural Networks (CNNs), RNNs form a powerful framework for comprehensive visual interpretation, with CNNs focusing on extracting spatial features, while RNNs capture the temporal dependencies, enhancing overall performance in visual understanding.

## Summary

Supervised and unsupervised learning paradigms form the foundation of the remarkable versatility of Convolutional Neural Networks (CNNs) and Recurrent Neural Networks (RNNs). CNNs, with their specialized multi-layered architecture, are particularly effective at handling spatial data, excelling in tasks such as image classification, object detection, and segmentation. Notable architectures like VGG and ResNet have set industry benchmarks in these areas. On the other hand, RNNs are specifically designed to process sequential data, making them indispensable for applications such as speech-to-text conversion and time series forecasting, where understanding temporal dependencies is crucial. When combined, these two paradigms complement each other to tackle more complex challenges. Hybrid models, such as convolutional RNNs, have emerged as groundbreaking solutions for intricate problems in fields like healthcare, finance, and autonomous systems, highlighting the transformative potential of deep learning across diverse industries.

## Exercise Questions

- What is the primary difference between supervised and unsupervised learning?
- How does labeled data affect the performance of supervised learning algorithms?
- What types of tasks are best suited for unsupervised learning?
- Can supervised learning be used in combination with unsupervised learning? If yes, how?
- What are some common evaluation metrics for supervised learning?
- What is the purpose of the convolutional layer in a CNN?
- How does a pooling layer contribute to the performance of a CNN?
- What are the roles of activation functions like ReLU in CNNs?
- Explain the difference between fully connected layers and convolutional layers in a CNN.
- Name and briefly describe one popular CNN architecture (e.g., AlexNet, VGGNet, ResNet).
- How does an RNN differ from a traditional feedforward neural network?
- What are the key limitations of basic RNNs, and how do LSTMs or GRUs address them?
- Why are RNNs particularly useful for sequential data?
- How is vanishing gradient a problem in training RNNs, and what solutions exist for it?
- Describe an application of RNNs in time series prediction. How does it work?

CHAPTER - 5

# Ensemble Learning and Model Combination Techniques

Ensemble learning refers to the technique of combining multiple machine learning models to achieve better predictive performance than any individual model. The core idea behind ensemble learning is that a group of weak models, when combined, can produce a stronger model with superior accuracy and generalization. This approach capitalizes on the concept of "wisdom of crowds," where the collective decision-making of multiple models leads to better results. Ensemble methods are widely used in various fields such as finance, healthcare, marketing, and more, as they offer improved robustness, accuracy, and reliability. There are several techniques within ensemble learning, the most commonly used being bagging, boosting, and stacking. Bagging (Bootstrap Aggregating) is a method where multiple models are trained independently on different subsets of the data, and their predictions are averaged or voted upon. This reduces the variance of the model and is particularly useful for high-variance, low-bias models like decision trees. Random Forest is a well-known example of a bagging technique, where multiple decision trees are created from random subsets of the data, and their predictions are aggregated for final decision-making.

Boosting is another popular ensemble technique that aims to improve the performance of weak models by focusing on the errors made by previous models. In boosting, models are built sequentially, with each subsequent model correcting the mistakes of the previous one. The final prediction is made by combining the weighted predictions of all the models. Algorithms such as AdaBoost, Gradient Boosting, and XGBoost are examples of boosting methods, known for their ability to turn weak learners into strong predictors, often used in competitions due to their high predictive power.Stacking, or stacked generalization, is a more advanced ensemble technique where multiple models (often of different types) are trained on the same data, and their predictions are combined using another model, known as a meta-learner or a second-level model. The meta-learner learns how to best combine the predictions of the individual base models, usually through methods like linear regression, decision trees, or other machine learning techniques. Stacking can handle complex relationships and often results in superior performance when compared to bagging and boosting.

The effectiveness of ensemble learning and model combination techniques is largely attributed to their ability to handle a variety of issues that may affect individual models, such as overfitting, bias, and variance. By combining models with different strengths and weaknesses, ensemble methods are more likely to produce robust, generalizable results. Furthermore, ensemble methods often reduce the risk of relying on a single model, which may perform poorly in certain situations or be prone to overfitting. Ensemble learning and model combination techniques have become crucial tools in the machine learning practitioner's toolkit. Whether it's bagging, boosting, or stacking, these methods allow practitioners to enhance the performance of their models, providing more accurate, stable, and reliable results. Given their proven success in a wide range of applications, ensemble techniques continue to be an active area of research and development, pushing the boundaries of what machine learning models can achieve.

## Ensemble Learning Works

The core principle of ensemble learning is based on the concept of the "wisdom of crowds," which posits that the collective judgment of a group is often more accurate than that of any individual within the group. In the realm of machine learning, this idea translates to the notion that aggregating the predictions of multiple models can yield more reliable and accurate outcomes than depending on a single model alone. There are several reasons why ensemble learning works:

**Diversity:** Ensemble learning flourishes when there is diversity among the individual models. When models make distinct errors on the same input, aggregating their predictions can effectively neutralize these errors, leading to a more precise overall outcome. By incorporating models with varying architectures, training data, or hyperparameters, ensemble learning harnesses the unique strengths of each model while reducing their individual weaknesses, resulting in a more robust and accurate prediction.

**Bias-Variance Trade off:** Ensemble learning is a powerful technique that addresses the bias-variance trade-off, a core challenge in machine learning. Models with high bias typically underfit the data, while those with high variance are prone to overfitting. By leveraging ensemble methods, we can combine multiple models, each with distinct bias-variance characteristics, to strike a more optimal balance. For instance, aggregating high-bias models helps lower the overall bias, while merging high-variance models can effectively reduce variance, resulting in improved generalization and model performance.

**Robustness:** Ensemble learning enhances prediction robustness by mitigating the effects of noise, outliers, and adversarial attacks. By combining the outputs of multiple models, it effectively reduces the influence of individual model errors, leading to more stable, consistent, and reliable predictions. This capability is especially crucial in real-world applications, where data can be noisy or vulnerable to adversarial manipulation.

### Many models versus one

Each model training algorithm is influenced by various factors, such as training data, hyperparameters, and other variables, which collectively impact the model's overall error. As a result, a single algorithm can generate different models, each with distinct levels of bias, variance, and irreducible error. By combining multiple diverse models, ensemble algorithms can reduce the total error rate while preserving the unique complexities and advantages of each individual model, such as a lower bias for specific data subsets. Research indicates that the greater the diversity among the models in an ensemble, the more accurate the final ensemble model tends to be. Ensemble learning can address challenges like overfitting in regression problems without sacrificing model bias. In fact, studies show that ensembles made up of diverse, under-regularized modelsthose that overfit their training dataoften outperform individual regularized models. Additionally, ensemble learning techniques can tackle issues related to high-dimensional data, offering an effective alternative to dimensionality reduction methods.

## Model Combination Schemes

### Max Voting

The max voting method is commonly employed for classification tasks. In this approach, multiple models make predictions for each data point, with each model providing a "vote" on the outcome. The final prediction is determined by the majority votei.e., the prediction that receives the most votes from the models. To illustrate, imagine you asked five colleagues to rate your movie on a scale of 1 to 5. If three colleagues rate it a 4 and two rate it a 5, the majority rating of 4 would be selected as the final score. Essentially, this method involves taking the mode of all the individual predictions, as demonstrated in Table 5.1. The result of max voting would look something like this:

**Table 5.1: Max voting method for 1 to 5 Colleague.**

| Colleague 1 | Colleague 2 | Colleague 3 | Colleague 4 | Colleague 5 | Final rating |
|---|---|---|---|---|---|
| 5 | 4 | 5 | 4 | 4 | 4 |

#### *Averaging*

Similar to the max voting technique, where multiple predictions are generated for each data point, the averaging method involves aggregating predictions from all models to derive a final outcome, as shown in Table 5.2. This approach calculates the mean of the predictions across all models and uses it to determine the final prediction. Averaging is applicable in both regression problems, where the goal is to predict continuous values, and classification problems, where it is used to estimate probabilities. For instance, in the example below, the averaging method would compute the average of all predicted values to arrive at the final result.

i.e. (5+4+5+4+4)/5 = 4.4

**Table 5.2: Individual ratings provided by five colleagues and the final average rating.**

| Colleague 1 | Colleague 2 | Colleague 3 | Colleague 4 | Colleague 5 | Final rating |
|---|---|---|---|---|---|
| 5 | 4 | 5 | 4 | 4 | 4.4 |

### *Weighted Average*

This method is an extension of the averaging approach, where each model is assigned a specific weight to indicate its relative importance in the prediction process. For example, if two of your colleagues are experts in a particular field while the others lack relevant experience, the responses from these two experts would be given greater weight in the final decision, as illustrated in Table 5.3.

The result is calculated as [(5*0.23) + (4*0.23) + (5*0.18) + (4*0.18) + (4*0.18)] = 4.41.

**Table 5.3:Individual weights and ratings provided by five colleagues**

<table>
<tr><th>Colleague 1</th><th>Colleague 2</th><th>Colleague 3</th><th>Colleague 4</th><th>Colleague 5</th><th colspan="2">Final rating</th></tr>
<tr><td>weight</td><td>0.23</td><td>0.23</td><td>0.18</td><td>0.18</td><td colspan="2">0.18</td></tr>
<tr><td>rating</td><td>5</td><td>4</td><td>5</td><td>4</td><td>4</td><td>4.41</td></tr>
</table>

## Voting Technique: A Glimpse

Voting is a key technique in ensemble learning, where the predictions from multiple models are combined to produce a final, more accurate prediction. The two primary forms of voting used in ensemble methods are hard voting, which relies on a majority rule for classification, and soft voting, where the predicted probabilities are averaged to determine the final outcome.

### *Hard Voting*

Hard voting, often referred to as majority voting, is a straightforward ensemble method where the predictions of each base model are counted, and the class with the highest number of votes is chosen as the final prediction. This technique is particularly effective for classification tasks, where the classes are distinct, mutually exclusive, and discrete. Let's discuss this with an example.

Suppose the task is to determine whether an email is spam or not, which is a binary classification problem. In this case, the two classes for classification are "Spam" (the negative class) and "Not Spam" (the positive class). To tackle this problem, we can utilize various algorithms to classify the emails. Let's assume we have applied five different models to classify the emails, and the resulting probabilities from each model are shown in Table 5.4 below:

**Table 5.4: The five different models to classify the classes.**

| Classifiers | Spam (y = 0) | Not Spam (y = 1) | Result |
|---|---|---|---|
| Classifier 1 | 56% | 44% | Spam |
| Classifier 2 | 49% | 51% | Not Spam |
| Classifier 3 | 60% | 40% | Spam |
| Classifier 4 | 45% | 55% | Not Spam |
| Classifier 5 | 39% | 61% | Not Spam |

***Source(https://medium.com)***

In this case, three classifiers out of five chose that the email was not spam. However, the email was marked as spam by two out of five people.

Based on the hard voting algorithm, the class that accumulates the highest number of votes is determined as the final prediction, as illustrated in Figure 5.1. Therefore, when the data is processed through the hard voting mechanism, it will classify spam as benign.

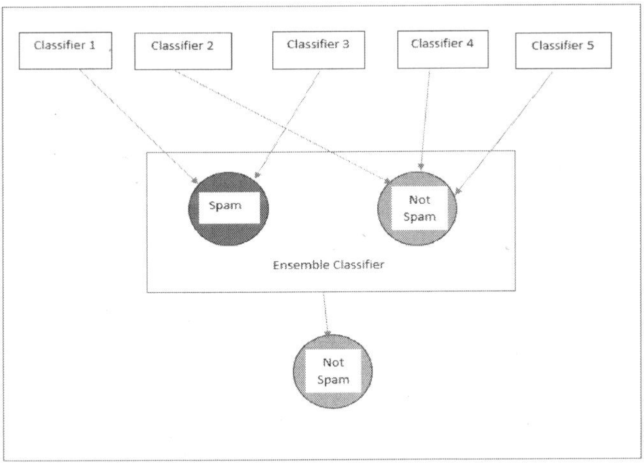


**Figure 5.1:Illustrates an Ensemble Classifier system.(Source: https:// medium.com)**

### *Soft Voting*

Soft voting, also known as weighted voting, involves considering the probability scores for each class from every base model and computing the weighted average of these probabilities to determine the final prediction. In this process, the average probability for each class is calculated, and the class with the highest weighted probability is selected as the winner. This method is applicable to both classification and regression tasks. Now, let's apply the soft voting mechanism to the email classification problem. To implement soft voting, we will compute the average probability score for each class across all models and choose the class with the highest average probability as the final prediction. Below is the step-by-step calculation:

Average Probability for "spam" class: (0.56 + 0.49 + 0.6 + .45 + .39) / 5 = 0.498

Average Probability for "Not spam" class: (0.44 + 0.51 + 0.4 + .55 + .61) / 5 = 0.502

Since the average probability for "Not spam" (0.502) exceeds that for "spam" (0.498), the soft voting ensemble model would classify the email as "Not spam."

In this example, soft voting enables us to harness the probability scores from each individual base model, facilitating a more nuanced decision-making process that taps into the collective expertise of all models. By considering the confidence level of each model, it generates a more refined prediction, which can significantly enhance overall performance and accuracy in real-world scenarios, as illustrated in Figure 5.2.

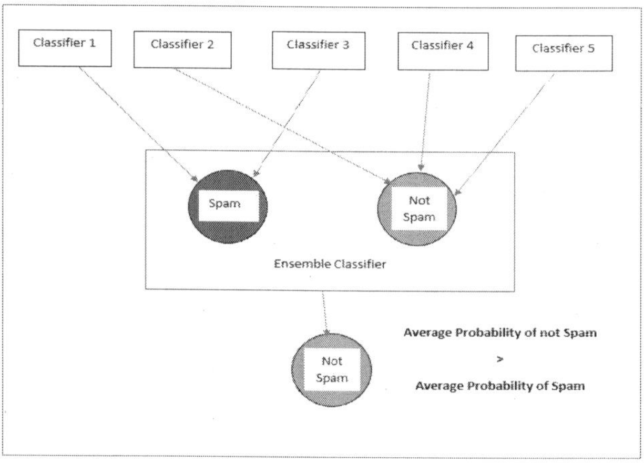


**Figure 5.2:Illustrates an Ensemble Classifier approach based on the average probabilities of predictions. Source (https://medium.com)**

## Voting-Error-Correcting Output Codes

Machine learning algorithms, such as logistic regression and support vector machines, are inherently designed for binary classification tasks, where only two classes are considered. To apply these models to multi-class (more than two classes) problems, they must either be adapted or substituted with alternative techniques. The Error-Correcting Output Codes (ECOC) method offers a solution by transforming a multi-class classification task into multiple binary classification problems, enabling the use of native binary classifiers directly. Unlike the one-vs-rest or one-vs-one strategies, which decompose multi-class problems into a fixed number of binary tasks, the ECOC technique encodes each class as a combination of an arbitrary number of binary classifiers. By utilizing an overdetermined representation, where additional classifiers are included, the technique enhances the model's ability to correct errors, ultimately improving predictive performance.

- Error-Correcting Output Codes (ECOC) is a powerful technique that allows binary classification models to be applied effectively to multi-class classification problems, enhancing their predictive capability.
- This guide demonstrates how to fit, evaluate, and utilize error-correcting output code classification models to make accurate predictions on multi-class datasets.
- Learn how to fine-tune and assess the performance of different hyperparameter settings, specifically the number of bits per class, when using error-correcting output codes for classification tasks.

Here is a brief explanation of how VEC-OC works:

**Multiple Classifiers:** VEC-OC involves the training of multiple classifiers, each of which is typically weak on its own, meaning they may not be highly accurate individually. These classifiers can either be the same type with variations in their training parameters or entirely different models, each contributing to the overall decision-making process.

**Error-Correcting Code:** Each class label is assigned a unique binary code, carefully designed to minimize the impact of classification errors. If a classifier incorrectly predicts a label, the system ensures that other classifiers can correct the mistake. This is achieved by assigning binary codes that are sufficiently distinct from one another, meaning they differ in multiple bits, providing a robust error-correction mechanism.

**Voting Mechanism:** After the classifiers generate their predictions (or votes), these are combined into a final decision. This prediction is usually determined by a majority vote or another aggregation method. By leveraging the redundancy of multiple classifiers, the system increases the probability of correctly identifying the right class, even if one or more classifiers make mistakes. This collective approach enhances the overall accuracy and robustness of the system.

**Error Correction:** When some classifiers make incorrect predictions (errors), the error-correcting properties of the code help ensure that the majority of votes remain accurate, resulting in a more precise final classification. This is especially valuable when individual classifiers tend to make mistakes but can still provide reliable outcomes when aggregated.

## Theoretical Foundations of ECOC

The theoretical foundation of Error Correcting Output Codes (ECOC) is rooted in error-correcting codes, which are integral to digital communication for detecting and correcting errors. In machine learning, ECOC leverages these codes to construct a resilient and reliable classification system, enhancing the model's ability to handle complex classification tasks and improving its robustness against misclassifications.

**Error-Correcting Codes:** Error-correcting codes are sophisticated mathematical constructs designed to introduce redundancy into data, enabling the detection and correction of errors during transmission or storage. Notable examples include Hamming codes and Reed-Solomon codes, which are specifically engineered to identify and correct a predetermined number of errors. The error correction capacity of these codes is determined by factors such as the length of the code and the level of redundancy incorporated.

**ECOC in Machine Learning:** In ECOC (Error-Correcting Output Codes), each class in a multi-class classification problem is assigned a distinct binary code, referred to as a codeword. These codewords are organized into a code matrix, where each row corresponds to a class, and each column represents a binary classifier. The binary classifiers are trained to differentiate between the various columns of the code matrix, effectively enabling the classification of data by interpreting the relationships between the codewords.

## Types of ECOC

There are various ECOC variations, each with unique properties and uses.

**One-vs-All (OvA):** In the One-vs-All approach, each individual class is compared against all other classes, resulting in a binary classification task for each class. This produces a code matrix where each column corresponds to a class, with the target class labeled as 1 and all others as -1. While this method is straightforward and easy to implement, it may not always provide the best performance, particularly for complex or imbalanced problems.

**One-vs-One (OvO):** In the One-vs-One approach, every pair of classes is compared individually, generating a code matrix where each column corresponds to a binary classifier for a specific class pair. While this method can offer higher accuracy, it also necessitates the training of a larger number of classifiers.

**Dense and Sparse Codes:** Dense codes employ a greater number of binary classifiers, which enhances error correction robustness but leads to a higher computational cost. In contrast, sparse codes utilize fewer classifiers, which reduces computational expenses, though it may come at the cost of some robustness in error correction.

## Applications of ECOC

### *Image Classification*

ECOC has become widely utilized in image classification tasks, particularly in scenarios where distinguishing between multiple classes is difficult due to the overlap between classes and the inherent variations within each class.

***Example: Handwritten Digit Recognition***

The MNIST dataset, which consists of images of handwritten digits (0-9), can benefit from the application of Error-Correcting Output Codes (ECOC) to enhance classification accuracy. In this approach, each digit is assigned a unique binary code, and a series of binary classifiers are trained to distinguish between different digit subsets. For example, one classifier may differentiate between even and odd digits, while another might separate digits less than 5 from those greater than or equal to 5. By combining the outputs of these multiple classifiers, ECOC improves the overall accuracy and robustness of digit recognition.

### *Text Classification*

In natural language processing, ECOC (Error-Correcting Output Codes) enhances text classification by decomposing the complex task of categorizing text into a series of simpler binary classification problems, thereby improving accuracy and efficiency.

#### *Example: News Article Classification*

Consider a scenario where the goal is to categorize news articles into distinct groups such as sports, politics, technology, and entertainment. The Error-Correcting Output Code (ECOC) method can be leveraged to create a series of binary classifiers, each designed to differentiate between pairs of categories or groups. For instance, one classifier could distinguish between sports and non-sports articles, while another may separate politics from non-politics articles. By aggregating the predictions of these binary classifiers, the overall classification accuracy for categorizing the news articles is significantly improved, leading to more precise and reliable results.

### *Bioinformatics*

ECOC (Error-Correcting Output Codes) is widely used in bioinformatics for tasks such as gene expression classification, where accurately distinguishing between different biological states or conditions is essential for understanding complex biological processes.

#### *Example: Cancer Type Classification*

In the field of cancer genomics, ECOC (Error-Correcting Output Codes) can be utilized to effectively classify different cancer types based on gene expression profiles. Each cancer type is represented by a distinct binary code, and a series of binary classifiers are trained to differentiate between various cancer categories. For example, one classifier might focus on distinguishing blood cancers from solid tumors, while another could differentiate between specific subtypes of solid tumors. This ensemble-based approach ensures highly accurate classification, contributing significantly to improved cancer diagnosis and personalized treatment strategies.

### *Speech Recognition*

ECOC (Error-Correcting Output Codes) can be highly advantageous in speech recognition tasks, particularly when it comes to effectively distinguishing between multiple phonemes or words, ensuring greater accuracy and robustness in the recognition process.

***Example: Phoneme Classification***

In speech recognition, accurately classifying phonemes—the distinct units of sound—is essential for effective processing. Error-Correcting Output Codes (ECOC) can be employed to assign unique binary codes to each phoneme, with multiple binary classifiers trained to distinguish between various phoneme subsets. This approach enhances the robustness and precision of phoneme recognition, significantly boosting the overall performance and reliability of speech recognition systems.

## Generating Diverse Learners

The base learners in an ensemble are generated by training individual models on various subsets of the training data or by employing different algorithms, architectures, or hyperparameters. The objective is to cultivate a diverse set of models that each make unique errors or possess complementary strengths. Now that we've covered the foundational ensemble techniques, let's delve into exploring the more advanced methods.

## Stacked Generalization

Stacking, also known as stacked generalization, is a heterogeneous parallel method that embodies the concept of meta-learning. Meta-learning involves training a meta-learner by combining the outputs of multiple base learners. In stacking, several base learners are trained on the same dataset, each utilizing a distinct training algorithm. These base learners generate predictions on an unseen dataset, which are then aggregated and fed into a final model—referred to as the meta-model in Figure 5.3. This meta-model is trained to optimize the final prediction by leveraging the collective insights from the individual base learners.

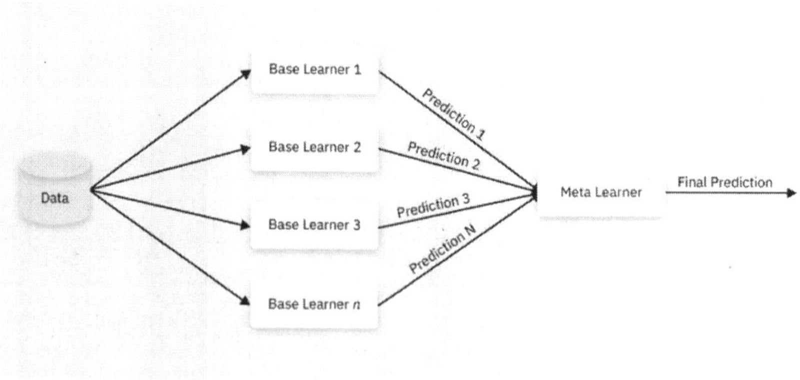


**Figure 5.3:Represents the input data used for training and prediction.**

**(Source: https://www.ibm.com )**

It is crucial to use a separate dataset from the one used to train the base learners when training the meta-learner. Training both the base learners and the meta-learner on the same dataset can lead to overfitting. To avoid this, it may be necessary to exclude certain data instances from the base learner's training set to serve as a test set, which will then be used as training data for the meta-learner. Research literature often recommends employing techniques like cross-validation to ensure that these datasets remain distinct and do not overlap. Similar to bagging, the scikit-learn ensemble module in Python offers various functions that facilitate the implementation of stacking techniques. The key steps in stacking are:

**Base Model Training:,**Train a diverse set of base models on the training data, utilizing various types such as decision trees, neural networks, and support vector machines. These models should be configured with different hyperparameters to capture a wide range of patterns and enhance the overall performance.

**Meta-Features Generation:** Leverage the trained base models to generate predictions on a validation set or through cross-validation. These generated predictions act as meta-features, which are then used to train the meta-learner.

**Meta-Learner Training:** Train a meta-learner model utilizing the meta-features derived in the previous step. The meta-learner is designed to intelligently combine the predictions from the base models, optimizing the final output for more accurate and reliable predictions.

**Prediction:** To generate predictions for new instances, begin by obtaining the predictions from the base models. Then, feed these predictions into the meta-learner, which will process them to deliver the final, consolidated prediction.

Stacking enables the meta-learner to understand the strengths and weaknesses of individual base models and determine the optimal way to combine their predictions. By incorporating a diverse range of base models, stacking captures various facets of the data, leading to enhanced prediction accuracy. The meta-learner itself can be any model capable of learning from the meta-features, such as logistic regression, decision trees, or neural networks. Stacking is especially effective when base models exhibit different strengths and weaknesses. For instance, combining models that are adept at identifying linear relationships with those that excel at capturing complex nonlinear patterns can significantly boost overall performance. However, successful stacking requires careful selection and fine-tuning of both the base models and the meta-learner to prevent overfitting and promote generalization. Overall, stacking offers numerous advantages in machine learning, including improved accuracy and robustness:

**Improved Predictive Performance:** Stacking enhances predictive accuracy by combining the outputs of multiple base models, effectively reducing both bias and variance in the final forecast. This technique enables the meta-model to leverage the strengths of each base model, allowing it to capture complex patterns that individual models might overlook, ultimately leading to improved performance and more reliable predictions.

**Model Diversity:** Stacking encourages the use of diverse base models, which can be trained with a range of algorithms, architectures, and hyperparameter configurations. This variety helps mitigate the risk of overfitting and enhances the stacked ensemble's resilience to different data patterns, resulting in a more robust and generalized model.

**Flexibility:** Stacking is a powerful and flexible technique that can be applied to a wide range of machine learning challenges, such as classification, regression, and time series forecasting. This strategy leverages multiple base models, including decision trees, support vector machines, neural networks, and others, to improve predictive performance by combining their strengths.

**Interpretability:** Stacking also helps uncover the significance of various base models and their individual predictions in shaping the final outcome. By examining the weights or contributions of each base model within the meta-model, we gain a deeper understanding of their relative importance and interpretability, offering valuable insights into how each model influences the overall prediction.

## *Blending*

Blending follows a similar methodology to stacking, but with a key distinction: it relies exclusively on a holdout (validation) set from the training data to generate predictions. Unlike stacking, which combines predictions from multiple models on the entire training set, blending restricts its predictions to the holdout set. These predictions, along with the holdout set itself, are then used to train a final model that is applied to the test set for evaluation.

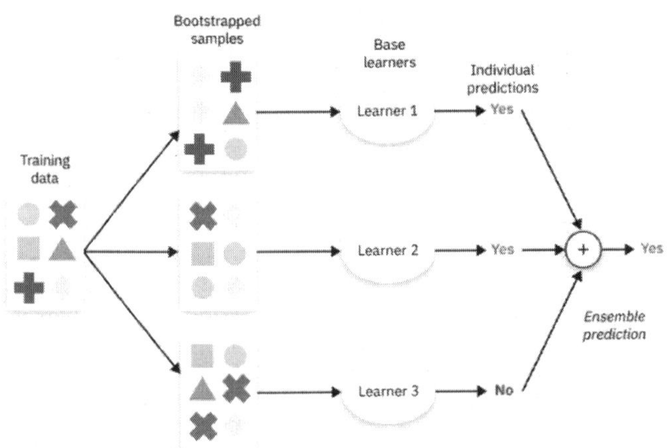


**Figure 5.4:Multiple subsets of the training data created using bootstrapping (random sampling with replacement). (Source: https:// www.ibm.com)**

### *Bagging*

Bagging, also known as Bootstrap Aggregating, is a homogeneous ensemble method that leverages multiple modified versions of a given training dataset to train several base learners using the same learning algorithm. This technique is implemented in Python through Scikit-learn's ensemble module, which includes functions such as the Bagging Classifier. Specifically, bagging employs bootstrap resampling to generate multiple new datasets from a single original training set, thereby enabling the training of several base learners.To elaborate, consider a training dataset containing n examples. Bootstrap resampling creates a new subsample dataset by randomly selecting n data instances from the original set. Some instances may be duplicated, while others may be excluded. These newly formed subsets are referred to as bootstrap samples. By repeating this process x times, x different iterations of the original dataset are created, each containing n samples. Each of these iterations is then used to train a separate base learner, all applying the same learning algorithm. Figure 5.4 illustrates this process.

### *Boosting*

Boosting algorithms are a type of sequential ensemble method that builds models iteratively. While there are several variations of boosting, they all adhere to a similar general framework. Initially, boosting trains a learner on a dataset, denoted asd. This first learner is typically weak, misclassifying many instances within the dataset. Similar to bagging, boosting then samples data from the original dataset to create a new dataset,$d_2$. However, unlike bagging, boosting places higher priority on the misclassified instances from the previous learner. A new learner is then trained on this new dataset,$d_2$. The process continues with a third dataset,$d_3$, which combines$d_1$ and $d_2$, prioritizing misclassified instances from the second learner as well as those where the first and second learners disagree. This iterative procedure repeatsn times to producen learners. Finally, boosting combines and assigns weights to all the learners to generate the final predictions, as illustrated in Figure 5.5.

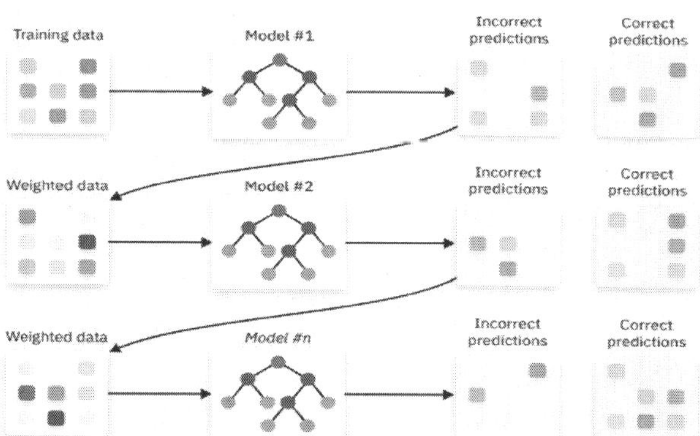


**Figure 5.5:Prediction aggregates results from all models, typically using weighted voting or summation. (Source: https://www.ibm.com)**

When generating a new dataset, boosting algorithms vary significantly in how they rank instances of incorrectly predicted data. This may be demonstrated by the most popular boosting techniques:

## Gradient Boosting

Gradient boosting is an ensemble learning technique that creates a robust final model by combining multiple weak learners, each trained on the same dataset. This method follows a stagewise approach, where the first weak learner does not directly train on the dataset; rather, it simply returns the mean of the target column. The residuals, or errors, from the first learner's predictions are then calculated and used as the target for training the second weak learner. This process is repeated iteratively, with each subsequent learner being trained on the residuals of the previous learner's output, progressively refining the model. The residuals are recalculated at each stage, guiding the next weak learner until the residuals reach zero, signalling that the model has effectively minimized the errors. For gradient boosting, the dataset must consist of numerical or categorical data, and the loss function used to generate residuals must be differentiable to ensure smooth updates during training.

### *XGBoost*

In addition to the traditional gradient boosting technique, XGBoost is another powerful machine learning approach within the boosting family. The full form of XGBoost is *eXtreme Gradient Boosting**, which represents a more advanced and optimized version of the original gradient boosting method. The primary distinction between XGBoost and GradientBoosting lies in its application of regularization techniques. XGBoost incorporates regularization to prevent overfitting, making it a more refined and robust variant of gradient boosting. As a result, XGBoost typically delivers superior performance compared to standard gradient boosting, often leading to faster execution times. Furthermore, XGBoost excels when handling datasets containing a mix of numerical and categorical variables, making it highly versatile in various machine learning tasks.

### *Adaboost*

AdaBoost is a powerful boosting algorithm that operates based on the stagewise addition method, where multiple weak learners are iteratively combined to form a strong learner. In AdaBoost, the value of the alpha parameter is inversely proportional to the error of the weak learner, meaning that a lower error results in a higher alpha value. Unlike Gradient Boosting in XGBoost, where the alpha parameter is specifically calculated based on the weak learner's errors, in AdaBoost, the alpha value is directly tied to the inverse of the learner's error, emphasizing the contribution of more accurate learners.

### *CatBoost*

The primary factor that distinguishes CatBoost from its competitors is the way it grows decision trees. Unlike many other algorithms, CatBoost constructs symmetric decision trees, enhancing its performance. Its exceptional ability to handle categorical data sets it apart, as it employs a unique technique tailored for such datasets. In CatBoost, categorical features are encoded based on the output columns, which means the weight of the output column is considered during both the training and encoding processes. This approach significantly boosts the model's accuracy when dealing with categorical data.

## Sequential Decision Trees

These principles lie at the heart of adaptability, where each tree adjusts its weights based on previously acquired accuracy data. As a result, the training process follows a sequential approach rather than a parallel one. In this method, the training and error measurement process is iteratively repeated for a specified number of iterations or until the error rate shows negligible change, as illustrated in Figure 5.6.

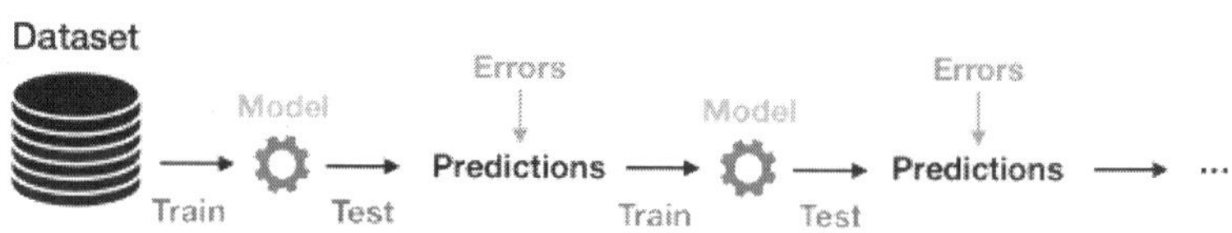


**Figure 5.6:The sequential learning of AdaBoost producing stronger learned model. (Source: https://builtin.com)**

## Boosting vs. bagging

Boosting is frequently compared to bagging, as they share some similarities, yet there are significant differences between the two. A detailed comparison of boosting and bagging is provided in Table 5.5 below:

## Algorithms based on Bagging and Boosting

Bagging and Boosting are among the most widely used and powerful techniques in machine learning. The following algorithms will be the primary focus of this discussion:

### *Bagging Meta-Estimator*

The Bagging meta-estimator is an ensemble learning algorithm that can be applied to both classification (Bagging Classifier) and regression (Bagging Regressor) tasks. It leverages the standard bagging technique, which involves creating multiple models from randomly sampled subsets of the training data and combining their predictions to improve accuracy and reduce overfitting.

**Table 5.5:Comparing boosting to bagging.**

| Aspect | Boosting | Bagging |
|---|---|---|
| Definition | Boosting combines weak learners to create a strong learner by focusing on misclassified data. | Bagging creates multiple models independently and combines their predictions to reduce variance. |
| Technique | Sequential, each model corrects errors made by the previous one. | Parallel, models are built independently. |
| Type of Learners | Typically uses weak learners (e.g., decision trees). | Uses the same type of model (usually decision trees). |
| Model Weighting | Models are weighted based on their performance, with more weight given to correct models. | All models have equal weight in the final prediction. |
| Error Correction | Focuses on misclassified data points, adapting in each iteration. | Reduces variance by averaging predictions across multiple models. |
| Overfitting | More prone to overfitting, especially with noisy data. | Less prone to overfitting due to averaging of models. |
| Speed | Slower due to sequential nature. | Faster since models are built in parallel. |
| Example Algorithms | AdaBoost, Gradient Boosting, XGBoost. | Random Forest, Bagged Decision Trees. |
| Final Prediction | Weighted sum of predictions. | Average of predictions (for regression) or majority vote (for classification). |

### *Random Forest*

Random Forest is a powerful ensemble machine learning algorithm that utilizes the bagging technique. It builds upon the bagging estimator by leveraging multiple decision trees as base estimators. What distinguishes Random Forest from traditional bagging is its approach of randomly selecting a subset of features at each node, ensuring that the best possible split is made based on this limited set of features. Here's a step-by-step breakdown of how a Random Forest model operates:

Bootstrapping involves generating random subsets from the initial dataset.

- At each node of the decision tree, only a randomly selected subset of features is considered for determining the optimal split.
- A separate decision tree model is trained on each subset of the data.
- The final prediction is obtained by averaging the predictions made by all individual decision trees.

In random forest, a subset of features and data can be used to build the decision trees. A subset of features is chosen at random for splitting at each node in the random forest sclera model, which specifically uses all features for decision trees.

## Mixture of Experts Revisited

The ability of a neural network to absorb and process information is constrained by the number of parameters it contains. As a result, the challenge of finding more efficient methods to expand model parameters without incurring significant computational overhead has become a central focus in deep learning research, particularly for complex, real-world applications such as autonomous driving systems. A mixture of experts is an ensemble learning technique that leverages multiple specialized neural networks, each focusing on a distinct portion of the training data, along with a gating network that assesses the entire input space to determine which expert is most suitable for a given input. This method involves dividing the input space into distinct subsets based on domain knowledge of the problem, training an expert model for each subset, and creating a gating model to determine which expert to rely on for specific predictions, ultimately combining their outputs. In traditional machine learning, all parameters of the model are activated for every input, resulting in high training costs as model complexity and data volume grow. By selectively activating only a subset of the network, this approach reduces computational demands and mitigates the interdependencies between network layers. This leads to improved generalization, greater model diversity, and more efficient training. Although initially applied with neural network experts and gating models, the concept is flexible and can be extended to any type of model. Thus, it shares significant similarities with stacked generalization and fits within the category of ensemble learning techniques known as meta-learning. The mixture of experts method represents a powerful and adaptable approach to ensemble learning.

- An intuitive approach to ensemble learning entails decomposing a complex task into smaller subtasks and assigning an expert model to handle each subtask individually.
- A "mixture of experts" is a method within ensemble learning that strategically tackles a predictive modeling problem by partitioning it into distinct subtasks, each addressed by a specialized expert model.
- The divide-and-conquer strategy is closely linked to the construction of decision trees, while the meta-learner approach is associated with the stacked generalization ensemble technique, where models are combined through a hierarchical learning process.

## Subtasks and Experts

Some predictive modeling tasks are inherently complex and require the handling of a wide range of tasks. To make such tasks more manageable, it is often beneficial to decompose the main task into several smaller subtasks. This approach enables effective and efficient predictive modeling without the need for excessive computational resources. For instance, consider an autonomous driving system where a machine learning model for image classification must analyze and categorize the behaviors of various dynamic and static objects across different locations and scenarios. Such a model is expected to be highly complex and scalable, with an immense number of parameters to accommodate all possible driving situations within the environment. By dividing this complex task into subtasks, and utilizing a managing or gating network to determine which expert to rely on for each input, we can significantly enhance the model's scalability. This approach enables the model to easily and effectively learn which expert to consult during inference for any new input. This strategy embodies the divide-and-conquer methodology, which is a cornerstone of many automated approaches to predictive modeling and problem-solving in general. Additionally, this concept can serve as the foundation for developing ensemble learning techniques. The subtasks may or may not overlap, and experts from related subdomains may be able to contribute to scenarios outside their primary area of expertise. This collaborative approach is fundamental to the "mixture of experts" technique, a key method in ensemble learning.

## Mixture of Experts

A Mixture of Experts (MoE) is an ensemble learning approach that leverages the concept of training specialized neural networks, or "experts," on different subsets of a predictive modeling task. This methodology, which has been extensively studied within the neural network community, focuses on decomposing the input space, allowing each expert to handle a distinct region of the data. A gating network plays a crucial role in this framework by selecting the most appropriate expert for a given input and then combining the outputs of multiple experts to make a final prediction, as illustrated in Figure 5.7.

There are four elements to the approach, which are as follows:

- Break down a task into smaller, manageable subtasks.
- Assign a specialized expert to handle each subtask.
- Implement a gating model to determine the most suitable expert for each specific task.
- Combine the predictions from the experts with the output of the gating model to generate a final prediction.

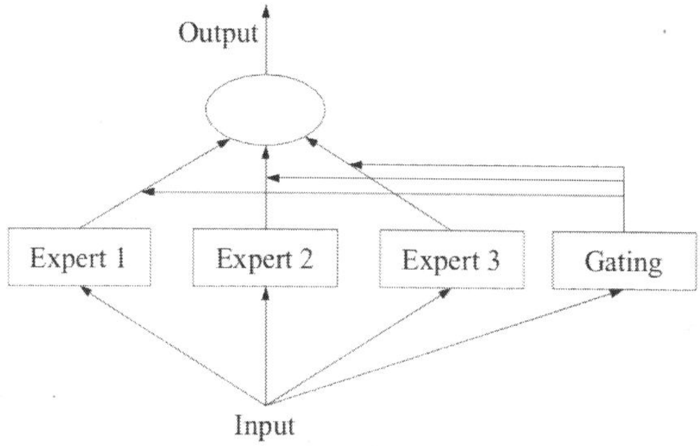


**Figure 5.7: Mixture of Experts Model with Expert Members and a Gating Network Taken from: Ensemble Methods. (Source: https://machinelearningmastery.com)**

## Subtasks

The first step in predictive modeling is to break down the problem into manageable subtasks. This often involves leveraging domain knowledge to segment the input space into distinct subspaces. For instance, in the context of autonomous driving, the dataset might be divided into various driving scenarios such as urban driving, highway driving, parking and valet operations, platooning, and autonomous delivery. In cases where the natural segmentation of the task is not immediately apparent, a more general and flexible approach can be adopted. For example, one could partition the input feature space by grouping related columns or separating examples based on distance metrics, outliers, inliers, or distribution characteristics. In a mixture of experts framework, a critical challenge lies in identifying the optimal way to divide the task and subsequently synthesizing a cohesive solution from the individual sub-solutions.

## Expert Models

The concept of a mixture of experts was originally conceived and explored within the domain of artificial neural networks. Traditionally, the "experts" in this framework are neural network models tasked with predicting a numerical value for regression tasks or a class label for classification tasks. However, it is important to note that any other model can be substituted in place of the expert. For instance, we can utilize neural networks not only to represent the gating functions but also to model the experts themselves. This approach leads to the formation of a mixture density network, where each expert processes the same input (data row) and generates its own prediction.

## Gating Model

A gating model is a distinct neural network trained in parallel with the expert models. Its primary function is to interpret the predictions made by each expert and help determine which expert should be trusted for a given input. This model, known as the gating network, is typically a neural network designed to make decisions based on the input space that is divided among the experts. The gating network has access to information regarding all expert contributions for a specific input, allowing it to efficiently decide which expert to rely on.

The gating network selects an expert for a particular input if that expert's squared error is lower than the weighted average squared error of all other experts. As a result, the probability of selecting that expert increases. If the gating network assigns a very low probability to any expert, the corresponding expert will receive a minimal gradient, meaning its parameters will be less impacted by that input. The gating network dynamically assigns weights based on the input, enabling the mixture of experts (MoE) to learn which portions of the feature space are best captured by each individual expert.

In essence, the mixture-of-experts framework can be viewed as a classifier selection algorithm, where each classifier is trained to specialize in a specific portion of the feature space. When applied to neural networks, the gating network and the expert models are trained simultaneously, allowing the gating network to learn how to trust each expert for making predictions. This training process is typically implemented using expectation-maximization techniques. The gating network often employs a SoftMax output layer, producing a probability-like confidence score for each expert. The overall training procedure aims to achieve two objectives: to optimize the gating function for a given set of experts, and to train the experts based on the distribution determined by the gating function.

## Pooling or Aggregating Method

Finally, the expert models must generate a prediction, which is accomplished through a pooling or aggregation mechanism. This process could be as straightforward as selecting the expert with the highest output or confidence, as determined by the gating network. Alternatively, a more sophisticated approach could involve computing a weighted sum that integrates each expert's predictions along with the confidence values estimated by the gating network. Other methods of utilizing the predictions and gating network outputs effectively may also be envisioned. The pooling or combining system may then either select the classifier with the highest weight or compute a weighted sum of the classifier outputs for each class, ultimately choosing the class with the highest weighted sum.

## Relationship With Other Techniques

The Mixture of Experts method, once more prominent, is now less widely used, perhaps due to its origins in the field of neural networks. However, over the past 25 years, the technique has seen significant advancements and exploration. A comprehensive overview of these developments can be found in the 2012 paper "Twenty Years of Mixture of Experts." Importantly, I encourage you to look beyond its historical context and consider the broader applications of this technique, particularly in how it could be applied to enhance your predictive modeling challenges.

## Mixture of Experts and Decision Trees

We can observe a connection between the mixture of experts model and Classification and Regression Trees (CART). Decision trees are constructed using a divide-and-conquer strategy applied to the feature space, where each split corresponds to a fixed value for an input feature, and each sub-tree can be seen as a separate sub-model. The concept of the mixture of experts has primarily been explored within the neural network community. In this context, researchers generally adopt a divide-and-conquer approach, aiming to learn a mixture of parametric models simultaneously and then use combining rules to derive a comprehensive solution. This method can be likened to a recursive decomposition strategy that breaks down the predictive modeling task into smaller subproblems, a concept often referred to as the hierarchical mixture of experts (HME).

The HME approach can be viewed as a variant of tree-based methods, with the key distinction being that the tree splits in HME are not hard decisions, but rather probabilistic or soft splits. Unlike decision trees, where task division is typically explicit and top-down, the mixture of experts model attempts to leverage all the expert submodels, rather than relying on a single model. Additionally, there are several other differences between HMEs and the CART method. In HME, a linear (or logistic regression) model is used at each terminal node, as opposed to a constant value in CART. The splits in HME can be multiway, rather than just binary, and they are based on probabilistic functions derived from a linear combination of inputs, unlike CART, where splits are determined by a single input feature.

However, these distinctions could lead to different approaches for a particular predictive modeling problem.

**For example:**

- Consider utilizing automated or general approaches to partition the feature space or problem into subtasks, enhancing the adaptability and broader applicability of the method.
- Explore both combinatory techniques that rely on the most reliable expert and those that aim to achieve a weighted consensus across multiple experts for more robust decision-making.

## Mixture of Experts and Stacking

The application of this technique is not confined solely to neural network models, as it can be extended to a wide range of standard machine learning techniques that aim to achieve similar outcomes. Consequently, the mixture of experts method belongs to a broader family of ensemble learning techniques, which also includes stacked generalization, or "stacking." Like the mixture of experts, stacking involves training a diverse set of machine learning models and subsequently using a higher-level model to optimally combine their predictions. This class of ensemble methods can be referred to as meta-learning models, which seek to learn how to best aggregate the outputs from multiple lower-level models.Meta-learning, in essence, is a process of "learning from learners" (i.e., classifiers). To develop a metaclassifier, the base classifiers are first trained (stage one), followed by the training of the metaclassifier (stage two). Unlike the mixture of experts, where the task is often decomposed into subtasks, stacking typically involves fitting all models to the same training dataset. Moreover, unlike the mixture of experts, the higher-level model in stacking does not receive the same input patterns as the lower-level models; rather, it takes the predictions from the lower-level models as input.Meta-learning approaches are particularly effective when certain classifiers consistently classify specific instances correctly or incorrectly. However, there is no reason why a hybrid model combining stacking and the mixture of experts could not be developed, potentially offering superior performance compared to either approach used alone for a particular predictive modeling task.

**For example:**

- Consider treating the lower-level models in a stacking ensemble as specialized experts, each trained on distinct perspectives of the training data. This approach might involve adopting a more flexible strategy for decomposing the problem into subproblems, where different data transformations or feature selection techniques are applied to each model.
- Explore the possibility of supplying the input pattern to the meta-model in stacking, aiming to adjust the weighting or contribution of the lower-level models based on the specific context of the prediction. This conditional approach could enhance the overall performance by tailoring the contributions of the models to the nuances of the current prediction scenario.

## Applications of Mixture of Experts (MoE)

MoEs are a commonly used technique in various machine learning domains because they have been in existence for the past 30 years.

### *Natural language processing (NLP)*

MoE (Mixture of Experts) introduces a revolutionary approach to training large models by enhancing efficiency, accelerating pre-training, and providing faster inference speeds. Unlike traditional dense models, where every parameter is utilized for all inputs, MoE leverages sparsity to activate only specific parts of the model based on the input, drastically reducing computational overhead. A prime example of this is Microsoft's translation API, Z-code. The MoE architecture in Z-code effectively scales to an enormous number of model parameters while maintaining a consistent level of computational resources.

### *Computer vision*

Google's V-MoEs, a sparse architecture built on Vision Transformers (ViT), demonstrate the powerful impact of Mixture of Experts (MoE) in advancing computer vision tasks. By dividing images into smaller patches and passing them through a gating or routing layer, V-MoEs can dynamically assign the most relevant experts to each patch, enhancing both performance and computational efficiency. One of the key advantages of this approach is its remarkable flexibility. You can reduce the number of experts selected per token to save time and computational resources, all without requiring additional training on the model's weights.

### *Recommendation systems*

The Mixture of Experts (MoE) model has proven highly effective in recommendation systems. For instance, Google researchers introduced an MMoE (Multi-Gate Mixture of Experts) based ranking system for YouTube video recommendations. In this approach, the task objective is first divided into two categories: engagement and satisfaction. Once a list of candidate videos is retrieved, the ranking system leverages candidate, user, and context features to predict the probabilities associated with these two categories of user behavior.

A key consideration in this method is that the MoE layer is not applied directly to the input data, due to the high dimensionality, which would result in substantial training and serving costs. MoEs have become widely adopted across various industries for diverse applications, as they decompose complex tasks into simpler subtasks, each solvable by a lightweight expert network. This decomposition enables parallelized training and fast inference, making MoEs particularly attractive for large-scale systems.

## Fine-tuning

Fine-tuning refers to the process of taking a pretrained machine learning model and further training it on a smaller, domain-specific dataset. The goal of fine-tuning is to preserve the core capabilities of the pretrained model while tailoring it to address specialized tasks or applications. By leveraging the power of an existing, sophisticated model, fine-tuning allows machine learning developers to efficiently create effective models for specific use cases. This method is particularly advantageous when computational resources are constrained or relevant data is limited. A well-fine-tuned model can outperform its original pretrained version in specific tasks by aligning more closely with the nuances of the target domain. For instance, a company integrating generative AI into its customer support system could fine-tune a large language model (LLM) using its own product data, policies, and historical customer interactions. This customization enhances the model's ability to generate more relevant, contextually accurate responses compared to a more general-purpose pretrained model.

## Fine-Tuning Work

Fine-tuning starts with a pretrained model that has already been trained on a large and diverse dataset, enabling it to learn a broad spectrum of features and patterns. For example, an image recognition model might be trained on millions of images, covering everything from landscapes and household objects to people.

During this initial training phase, the model learns to generalize by identifying underlying patterns and features across a variety of data. Over time, it becomes proficient at interpreting new inputs. For instance, a model trained on a vast array of images might gradually learn to detect whether a photo contains a bird after analyzing thousands of bird images. Despite their impressive ability to generalize, off-the-shelf pretrained models often fall short when applied to niche tasks. A model trained on general images can identify a bird in an image, but it might struggle to differentiate between species, which would be a critical issue when building an app to help birdwatchers identify their sightings. Creating a specialized model from scratch for such a niche application would be computationally expensive and resource-intensive, making it impractical for smaller developers.

This is where fine-tuning becomes indispensable. It leverages the foundational knowledge already embedded in a pretrained model and adapts it for a specific task. Fine-tuning effectively bridges the gap between the general knowledge learned in the initial training and the expertise needed for specialized use cases. To fine-tune a model, developers curate or select a smaller, task-specific dataset tailored to their needssuch as a collection of bird images for a birdwatching app. While these fine-tuning datasets typically consist of hundreds or thousands of images, they are still much smaller than the extensive dataset used for the model's original training. Once the data is collected and preprocessed, the developer fine-tunes the pretrained model by continuing the training process. The earlier layers of the neural network, which capture basic features like textures in images or vector embeddings in text, usually remain unchanged or are "frozen," while the later layers are adjusted or enhanced to better capture the nuances of the new dataset. This process allows the model to retain its valuable foundational knowledge while adapting to the specific task. To preserve this balance, model developers often use a lower learning rate—a hyperparameter that controls how much the model's weights are adjusted during training. This precaution ensures that fine-tuning does not make drastic changes to the model's previously learned knowledge, allowing the model to improve without losing its prior capabilities.

## Fine-tuning vs. training

Fine-tuning, although often associated with model training, is a distinct process from what is traditionally referred to as "training." To avoid confusion, data scientists typically differentiate the two by referring to the latter as pre-training in this context.

### *(Pre-)Training*

At the start of the training process (or, in this case, pre-training), the model has no prior knowledgeit has yet to "learn" anything. Training begins with the random initialization of the model's parameters, which include the varying weights and biases applied to the mathematical operations at each node of the neural network. Training unfolds iteratively in two key phases: First, during the forward pass, the model generates predictions for a batch of inputs from the training dataset. A loss function then calculates the discrepancy (or "loss") between the model's predictions and the correct answers, known as the ground truth. In the second phase, backpropagation occurs, where an optimization algorithmtypically gradient descentis employed to adjust the model's weights throughout the network in order to minimize the loss. These weight adjustments are the model's way of "learning." This iterative process is repeated over multiple training epochs until the model reaches a level of proficiency deemed sufficient.Conventional supervised learning, commonly used for pre-training models in computer vision tasks such as image classification, object detection, and image segmentation, relies on labeled data. Labels (or annotations) provide both the range of possible answers and the ground truth for each sample. On the other hand, large language models (LLMs) are typically pre-trained through self-supervised learning (SSL), in which they learn from pretext tasks designed to derive ground truth from the inherent structure of unlabeled data. These pretext tasks help the model acquire knowledge that is valuable for subsequent, downstream tasks. They typically take one of two approaches:

***Self-prediction:,***Assigning the model the task of reconstructing the original input after masking a portion of it. This is the most common way that LLMs are trained.

***Contrastive learning:*** Models are trained to discover distinct embeddings for unrelated inputs and similar embeddings for related inputs. Computer vision models like Contrasting Language-Image Pretraining (CLIP), which are made for few-shot or zero-shot learning, make extensive use of this.

Thus, SSL eliminates the need to annotate millions or billions of data points, enabling the use of incredibly large datasets for training. Although this saves a great deal of work, it still uses a lot of computer power.

## Fine-tuning large language models

Fine-tuning is a critical phase in the development of large language models (LLMs), enabling the raw linguistic power of base foundation models to be adapted for a diverse range of use cases, from chatbots and coding assistants to applications across creative and technical domains. LLMs are initially pre-trained through self-supervised learning on vast amounts of unlabelled data, a process that equips them with general language generation capabilities. Autoregressive models like OpenAI's GPT, Google's Gemini, and Meta's Llama are trained to predict the next word(s) in a sequence, repeating this process until the completion of a sample. During pre-training, the model is given the start of a sentence from the training corpus and continuously predicts the subsequent word(s), using the actual next word as the ground truth for each prediction.

While this pre-training endows the models with impressive text generation skills, it does not imbue them with a true understanding of a user's intent. Essentially, autoregressive LLMs do not "answer" prompts; rather, they append text to them. Without specific input through prompt engineering, a pre-trained, non-fine-tuned LLM will simply generate grammatically coherent predictions based on the prompt's initial sequence. For instance, when prompted with "teach me how to make a resumé," the model might respond with "using Microsoft Word" — a valid continuation, but not aligned with the user's deeper intent. While the model may have a wealth of knowledge on resumé writing drawn from its pre-training data, this knowledge might not be readily accessible or effectively applied without fine-tuning.

The fine-tuning process is therefore indispensable, not only in adapting foundation models to specific business needs, tones, and use cases but also in refining them for practical, real-world applications. It ensures that LLMs can go beyond basic text generation, transforming them into powerful tools capable of providing highly relevant and context-aware responses.

## Instruction Tuning

Instruction tuning is a specialized form of supervised fine-tuning (SFT) commonly applied to enhance large language models (LLMs) for chatbot applications. This process adapts the LLM to generate responses that more effectively address user queries, or in other words, to better adhere to instructions. Instruction tuning relies on labeled examples structured in a (prompt, response) format, where the prompts are task-oriented instructions, such as "translate the following sentence from English to Spanish" or "classify the following sentence as Positive or Negative." These examples guide the model on how to respond to a wide range of use cases, including question answering, summarization, and translation.

By updating the model's weights to reduce the discrepancy between the model's outputs and the labeled responses, the LLM learns to generate more appropriate and precise answers to prompts. For instance, when given a prompt like "teach me how to write a resumé," the training data for SFT would include various (prompt, response) pairs that demonstrate the correct way to respond to "teach me how to" requests. Instead of simply completing the sentence, the model would learn to offer structured, step-by-step guidance. This process helps the model follow instructions more effectively across a broad spectrum of tasks.

## Cascading

Cascading in ensemble learning is a strategy where multiple models are arranged in a sequential order to enhance predictive accuracy. The core concept behind cascading is to begin with simpler, faster models that efficiently handle easy cases, and progressively deploy more sophisticated models to address instances where the simpler models fall short. This approach is particularly effective in scenarios where some instances are straightforward to classify, while others are more challenging. The simpler models filter out the easily classifiable cases, allowing the more complex models to concentrate on the harder-to-classify ones.

In a typical cascading ensemble, the process is divided into several stages. The first stage involves applying a basic, efficient modelusually a simple classifierthat accurately classifies a large portion of the dataset. For the remaining, more difficult-to-classify instances, more advanced models are progressively applied in the following stages. This method significantly reduces computational costs and accelerates classification by invoking more complex models only when necessary.

One of the key advantages of cascading is its ability to boost the ensemble's overall accuracy by directing computational resources toward the most challenging cases, thereby optimizing performance without sacrificing efficiency. Cascading is frequently utilized in applications like object detection, where simpler models can easily identify certain features, while more complex models are required to resolve ambiguous or intricate instances. A prime example of cascading in ensemble learning is the Viola-Jones object detection framework, which applies a series of increasingly complex classifiers (using Haar features) in stages to detect objects like faces in images. This cascading structure ensures that the system remains fast by applying complex classifiers only when essential.

## Summary

Ensemble learning in machine learning improves predictive performance and robustness by integrating the strengths of multiple models. Techniques like bagging help minimize variance, while boosting enhances accuracy by sequentially addressing errors. Advanced strategies such as stacked generalization and cascading further refine decision-making by either synthesizing model outputs or leveraging sequential processes. Overall, ensemble learning offers a robust and versatile approach to solving complex predictive problems across a wide range of applications.

## Exercise Questions

- What is the main goal of combining multiple learners in machine learning?
- How does generating diverse learners improve ensemble performance?
- What are the key differences between homogeneous and heterogeneous ensemble methods?
- What is the principle behind voting in ensemble methods?
- How do error-correcting output codes (ECOC) help in multi-class classification?
- What is the role of base learners in bagging?
- How does boosting address model errors iteratively?
- What is the significance of assigning weights to learners in boosting?
- How does the mixture of expert's approach divide the problem space?
- What is stacked generalization, and how does it optimize meta-learning?
- Why is fine-tuning essential for improving ensemble performance?
- What is cascading, and how does it structure multiple models in sequence?
- How does diversity among base models contribute to ensemble robustness?
- What are the main limitations of bagging compared to boosting?
- In what scenarios is stacked generalization most beneficial?

CHAPTER - 6

# Introduction to Machine Learning

Machine Learning (ML) is a subfield of artificial intelligence (AI) that focuses on the development of algorithms that allow computers to learn from and make decisions based on data. Unlike traditional software development, where explicit instructions are written for each task, ML systems identify patterns and relationships within data to make predictions, classify information, or automate decision-making processes. This approach enables machines to improve their performance over time as they are exposed to more data, allowing them to handle complex tasks such as image recognition, speech processing, and even playing strategic games like chess. The core principle of machine learning is its ability to learn from experience. By using historical data as input, ML models train themselves to identify patterns and trends. Once a model has been trained, it can generalize this knowledge to make predictions about new, unseen data. This process is often broken down into three main categories: supervised learning, unsupervised learning, and reinforcement learning. In supervised learning, models are trained on labeled data, while unsupervised learning deals with unstructured data without predefined labels. Reinforcement learning, on the other hand, is used in situations where an agent learns by interacting with an environment and receiving feedback.

Supervised learning is one of the most widely used approaches in machine learning. In this approach, the model is provided with a set of input-output pairs, and the goal is to learn a mapping from inputs to outputs. This method is particularly effective in tasks such as image classification, spam detection, and regression analysis. The key to successful supervised learning lies in the quality and quantity of the labeled data provided for training. Well-labeled data helps the model learn more effectively, leading to higher accuracy in its predictions. In contrast, unsupervised learning does not require labeled data. Instead, the model tries to identify hidden structures or patterns within the data on its own. This type of learning is useful for clustering similar data points together or for dimensionality reduction in complex datasets. Popular algorithms for unsupervised learning include k-means clustering and principal component analysis (PCA), which help in identifying meaningful groupings or reducing the number of variables in a dataset without losing important information.

Reinforcement learning is inspired by behavioral psychology, where agents take actions in an environment to maximize some notion of cumulative reward. This type of learning is commonly used in robotics, game playing, and autonomous systems, such as self-driving cars. Reinforcement learning algorithms are designed to improve their decision-making ability over time by receiving feedback from their environment and learning from both successful and unsuccessful actions. The applications of machine learning are vast and continue to grow rapidly across various industries. In healthcare, ML is used to predict patient outcomes, assist in diagnostics, and personalize treatment plans. In finance, it helps detect fraudulent activities and optimize investment strategies. From personalized recommendations on e-commerce websites to natural language processing tools like chatbots and voice assistants, machine learning is revolutionizing how businesses and individuals interact with technology. As the field continues to advance, we can expect even more innovative applications that will reshape industries and enhance everyday life.

**Figure 6.1: Concept of Machine Learning.**

## Types of Machine Learning (ML)

Machine Learning (ML) can be broadly categorized into three main types based on the nature of the learning process and the type of data used (Table 6.1).

**Table 6.1: Types of Machine Learning:**

| Type of ML | Description | **Examples** |
|---|---|---|
| Supervissssed Learning | Model learns from labeled data (input-output pairs). | Spam detection, Image recognition, Fraud detection |
| Unsupervised Learning | Model identifies patterns in unlabeled data. | Customer segmentation, Anomaly detection |
| Reinforcement Learning | Model learns by interacting with an environment and receiving rewards. | Game playing (AlphaGo), Robotics, Self-driving cars |

- These types are:

### 1. Supervised Learning

In supervised learning, the algorithm is trained on a labeled dataset, where each input data point (features) is paired with its corresponding output (labels). The model learns to establish a relationship between inputs and outputs by iteratively adjusting its parameters to minimize the discrepancy between predicted and actual outputs, thereby refining its ability to make accurate predictions.

- Applications: Spam email detection, sentiment analysis, and house price prediction.
- Common Algorithms: Linear regression, logistic regression, support vector machines, and neural networks.

### 2. Unsupervised Learning

Unsupervised learning focuses on analyzing unlabelled data, where the algorithm uncovers hidden patterns, structures, or clusters within the data without the need for predefined labels or explicit guidance.

- Applications: Customer segmentation, anomaly detection, and data compression.
- Common Algorithms: K-means clustering, hierarchical clustering, and principal component analysis (PCA).

### 3. Reinforcement Learning (RL)

Reinforcement learning is a process where an agent is trained to make a series of decisions through interactions with its environment. The agent learns by receiving feedback—either rewards or penaltiesbased on the consequences of its actions, refining its strategy over time to maximize positive outcomes.

- Applications: Robotics, game playing (e.g., AlphaGo), and autonomous vehicles.
- Key Concepts: Agent, environment, rewards, and policy optimization.

These types of machine learning form the cornerstone of intelligent system development, with each one designed to tackle specific challenges and tailored to address a wide range of problem domains.

## Linear models (SVMs and Perceptions, logistic regression)

Linear models are core techniques in machine learning, widely applied to both classification and regression tasks. They operate by identifying a linear relationship between the input features and the output, making them a powerful starting point for predictive modeling. As illustrated in Table 6.2, a comparison of linear models highlights their foundational role in the field. These models not only provide valuable insights into more complex algorithms but also serve as essential benchmarks for evaluating performance across various tasks.

**Table 6.2: Linear Models**

| Model | Type of Model | Objective | Decision Boundary | Learning Algorithm |
|---|---|---|---|---|
| **Support Vector Machine (SVM)** | Supervised, classification | Classify data into two classes by finding a hyperplane with the maximum margin. | Linear (if using a linear kernel) or non-linear (if using non-linear kernels like RBF). | Quadratic programming (Convex optimization). |
| **Perceptron** | Supervised, classification | Find a linear decision boundary to separate two classes. | Linear | Stochastic gradient descent |
| **Logistic Regression** | Supervised, classification | Predict probabilities of class membership, then classify based on threshold. | Linear | Gradient descent or Newton's method |

### 1. Support Vector Machines (SVMs)

SVMs are strong supervised learning algorithms that are mainly employed for classification, though they are also capable of handling regression tasks.

**Core Idea:** Support Vector Machines (SVMs) strive to identify the optimal hyperplane that best separates data points from different classes while maximizing the margin. This margin represents the largest possible distance between the hyperplane and the closest data points, known as support vectors, from each class.

**Linear SVMs:** When the data can be separated linearly, these are employed. In 2D, the algorithm looks for a straight line; in higher dimensions, it looks for a hyperplane that separates the classes.

**Kernel Trick:** SVMs can convert non-linear data into a higher-dimensional space that is separated by linearity by using kernel functions (such as polynomial kernels or the radial basis function).

**Applications:** Face detection, text categorization, and bioinformatics.

## 2. Perceptrons

One of the most basic kinds of artificial neural networks, the perceptron is made for tasks involving binary classification.

**Core Idea:** A perceptron generates a binary decision (such as 0 or 1) after using a weighted sum of input features and passing it through a threshold function.

**Learning Algorithm:** Using a simple rule, the perceptron modifies its weights in proportion to the input and the error if the prediction is incorrect.

**Limitations:** Perceptrons are limited to classifying linearly separable data. In situations like XOR, where classes can't be divided by a straight line, it fails.

**Applications:** Early uses involved simple pattern recognition exercises.

## 3. Logistic Regression

Logistic regression is a statistical technique primarily employed for binary classification. Despite its name, it functions as a classification algorithm rather than a regression method.

**Core Idea:** Logistic regression models the likelihood of a binary outcome (e.g., 0 or 1) by utilizing a sigmoid function, which transforms any real-valued input into a probability value within the range [0, 1]. The classification decision is based on a threshold, commonly set at 0.5, which defines the decision boundary between the two possible outcomes.

## Equation:

$$P(y = 1|x) = \frac{1}{1+e^{-(w^T x+b)}},$$

where $w^T x$+bis the linear combination of weights and input features.

**Optimization:** It reduces a loss function (often cross-entropy loss) using algorithms such as Gradient Descent.

**Extensions:** By using methods like one-vs-all or softmax regression, logistic regression can be expanded to multiclass classification.

**Applications:** Credit scoring, disease diagnosis, and marketing analytics.

***Example:***

Here's an example illustrating how each linear model works with a simple classification problem:

**Problem:** Classify emails as Spam or Not Spam by analyzing features such as the frequency of specific keywords, email length, and the presence of attachments.

### 1. Support Vector Machines (SVMs)

- Input Data: Numerical features extracted from emails, e.g.,
- Keyword Frequency = 3
- Email Length = 100 words
- Attachments = Yes (encoded as 1).
- SVM Process:In the feature space, SVM locates a hyperplane that most effectively distinguishes between "Spam" and "Not Spam" emails with the largest margin. For example:
- Spam: Keyword Frequency > 5 and Email Length < 50.
- Not Spam: Otherwise.
- Outcome:It is categorized as spam if the provided email features are located on the "Spam" side of the hyperplane.

### 2. Perceptron

- Input Data: Similar numerical features.
- Perceptron Process:A linear combination of the features is computed:
- **Perceptron Process:** A linear combination of the features is computed:
- Output=$w_1$×Keyword Frequency+$w_2$×Email Length+$w_3$×Attachments+Bias
- If the output exceeds a threshold (e.g., 0), classify the email as Spam; otherwise, classify it as Not Spam.
- **Outcome:** If 3×3+0.1×100+5×1−20>03 the email is classified as Spam.

### 3. Logistic Regression

- Input Data: Same features as above.
- Logistic Regression Process:
- Compute the linear combination of features:
- Compute the linear combination of features: z=w1×Keyword Frequency+w2×Email Length+w3×Attachments+Bias
- Use the sigmoid function to calculate the probability of the email being Spam:
- P(Spam): $= \frac{1}{1+e^{-z}}$.

- If (Spam)>0.5, classify the email as Spam; otherwise, classify it as Not Spam.
- Outcome: If$P$ (Spam)=0.78, the email is classified as Spam because the probability exceeds 0.5.

### *Comparison of Results:*

For the same features:

- SVM: Spam.
- Perceptron: Spam.
- Logistic Regression: Spam with a confidence of 78%.

The examples provided demonstrate how linear models can use their special advantages to solve a simple binary classification problem in a novel way.

## Intro to Neural Nets

Neural Networks (NNs) are advanced computational systems modeled after the human brain's architecture, particularly its intricate network of neurons. These models consist of multiple layers of interconnected "neurons" or nodes that process and transmit information. The input data is initially received by the first layer, which then passes through several hidden layers. Each of these layers applies various mathematical transformations, with each neuron processing the data by applying a weight, a bias, and an activation function, which introduces non-linearity into the system. This non-linearity allows the network to learn and capture intricate patterns and relationships within the data.

The final output layer of the network generates predictions or classifications, depending on the specific task it is designed to perform. Neural networks serve as the backbone of deep learning, a powerful subset of machine learning, and have revolutionized the approach to solving complex problems across various domains. They excel in tasks such as image recognition, natural language processing, and autonomous driving by effectively identifying complex patterns in large datasets.

By learning from vast amounts of labeled data, neural networks continuously refine their capabilities through training techniques like backpropagation. This iterative learning process enables them to generalize from existing data and improve their performance over time. As a result, neural networks have become indispensable tools for working with unstructured data, including images, text, and speech, and are at the forefront of many cutting-edge applications.

## Structure of a Neural Network

As seen in the Figure 6.2 below, ANNs consist of three essential layers: input layers, hidden layers, and the output layer.

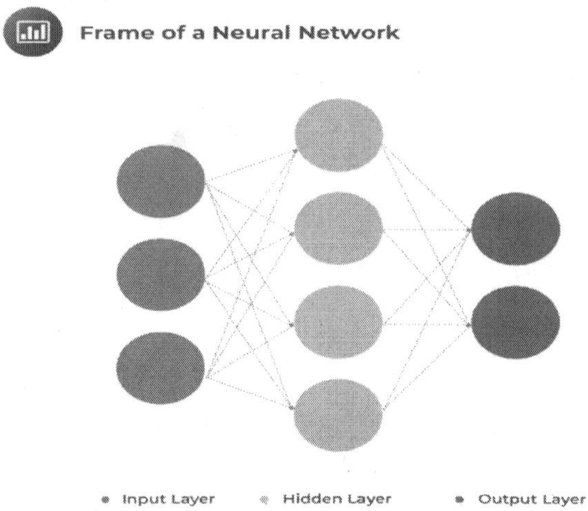


**Figure 6.2: Three Essential Layers [Source: analystprep]**

### 1. Input Layer

The input layer serves as the initial gateway through which raw data enters the neural network. Each neuron within this layer corresponds to a specific feature or variable from the input dataset. For instance, in an image recognition task, the individual pixels of an image may act as the features, while in a financial application, attributes such as age, income, and loan amount could represent the input variables. Notably, the input layer does not engage in any computation or transformation of the data; rather, it functions solely to pass the information forward to the subsequent layers for further processing.

### 2. Hidden Layers

Hidden layers are the fundamental components that drive computations in a neural network. Each neuron within these layers receives inputs, calculates a weighted sum, adds a bias term, and applies an activation function (such as ReLU, sigmoid, or tanh) to introduce non-linearity. This non-linearity allows the network to learn and model complex relationships within the data. In deep learning, multiple hidden layers are stacked to progressively extract more abstract and high-level features, which is why these architectures are referred to as Deep Neural Networks (DNNs). This hierarchical feature extraction enables the network to tackle increasingly complex tasks with greater accuracy and depth.

### 3. Output Layer

The output layer generates the final prediction of the neural network. The number of neurons in this layer is determined by the specific requirements of the task at hand. For binary classification, the output layer typically consists of a single neuron with a sigmoid activation function, producing a probability value. In contrast, for multiclass classification, the output layer usually contains multiple neurons with a softmax activation function, which calculates the probability for each class. For regression tasks, the output layer generates a continuous value, either without an activation function or using a linear activation to produce the desired output.

## Working of a Neural Network

Representation of the flowchart in block format to help visualize the working of a neural network (Figure 6.3).

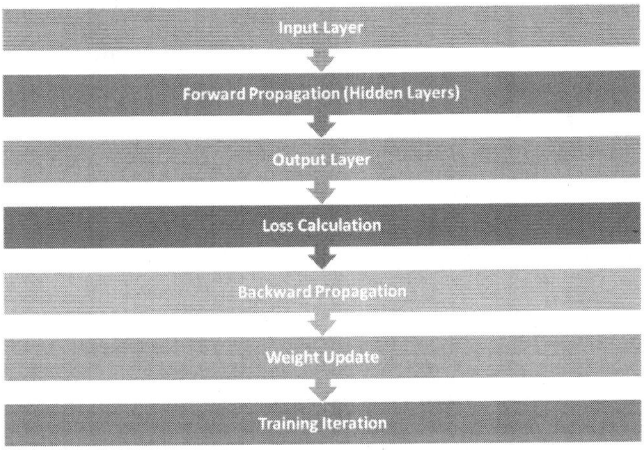


**Figure 6.3: Working of Flowchart.**

Working Principle of Artificial Neural Networks, as mention in below Figure 6.4.

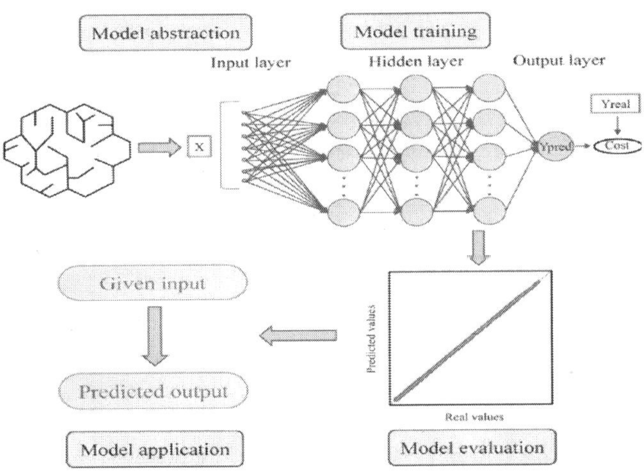


**Figure 6.4: Working Principle of Artificial Neural Networks [Source: researchgate]**

### 1. Forward Propagation

Forward propagation refers to the process of passing input data through a neural network to generate predictions. During this process, each neuron computes a weighted sum of its inputs, adds a bias term, and applies an activation function to produce an output. This output is then passed on to the next layer, and the calculation continues through all layers, from the input to the output layer. For instance, in an image recognition task, the input data (pixel values) undergoes multiple transformations in each layer, with the final output layer providing the predicted class label (e.g., "cat" or "dog").

### 2. Loss Calculation

Loss calculation quantifies the discrepancy between a network's predictions and the actual outcomes. The loss function is used to evaluate the error in the network's predictions. For classification tasks, cross-entropy loss is often employed, while mean squared error is the standard for regression tasks. For instance, if the model predicts a 0.8 probability for "Spam" but the true label is 1 (Spam), the loss function computes the difference between the predicted and actual values to assess the model's accuracy.

### 3. Backward Propagation (Backpropagation)

Backward propagation, also known as backpropagation, is a key process in training neural networks where the network's weights are updated to minimize the loss function. This involves computing the gradient of the loss with respect to each weight by applying the chain rule of calculus. The gradients provide crucial information to adjust the weights and biases in a way that reduces the loss. For example, if a particular weight has a large impact on the error, it will be adjusted in proportion to its contribution during the update step, ultimately improving the model's accuracy.

### 4. Training Iteration

A single training iteration consists of the full cycle of forward propagation, loss calculation, and backward propagation. Through multiple iterations (or epochs), the network progressively enhances its predictions by reducing the loss. For instance, after 1,000 epochs, a neural network trained for image classification might increase its accuracy from 60% to 95%.

## Types of Neural Networks

### 1. Feedforward Neural Networks (FNN)

Feedforward neural networks (FNNs) are the most basic type of neural network, characterized by the unidirectional flow of information—from input to output. These networks are well-suited for fundamental tasks like classification and regression. A classic example of their application is predicting house prices based on factors such as size, location, and other relevant features. While FNNs are simple and efficient for such tasks, they may struggle to capture more complex relationships, such as temporal or spatial dependencies within the data.

### Structure of a Feedforward Neural Network

- Input Layer: The input layer consists of neurons that receive and process the initial data. Each neuron in this layer represents a distinct feature or attribute of the input data, acting as the gateway for information to enter the network.
- Hidden Layers: One or more hidden layers are situated between the input and output layers. These layers are essential for uncovering intricate patterns and relationships within the data. Each neuron in a hidden layer calculates a weighted sum of its inputs, which is then passed through a non-linear activation function to introduce complexity and enable learning of non-linear patterns.
- Output Layer: The output layer produces the final result or prediction of the network. The number of neurons in this layer corresponds to the number of categories in a classification task or the number of output variables in a regression task, delivering the network's ultimate decision or estimate.

The weights assigned to each neuronal connection in these layers are modified during training in order to reduce prediction error(Figure 6.5).

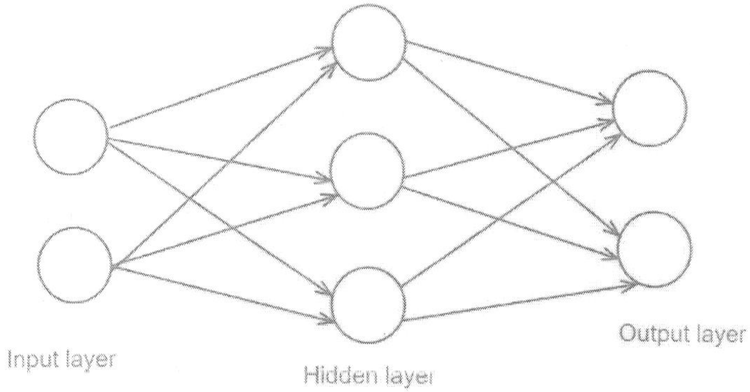


**Figure 6.5: Feed Forward Neural Network [Source: geeksforgeeks]**

### Working

Feedforward Neural Networks are the most basic form of artificial neural networks, where information moves unidirectionally—from the input layer, through one or more hidden layers, and finally to the output layer. These networks are characterized by the absence of feedback loops, meaning the output is not fed back into the network, ensuring a straightforward flow of data.

- Step-by-Step Working of FNN

### 1. Input Layer

The input layer receives raw data features, such as numerical values, images, or text, with each input node representing a single feature of the data. For example, in a dataset where each sample consists of three features, the input layer will have three neurons, one for each feature. The input layer's role is limited to forwarding the input data to the subsequent layers without performing any computation.

### 2. Weighted Sum Calculation

- In the hidden layer(s), each neuron computes a weighted sum of its inputs:

$$z = \sum (w_i \cdot x_i) + b$$

- $w_i$: Weight associated with the input $x_i$
- b: Bias term (allows the model to fit the data better by shifting the activation function)

### 3. Activation Function

An activation function is applied to the weighted sum in order to add non-linearity.

***Common activation functions:***

- ReLU (Rectified Linear Unit): Outputs max (0, z) to allow the network to learn complex patterns.
- Sigmoid: Outputs values between 0 and 1, used in binary classification tasks.
- Tanh: Outputs values between -1 and 1, often used when data is centered.

This change allows the network to simulate complicated relationships connecting the target and input features.

### 4. Output Layer

The output layer is reached once the data has passed through one or more hidden layers.

Predictions are generated by the output layer. The task determines how many neurons are present in this layer:

- Binary Classification: 1 neuron with sigmoid activation.
- Multiclass Classification: One neuron per class with SoftMax activation.
- Regression: 1 neuron with a linear activation function.

### 5. Loss Calculation

A loss function is used to compute the error between the network's output and the true labels:

- Cross-Entropy Loss: Used for classification problems.
- Mean Squared Error (MSE): Used for regression problems.

### 6. Backpropagation and Weight Update

The network employs backpropagation to compute the gradients of the loss function relative to the weights. An optimization algorithm, such as Stochastic Gradient Descent or Adam, then updates the weights and biases in order to minimize the loss and improve the model's performance.

### 7. Training Iterations (Epochs)

This cycle of forward propagation, loss calculation, and backpropagation is repeated across multiple epochs. With each iteration, the network refines its weights, gradually enhancing its ability to make more accurate predictions.

## 2. Convolutional Neural Networks (CNN)

Convolutional Neural Networks (CNNs) are specifically designed to process image and video data. These networks utilize convolutional layers to detect spatial patterns, such as edges, textures, and shapes, within images. For example, in a face recognition system, CNNs might first identify key facial features like eyes and mouths, then combine these features to accurately recognize a face. CNNs are extensively employed in various computer vision applications, including object detection, medical imaging, and autonomous vehicle navigation (Figure 6.6).

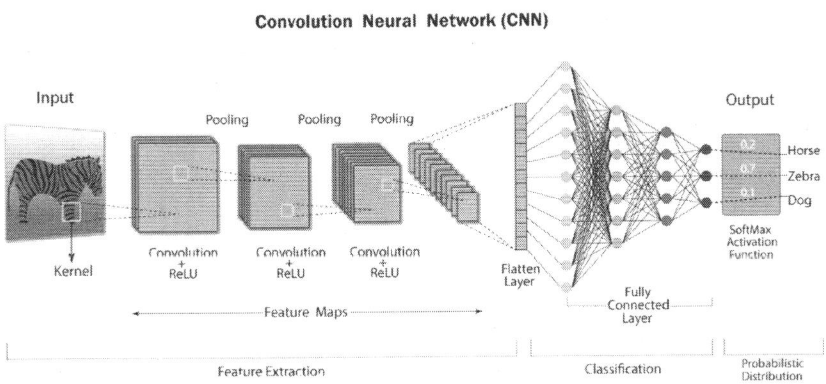


**Figure 6.6: Convolutional Neural Network — CNN architecture.**

Convolutional Neural Networks (CNNs) are distinguished by their capability to learn spatial hierarchies of features, progressively identifying simple patterns in the initial layers and evolving into more complex representations in deeper layers.

Key innovations such as parameter sharing and local connectivity contribute to their computational efficiency, making CNNs particularly well-suited for visual tasks. The wide-ranging applications of CNNs include image classification, object detection, medical imaging, facial recognition, and autonomous driving, among others. Their versatility, scalability, and remarkable accuracy have solidified their indispensable role in the field of modern deep learning.

## Components and working of CNN

### 1. Input Layer

The input layer serves as the entry point for data into a Convolutional Neural Network (CNN), where raw inputs, such as images, are introduced. These images are represented as multi-dimensional arrays, or tensors, with the dimensions corresponding to height, width, and depth—such as color channels (e.g., RGB). For example, a 28×28 grayscale image is depicted as a matrix containing 784-pixel values, whereas a color image includes an additional depth dimension, represented as 28×28×3. Before the data is fed into the network, preprocessing steps like normalization are applied, which involves scaling pixel values to a range between 0 and 1, ensuring the input is standardized for more efficient and effective model training.

### 2. Convolutional Layers

The input layer serves as the entry point for a Convolutional Neural Network (CNN), where raw data, such as images, are introduced to the network. These images are represented as multi-dimensional arrays, or tensors, with their dimensions corresponding to height, width, and depth (e.g., color channels like RGB). For example, a 28×28 grayscale image is depicted as a matrix containing 784-pixel values, while a color image includes an additional depth dimension, such as 28×28×3 for RGB. Before the data is fed into the network, preprocessing steps like normalization (scaling pixel values between 0 and 1) are applied, ensuring that the input is standardized for more efficient and effective training.

### 3. Activation Function

Activation functions inject non-linearity into the neural network, allowing it to learn and model complex, intricate patterns. After performing the convolution operation, an activation function like ReLU (Rectified Linear Unit) is applied to the feature maps. ReLU modifies all negative values, replacing them with zeros, which prevents the model from merely learning linear transformations. While other activation functions such as sigmoid or tanh are used in specific contexts, ReLU is favored due to its computational efficiency and its effectiveness in mitigating issues like vanishing gradients.

## 4. Pooling Layers

Pooling layers play a crucial role in reducing the spatial dimensions of feature maps while retaining the most essential information. This process enhances the model's computational efficiency and improves its robustness against variations in input, such as shifts or distortions. Two common types of pooling are max pooling, which selects the maximum value from each region of the feature map, and average pooling, which computes the average value. For instance, applying max pooling to a 4×4 feature map with a 2×2 window yields a 2×2 output. By simplifying the representation, pooling layers help the model concentrate on the most salient features, thereby improving its ability to generalize.

## 5. Flattening

After passing through several convolutional and pooling layers, the feature maps remain in a multi-dimensional format. Flattening converts these multi-dimensional maps into a one-dimensional vector, preparing them for input into fully connected layers. For example, a 7×7×64 feature map is transformed into a 1×3136 vector. This flattening step effectively bridges the gap between the feature extraction process and the subsequent classification or regression tasks, which are handled by the dense layers.

## 6. Fully Connected Layers

The fully connected layer, also referred to as a dense layer, processes the flattened input vector, performing advanced reasoning to generate predictions. Each neuron in this layer is intricately connected to all neurons from the preceding layer, enabling comprehensive data integration. The dense layer calculates a weighted sum of the inputs, applies an activation function to introduce non-linearity, and produces the resulting output. In classification tasks, the final layer often utilizes a softmax function to transform the output into a set of probabilities, each corresponding to a specific class. For example, in image classification, the output would represent the probability distribution across categories such as cats, dogs, or cars, indicating the likelihood of the input belonging to each respective class.

## 7. Loss Calculation

The loss function quantifies the disparity between the model's predicted output and the actual target values. In classification tasks, cross-entropy loss is widely employed to penalize incorrect predictions, while for regression tasks, mean squared error (MSE) is the standard metric. The calculated loss value serves as a critical signal during the training process, directing the model to refine its parameters and progressively minimize errors, thereby enhancing its performance over time.

## 8. Backpropagation and Optimization

Backpropagation is a fundamental process in neural networks that involves computing the gradients of the loss function with respect to the model's weights and biases. These gradients guide the adjustment of the parameters to reduce the error or loss. Optimization algorithms, such as Stochastic Gradient Descent (SGD) and Adam, are essential for efficiently updating the weights. Through iterative refinements of these parameters, the model progressively improves its ability to make accurate predictions, ultimately converging towards an optimal solution.

### 3. Recurrent Neural Networks (RNN)

Recurrent Neural Networks (RNNs) are specifically designed to process sequential data, where the order of inputs is crucial, such as in time series, audio, and text. They leverage feedback loops to retain memory of past inputs, enabling them to capture contextual relationships. For instance, in text generation, an RNN retains the context of preceding words to accurately predict the next word. Variants like Long Short-Term Memory (LSTM) networks and Gated Recurrent Units (GRUs) address the issue of vanishing gradients in traditional RNNs, enhancing their ability to manage long-term dependencies (Figure 6.7).

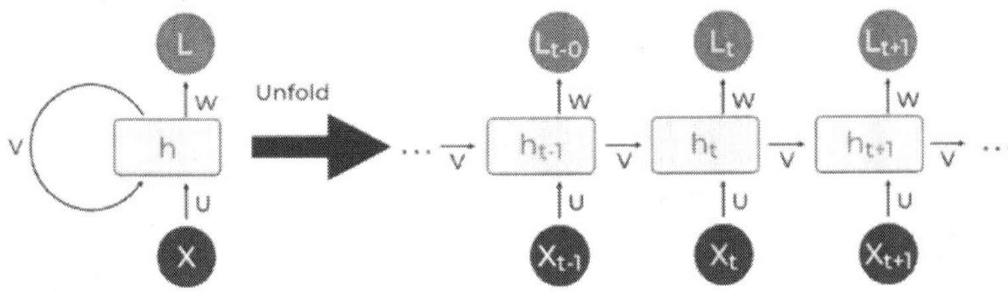


**Figure 6.7: Recurrent Neural Network [Source: geeksforgeeks].**

Features of RNNs

### 1. Sequential Data Handling

RNNs process input data in a sequential manner, step by step, retaining a "memory" of previous computations. This approach enables the network to capture temporal dependencies and relationships between data points, allowing it to recognize patterns and identify intricate connections within a sequence over time.

*Example:* In natural language processing, RNNs can predict the next word in a sentence based on the preceding words.

### 2. Hidden States

The hidden state is a crucial component of Recurrent Neural Networks (RNNs), enabling them to retain and recall past information. At each time step, the hidden state is updated by incorporating both the current input and the previous hidden state. This recurrent structure imbues the network with a form of memory, allowing it to effectively store and leverage historical data for future predictions or tasks.

$$h_t = f(W_{xh}x_t + W_{hh}h_{t-1} + b_h)$$

Mathematically:

Where:

- $h_t$: Current hidden state
- $x_t$: Current input.
- $Wx_h$ and $W_{hh}$: Weight matrices.
- $b_h$: Bias term.
- f: Activation function (commonly tanh or ReLU)

**3. Outputs**

The outputs of RNNs depend on the task:

- Many-to-Many: Generates a result at every time interval (machine translation, for example).
- Many-to-One: Produces a single output that summarizes the entire sequence (sentiment analysis, for example).
- One-to-Many: Uses a single input to produce a series of outputs(e.g., music generation).

Summarizing the challenges, enhanced variants, and applications of Recurrent Neural Networks (Table 6.3).

**Table 6.3:Challenges, Enhanced Variants, and Applications of RNNs.**

| Category | Description |
|---|---|
| **Challenges of RNNs** | 1. **Vanishing/Exploding Gradient Problem**: RNNs struggle with long-range dependencies as gradients can either vanish or explode during backpropagation. |
| | 2. **Slow Training**: Training RNNs is computationally intensive, requiring sequential processing. |
| | 3. **Difficulty in Handling Long Sequences**: RNNs can struggle with long-term dependencies as the signal gets lost as it moves through multiple time steps. |
| | 4. **Overfitting**: Due to the large number of parameters, RNNs can overfit on small datasets without proper regularization. |

| | |
|---|---|
| **Enhanced Variants of RNNs** | 1. **Long Short-Term Memory (LSTM)**: Addresses the vanishing gradient problem by introducing gates to control the flow of information. |
| | 2. **Gated Recurrent Unit (GRU)**: A simpler alternative to LSTM that uses fewer gates but still solves vanishing gradient issues. |
| | 3. **Bidirectional RNN (BiRNN)**: Uses two RNNs, one processing the sequence from left to right and the other from right to left, improving context understanding. |
| | 4. **Attention Mechanisms**: Enhances RNNs by allowing the network to focus on relevant parts of the input sequence, improving long-range dependency handling. |
| **Applications of RNNs** | 1. **Speech Recognition**: RNNs are used to transcribe spoken language into text by capturing sequential patterns in audio data. |
| | 2. **Natural Language Processing (NLP)**: Used in tasks like machine translation, sentiment analysis, and language modeling by understanding the sequence of words in a sentence. |
| | 3. **Time Series Prediction**: RNNs are used for predicting stock prices, weather forecasting, and other time-based data. |
| | 4. **Music Generation**: RNNs can generate new music sequences by learning from existing musical compositions. |
| | 5. **Image Captioning**: RNNs are employed to generate captions for images by first processing the image through a CNN and then generating a sequence of words as a caption using an RNN. |

### 4. Generative Adversarial Networks (GANs)

Generative Adversarial Networks (GANs) comprise two neural networks a generator and a discriminator that engage in a competitive process. The generator produces synthetic data, while the discriminator assesses its authenticity. By learning from a dataset of real-world images, GANs can generate highly realistic visuals. These networks are commonly applied in tasks such as image synthesis, style transfer, and video generation, where the goal is to create or modify media that closely resemble real-world content.

## Key Components of GANs

### 1. Generator

**Purpose:** The purpose of the generator is to produce artificial data from an initial input or random noise. It makes an effort to provide the discriminator with data which is as realistic as possible.

**Working:** The generator converts random noise into data (such as text, images, etc.) that resembles the actual data distribution. The intended outcome is for the generated data to be identical to the original data.

- Mathematical Representation:G(z)=Fake Data
- Where $z$ is the input noise, and ($z$) is the output of the generator (the fake data).

## 2. Discriminator

**Purpose:** The discriminator's job is to tell the difference between authentic and fraudulent data. After training, it is taught to give real data a high probability and fake data a low probability.

**Working:** The discriminator receives both real data (from the training set) and fake data (generated by the generator). Its task is to distinguish between real and fake data, providing valuable feedback to the generator to refine its output and improve the generation process.

Mathematical Representation:($x$) =Real or Fake

Where

- $x$ is the input data, and
- $D(x)$ is the probability that
- $x$ is real (or fake).

## 3. Adversarial Process

How It Works: In a hostile environment, the discriminator and generator are trained concurrently:

- The generator is designed to create data that closely resembles real data, making it as convincing as possible to the discriminator.
- The discriminator is trained to effectively differentiate between authentic and fabricated data.
- Throughout the training process, the generator improves its ability to generate realistic data, while the discriminator sharpens its skill in detecting counterfeit data.

This adversarial training leads to a min-max game:

$$\min_G \max_D \mathbb{E}_{x\sim p_{\text{data}}}[\log D(x)] + \mathbb{E}_{z\sim p_z}[\log(1 - D(G(z)))]$$

Where:

- $P_{\text{data}}$ is the real data distribution.
- $p_z$ is the distribution of the random noise input to the generator

## Challenges in GANs

Generative Adversarial Networks (GANs), despite their remarkable capabilities, encounter several significant challenges that can hinder their effective deployment. One of the most prominent issues is training instability. GANs rely on a competitive adversarial process between the generator and discriminator, making it difficult to maintain a balance where both networks enhance simultaneously. If one network becomes disproportionately stronger than the other, it can result in suboptimal outcomes or even cause the training process to collapse. Another critical challenge is mode collapse, where the generator produces a limited set of outputs instead of a diverse range of high-quality data. This becomes especially problematic when the objective is to generate a broad spectrum of realistic and varied samples. Furthermore, evaluating GANs poses its own set of difficulties. Traditional performance metrics, such as accuracy, are not applicable since GANs generate data rather than classify or predict it. This makes it inherently subjective to assess the quality of their output, complicating the process of comparing results across different models or identifying the "best" model without relying on human judgment.

## Applications of GANs

Despite the challenges they face, GANs have demonstrated immense potential across a wide variety of applications. In the realm of image generation, GANs excel at producing highly realistic images that closely replicate real-world objects, such as creating lifelike synthetic faces or virtual environments. One of the most exciting developments is in image-to-image translation, where GANs can seamlessly transform images from one style or format to another—such as converting rough sketches into photorealistic images or adding color to black-and-white photographs. Additionally, GANs play a pivotal role in super-resolution tasks, enhancing low-resolution images to a higher quality, which proves invaluable in fields like medical imaging and satellite photography. In situations where data is limited, GANs can perform data augmentation by generating synthetic samples, improving machine learning models when real-world data is scarce. Furthermore, GANs are making waves in the fashion and design industries, from generating innovative clothing designs and forecasting trends to enabling virtual clothing try-ons for e-commerce platforms.

### 5. Autoencoders

Autoencoders are specialized neural networks that learn to encode data into compact representations and then decode it to reconstruct the original input. These networks are primarily used in unsupervised learning tasks, such as anomaly detection and dimensionality reduction. For instance, an autoencoder trained on normal network traffic can identify irregularities, such as potential cyberattacks, by recognizing deviations from the learned patterns (see Figure 6.8).

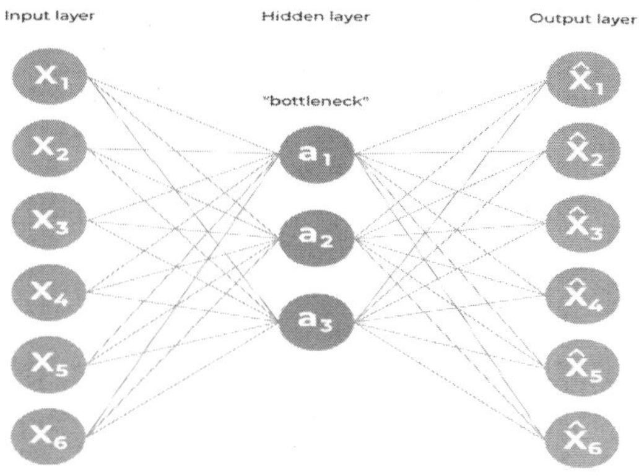


**Figure 6.8: Architecture of Autoencoder [Source: geeksforgeeks].**

## Components of Autoencoders

### 1. Encoder

The encoder processes the input data and compresses it into a compact, dense representation known as the latent space or bottleneck layer. This compressed form retains the most critical features of the data while significantly reducing its dimensionality. Typically, the encoder is composed of multiple layers of neurons that progressively reduce the input's dimensionality, ultimately producing the compressed representation.

Mathematical Representation:

$$h = f_{\text{encoder}}(x)$$

Where

- $x$ is the input, and
- h is the encoded representation.

### 2. Latent Space (Bottleneck)

The latent space acts as a compressed representation of the input data, capturing the most salient features or patterns identified by the encoder. Typically, smaller in size than the original input, the latent space challenges the model to learn a more compact and efficient representation. The effectiveness of this latent space plays a crucial role in the model's ability to accurately reconstruct the original input.

### 3. Decoder

The decoder processes the compressed latent space representation and seeks to reconstruct the original input data. Its primary objective is to generate an output that closely resembles the original input. Functioning as a neural network, the decoder mirrors the encoder's architecture, but in reverse, progressively expanding the dimensions until the output aligns with the original input.

Mathematical Representation:

$$x\hat{}=f_{\text{decoder}}(h)$$

Where

- x^ is the reconstructed data, and
- h is the latent representation.

### 4. Loss Function

The purpose of measuring the autoencoder's performance is to evaluate how accurately it reconstructs the input data. Typically, a loss function such as Mean Squared Error (MSE) is used to quantify the discrepancy between the input and its reconstructed output. During the training process, the autoencoder's parameters (weights) are iteratively adjusted to minimize this loss function, gradually enhancing the quality of the reconstruction and improving its accuracy over time.

Mathematical Representation:

$$(x,x\hat{})=\|x-x\hat{}\|^2$$

Where

- x is the original input, and
- x^ is the reconstructed output.

## Types of Autoencoders

**Vanilla Autoencoders:** The basic form of an autoencoder comprises an encoder and a decoder network, both constructed with fully connected layers. These autoencoders are typically employed for fundamental tasks such as data compression and noise reduction.

**Variational Autoencoders (VAEs):** A probabilistic extension of the autoencoder, where the latent space is represented as a distribution instead of a fixed vector. Variational Autoencoders (VAEs) are particularly useful for generative tasks, as they enable smooth and continuous sampling from the latent space, fostering more diverse and realistic data generation.

**Denoising Autoencoders:** These models are specifically trained to eliminate noise from input data. During training, they are exposed to noisy data and learn to reconstruct the original, clean version. This ability makes them highly effective for tasks such as image denoising, where removing unwanted distortions is crucial.

**Sparse Autoencoders:** These autoencoders impose a sparsity constraint on the latent space, compelling the majority of neurons in the hidden layers to remain inactive. As a result, this encourages the model to learn more meaningful and efficient features.

**Convolutional Autoencoders:** These autoencoders leverage convolutional layers rather than fully connected layers, making them especially well-suited for tasks involving image data, where capturing local features and understanding spatial hierarchies is crucial for accurate analysis.

## Applications of Autoencoders

Autoencoders are powerful and widely utilized in a variety of applications, particularly in domains that demand efficient data compression and advanced representation learning. A primary use case is data compression, where autoencoders learn to encode input data into a more compact, lower-dimensional space, effectively reducing storage needs while retaining key features. This approach proves invaluable in image and video compression. Another prevalent application is denoising, in which denoising autoencoders are trained to eliminate noise from corrupted data, thereby reconstructing its clean version. This technique has significant practical implications across fields such as image processing, signal processing, and medical imaging, enhancing data quality and reliability.

Autoencoders play a crucial role in dimensionality reduction by efficiently compressing the input data, retaining only the most essential features, much like traditional techniques such as Principal Component Analysis (PCA). This ability makes them particularly useful for data pre-processing before applying other machine learning models. In the realm of anomaly detection, autoencoders are adept at identifying outliers or unusual patterns by training on normal data and using reconstruction errors to flag anomalies. This method finds applications across various fields, including fraud detection, network security, and industrial fault detection. Additionally, Variational Autoencoders (VAEs) are employed in image generation tasks, where they can create entirely new data samples that closely resemble the original input, making them invaluable for creative industries such as art generation, fashion design, and more. Moreover, autoencoders are also widely used for feature extraction, simplifying complex data and identifying meaningful features that enhance the performance of other machine learning algorithms.

## Challenges in Autoencoders

Autoencoders offer a wide range of applications, but they also present several challenges that can impact their effectiveness. One of the most prominent issues is overfitting, particularly when the model is overly complex compared to the available dataset. Overfitting occurs when the autoencoder becomes highly adept at reconstructing the training data but struggles with generalizing to unseen data, undermining its ability to perform well in real-world scenarios. To mitigate this, strategies like regularization (e.g., dropout), early stopping, or employing simpler model architectures are commonly used.Another significant challenge is the computational complexity involved in training autoencoders, particularly deep or convolutional variants. These models can be resource-intensive, demanding considerable processing power and time, especially when handling high-dimensional datasets. Furthermore, tuning hyperparameters, such as the size of the latent space, can be both intricate and time-consuming, requiring careful experimentation to achieve optimal results.

Interpretability is also a key concern, especially with more complex models like Variational Autoencoders (VAEs). While autoencoders are capable of learning compressed representations of data, understanding the specific features or patterns captured within the latent space is not always straightforward. This lack of transparency makes it difficult to explain the model's behavior and decisions. Additionally, selecting the right architecturesuch as the appropriate number of layers or neurons for a given taskcan be a challenge, as performance is highly sensitive to these design choices. Lastly, there is the delicate balance between compression and reconstruction quality: if the latent space is too small, critical information may be lost, whereas an overly large latent space may lead to overfitting or unnecessary complexity, ultimately reducing the model's effectiveness.

## Application of Neural networks

Neural networks have become integral across a variety of industries due to their remarkable ability to model complex patterns and deliver highly accurate predictions. In fields like image recognition and computer vision, Convolutional Neural Networks (CNNs) are extensively used for tasks such as facial recognition, object detection, and medical image analysis. These networks play a pivotal role in diagnosing diseases like cancer by analyzing medical images, and they are essential in autonomous vehicles for recognizing pedestrians, traffic signs, and obstacles. In natural language processing (NLP), neural networks power systems such as virtual assistants (e.g., Siri, Alexa) and translation services (e.g., Google Translate), enabling advanced tasks like machine translation, sentiment analysis, and text summarization. Additionally, neural networks are fundamental to speech recognition, driving voice-controlled systems and transcription services that convert spoken language into text.Beyond these, neural networks are crucial to the development of autonomous vehicles, processing sensor data to help navigate and understand the surrounding environment. In healthcare, they support disease diagnosis through medical imaging, predict patient outcomes, and enable personalized treatment plans. In the financial sector, they are employed for fraud detection, stock market trend predictions, and risk management by analyzing vast datasets of financial transactions. The field of robotics also benefits significantly, with neural networks enabling robots to perform complex tasks such as object manipulation, pathfinding, and human-robot interaction. Marketing and customer insights are revolutionized by neural networks through customer segmentation, targeted advertising, and behavior prediction, offering enhanced personalized experiences in e-commerce and social media platforms.

Neural networks are also pivotal in fraud detection, identifying suspicious transactions in real-time, and in climate forecasting, where they predict weather patterns and environmental changes by processing data from diverse sources. Additionally, the power recommendation systems on platforms like Amazon and Netflix, offering personalized content and product suggestions based on user preferences and historical behavior. These wide-ranging applications highlight how neural networks are transforming industries by enabling systems to learn from complex data, improve over time, and drive innovations in automation, personalization, and decision-making. As technology continues to evolve, the potential applications of neural networks will expand, further reshaping the future of many sectors.

## What a Shallow Network Computes

A shallow neural network is a type of neural network that contains only a single hidden layer between the input and output layers. While it is simpler than deep neural networks, which have multiple hidden layers, a shallow network is still capable of approximating complex functions. However, its ability to model intricate patterns is more limited compared to the more powerful architectures of deeper networks. Here's what a shallow network computes:

### 1. Linear Decision Boundaries

In a shallow neural network with a single hidden layer, each neuron applies a linear transformation to its inputs. The network's output is derived from a weighted sum of these transformations, followed by an activation function such as sigmoid or ReLU. As a result, the shallow network can model linear decision boundaries or simple linear relationships between inputs and outputs. However, when the data demands more complex decision boundaries or nonlinear mappings, a shallow network struggles to capture these intricate patterns, limiting its ability to perform effectively.

### 2. Combinations of Inputs

Although a shallow network primarily captures linear relationships, its hidden layer neurons enable it to compute and process combinations of inputs. These combinations are weighted, transformed, and then passed on to the output layer. This process allows the network to model nonlinearity by representing the data in a more complex manner than a simple linear model could. The hidden layer functions as a feature extractor, learning more abstract representations of the input data, albeit with limitations in the depth and sophistication of the features it can learn.

### 3. Simple Classification Tasks

A shallow neural network is capable of handling straightforward classification tasks where the data is linearly separable. For instance, it can effectively classify data points into distinct categories when there exists a clear boundary that separates the classes. In the case of binary classification, a shallow network with a single hidden layer can perform well, especially when the classes are simple, non-complex, and do not overlap significantly.

### 4. Approximation of Nonlinear Functions

While shallow networks have inherent limitations, they can still approximate certain nonlinear functions effectively. By fine-tuning the weights and biases, shallow networks are capable of modeling relatively simple nonlinear relationships. However, their capacity to approximate more complex functions is restricted. For more intricate tasks, such as image recognition or natural language processing, deeper networks are generally required to achieve superior performance and capture the full complexity of the problem.

### Limitations of Shallow Networks

Complexity Limitations: Shallow networks are constrained in their capacity to capture sophisticated abstractions within data. While they can approximate basic functions, they struggle with more intricate tasks, particularly those involving vast amounts of unstructured data such as images, audio, and text. Furthermore, their ability to generalize is often limited, especially when dealing with complex, high-dimensional relationships, resulting in poor performance on unseen data.

## Training a Network

The process of modifying the model's weights and biases in order to reduce the error (or loss) between the target values and the predicted output is known as training a neural network. This process typically involves several key steps:

**Initialization of Weights:** The training process starts by initializing the network's weights and biases. The weights are commonly initialized either randomly or through specific techniques such as Xavier initialization or He initialization, which are designed to mitigate challenges like vanishing or exploding gradients. On the other hand, biases are generally initialized to small constant values, frequently set to zero, to maintain stability during the early stages of training.

**Forward Propagation:** During forward propagation, the input data is passed sequentially through each layer of the network, ultimately producing an output. At each layer, a linear transformation is applied to the inputs by multiplying them with weights and adding biases. This is followed by an activation function (such as ReLU, Sigmoid, or Tanh), which introduces non-linearity to the model. This process is repeated across all layers, with each layer refining the information, until the final output layer is reached, generating the predicted result.

- Input Layer: The network receives the input data.
- Hidden Layers: Each hidden layer processes the input and applies an activation function to learn patterns and features.
- Output Layer: The final layer produces the predicted output of the network.

**Loss Calculation:** After the network generates an output, the subsequent step is to compute the loss (or error). This is achieved by measuring the discrepancy between the predicted output and the actual target values, using a loss function (also referred to as a cost function). Common loss functions include:

- Mean Squared Error (MSE) for regression tasks
- Cross-Entropy Loss for classification tasks
- The loss function quantifies how well the network's predictions match the target values. A lower loss indicates better performance.

**Backward Propagation (Backpropagation):** Backpropagation is a fundamental algorithm for training neural networks. It efficiently computes the gradients of the loss function in relation to the network's weights and biases. This process enables the network to adjust its parameters systematically, optimizing them to reduce the loss and improve its predictive accuracy over time.

- **Gradient Calculation:** By applying the chain rule of calculus, gradients are computed layer by layer, beginning from the output layer and propagating backward through the network. This process enables the network to assess the contribution of each weight to the overall error, allowing for precise adjustments during the learning process.
- **Error Propagation:** The errors from the output are transmitted back through the network, allowing the weights to be adjusted in a manner that minimizes the overall error, optimizing the model's performance.

**Weight Update (Optimization):** After calculating the gradients, the next step is to adjust the weights in order to minimize the loss. This is achieved through an optimization algorithm, with Stochastic Gradient Descent (SGD) being the most widely used method. Optimization algorithms work as follows:

- Gradient Descent: The weights are updated in the gradient's negative direction, which minimizes the loss.
- Learning Rate: The magnitude of the step taken towards the gradient is governed by the learning rate. A smaller learning rate may result in slow convergence, whereas a larger learning rate could cause the algorithm to overshoot the optimal solution.

There are variations of gradient descent:

- **Batch Gradient Descent:** Weights are updated using the complete dataset.

- **Stochastic Gradient Descent (SGD):** Weights are updated one data point at a time.
- **Mini-Batch Gradient Descent:** Utilizing a tiny portion of the dataset (mini-batch), weights are updated.
- To increase convergence and efficiency, sophisticated optimizers like Adam or RMSprop combine the advantages of SGD and momentum.

**Iteration/Epochs:** Training a neural network involves multiple iterations, commonly referred to as epochs. An epoch represents a full pass through the entire dataset. During each epoch, the network executes forward propagation, calculates the loss, backpropagates the error, and adjusts the weights accordingly. As the network progresses through each epoch, it refines its predictions, leading to increased accuracy and a reduction in the loss function.

**Epochs:** The total number of times the entire dataset is processed through the network during training is referred to as the number of epochs. While increasing the number of epochs typically enhances learning, an excessive number of epochs can lead to overfitting, where the model becomes too specialized to the training data and performs poorly on unseen data.

**Evaluation:** After the training process, the model is evaluated on a separate validation set to assess its ability to generalize. This step is crucial for determining how well the model will perform on unseen data. Based on its performance on the validation set, the model may undergo further refinement, such as adjustments to the learning rate or modifications to its architecture, to improve its overall effectiveness.

**Stopping Criteria:** Training stops when one of the following conditions is met:

- The model demonstrates satisfactory performance on the validation set, indicating effective generalization to unseen data.
- The loss curve has plateaued, suggesting that additional training does not lead to significant improvements in model performance.
- The maximum number of epochs or iterations has been reached, completing the training process.

**Overfitting and Regularization:** During the training process, it is essential to continuously monitor the network for indications of overfitting, a condition where the model becomes excessively customized to the training data, leading to poor performance on unseen data. To mitigate this risk and promote better generalization, regularization techniques such as dropout, L2 regularization, and early stopping are employed, helping the model maintain its ability to perform effectively on new, unseen data.

**Testing and Deployment:** Once the network has been trained and evaluated, it should be tested on an independent test set to verify its ability to generalize effectively to new, unseen data. Following this, the model is prepared for deployment in real-world applications, where it can accurately make predictions on fresh, previously unencountered data.

## Loss Functions

A loss function, also known as a cost function, is a fundamental element in machine learning and neural networks. It quantifies the discrepancy between a model's predicted output and the true target values, often referred to as the ground truth. The objective during model training is to minimize this loss function, thereby refining the model's predictions to more closely align with the actual values. The choice of loss function varies depending on the specific type of machine learning task, such as regression or classification, as different tasks require different approaches to measuring error.

### 1. Mean Squared Error (MSE)

- Used for: Regression tasks
- Formula:

$$MSE = \frac{1}{n}\sum_{i=1}^{n}(y_i - \hat{y}_i)^2$$

- Where yi is the true value and y^ is the predicted value for the i-th data point, and n is the number of data points.

The Mean Squared Error (MSE) measures the average of the squared differences between the true values and the predicted values. By squaring the errors, this loss function imposes a significant penalty on large deviations, making it particularly sensitive to outliers. MSE is commonly employed in regression tasks due to its ability to offer a smooth and continuous gradient, facilitating efficient optimization. Additionally, its sensitivity to large errors makes it effective for minimizing substantial discrepancies in predictions.

### 2. Mean Absolute Error (MAE)

- Used for: Regression tasks
- Formula:

$$MAE = \frac{1}{n}\sum_{i=1}^{n}|y_i - \hat{y}_i|$$

- Where $y_i$ is the true value, $y^\wedge_i$ is the predicted value, and nnn is the number of data points.

The Mean Absolute Error (MAE) quantifies the average of the absolute differences between the actual and predicted values. Unlike Mean Squared Error (MSE), which squares the differences, MAE avoids exaggerating larger discrepancies, making it less sensitive to significant errors. As a result, MAE offers greater robustness in the presence of outliers.

### 3. Cross-Entropy Loss (Log Loss)

- Used for: Classification tasks (especially binary and multi-class classification)
- Binary Cross-Entropy Formula:

$$\text{Binary Cross-Entropy} = -\frac{1}{n}\sum_{i=1}^{n}\left[y_i \cdot \log(\hat{y}_i) + (1 - y_i) \cdot \log(1 - \hat{y}_i)\right]$$

- Where $y_i$ is the true label (0 or 1), and $y\hat{}_i$ is the predicted probability for class 1.

Multi-Class Cross-Entropy:

$$\text{Categorical Cross-Entropy} = -\sum_{i=1}^{n}\sum_{c=1}^{C} y_{ic} \cdot \log(\hat{y}_{ic})$$

- Where C is the number of classes, $y_i c$ is the true label for class c, and $y\hat{}_{ic}$ is the predicted probability for class ccc.

Cross-entropy loss is a widely used objective function in classification tasks. In binary classification, it measures the difference between the true label and the predicted probability using a logarithmic scale. For multi-class classification, this concept is extended to compute the loss across all possible classes. Cross-entropy is especially valuable for probabilistic models, as it assigns a higher penalty to predictions that significantly diverge from the true label's probability distribution. This makes it an effective and robust loss function for a variety of classification problems, including image classification and text categorization.

### 4. Hinge Loss

Used for: Support Vector Machines (SVMs) and binary classification

Formula:

$$\text{Hinge Loss} = \sum_{i=1}^{n} \max(0, 1 - y_i \cdot \hat{y}_i)$$

- Where $y_i$ is the true label (-1 or +1) and $y\hat{}_i$ is the predicted output.

Hinge loss is primarily used in Support Vector Machine (SVM) models to maximize the margin between distinct classes. For correctly classified samples that are far from the decision boundary, the loss is 0. However, if a sample is misclassified or falls within the margin, the loss increases linearly. This loss function drives the model to not only correctly classify points but also to do so with as large a margin as possible, ensuring better generalization and robustness.

## 5. Huber Loss

Used for: Regression tasks, especially when dealing with outliers

- Formula:

$$L_\delta(y, \hat{y}) = \begin{cases} \frac{1}{2}(y - \hat{y})^2 & \text{for } |y - \hat{y}| \leq \delta \\ \delta \cdot \left(|y - \hat{y}| - \frac{1}{2}\delta\right) & \text{for } |y - \hat{y}| > \delta \end{cases}$$

- Where y is the true value, y^ is the predicted value, and δ is a threshold parameter.

The Huber loss function is a hybrid of Mean Squared Error (MSE) for small errors and Mean Absolute Error (MAE) for larger ones. This combination allows it to maintain the advantages of both, while being less sensitive to outliers than MSE. As a result, Huber loss is more robust when dealing with data that contains outliers. Specifically, for errors smaller than a threshold(delta), it behaves like MSE, penalizing small discrepancies quadratically. For errors larger than(delta), it transitions to behave like MAE, providing a linear penalty that reduces the influence of large outliers.

## 6. Kullback-Leibler Divergence (KL Divergence)

Used for: Comparing two probability distributions

- Formula:

$$D_{KL}(P||Q) = \sum_i P(x_i) \cdot \log\left(\frac{P(x_i)}{Q(x_i)}\right)$$

- Where P and Q are two probability distributions.

KL Divergence (Kullback-Leibler Divergence) quantifies the extent to which one probability distribution deviates from a second, reference probability distribution. It plays a crucial role in various machine learning tasks, including variational inference, generative models (such as GANs), and model calibration. By penalizing the divergence between predicted and true distributions, KL Divergence encourages the model to generate outputs that closely align with the actual distribution, thereby improving model accuracy and robustness.

## 7. Cosine Similarity Loss

Used for: Text classification, document similarity

- Formula:

$$\text{Cosine Similarity} = \frac{A \cdot B}{||A|| \cdot ||B||}$$

- Where, A and $B$ are vectors representing two items.

Cosine similarity is a metric that measures the cosine of the angle between two vectors within a multi-dimensional space. In machine learning, it is frequently employed to evaluate the similarity between two text documents or data points. The cosine similarity loss function works by minimizing the angle between the predicted and actual vectors, guiding models to optimize predictions by emphasizing the similarity between items. This approach helps improve the accuracy of models by focusing on the relationship between features, rather than their absolute values.

**Note:**

- Mean Squared Error (MSE) and Mean Absolute Error (MAE) are commonly used in regression tasks to assess the disparity between predicted and actual values, with MSE emphasizing larger errors and MAE offering a more robust evaluation.
- Cross-Entropy Loss is typically applied in classification tasks, where it measures the difference between predicted probabilities and the true class labels, helping to optimize model performance in categorical predictions.
- Hinge Loss is primarily used in Support Vector Machines (SVMs) for classification problems, focusing on maximizing the decision margin between different classes for better classification accuracy.
- Huber Loss integrates the benefits of both MSE and MAE, providing robustness to outliers by combining the squared error for small differences and absolute error for larger discrepancies.
- Kullback-Leibler (KL) Divergence quantifies the difference between two probability distributions, making it essential for tasks such as training generative models and measuring how one distribution diverges from another.
- Cosine Similarity Loss is employed when measuring the similarity between two vectors, often used in tasks like natural language processing (NLP) and recommendation systems, where the orientation of the vectors matters more than their magnitude.

## Back Propagation and Stochastic Gradient Descent

### Backpropagation

Backpropagation is a fundamental algorithm used to train neural networks, enabling them to learn and improve from the errors made in their predictions. The process starts with a forward pass, where input data is fed through the network to generate an output. The difference between the predicted and actual values is then calculated using a loss function. During the backward pass, backpropagation employs the chain rule of calculus to compute the gradient of the loss function with respect to each weight in the network. These gradients reveal how much each weight contributes to the overall error. By iteratively adjusting the weights in the direction that minimizes this error, the neural network fine-tunes its parameters, gradually improving its ability to make more accurate predictions.

### Stochastic Gradient Descent (SGD)

Stochastic Gradient Descent (SGD) is an efficient optimization technique used to update the parameters of a model in order to minimize the loss function. In contrast to batch gradient descent, which calculates gradients using the entire dataset, SGD updates the model's weights after processing each individual data point or a small batch of data. This approach makes SGD faster and more memory-efficient, particularly when dealing with large datasets. The update process involves computing the gradient of the loss function with respect to the model's weights and adjusting the weights in the direction of the negative gradient. While SGD introduces some noise due to its inherent variance, this randomness can actually be beneficial by helping the algorithm escape local minima and discover better global solutions. Variants of SGD, such as mini-batch SGD, momentum-based methods, and adaptive learning techniques, enhance its stability and speed up convergence. When combined with backpropagation, SGD serves as a foundational technique in neural network training, enabling models to effectively learn complex patterns from data.

## Neural Networks as Universal Function Approximates

Neural networks are frequently described as universal function approximators, a concept derived from the universal approximation theorem. According to this theorem, a neural network with at least one hidden layer and a non-linear activation function has the potential to approximate any continuous function with arbitrary precision, provided it has an adequate number of neurons and properly adjusted weights. In essence, this means that neural networks, in theory, possess the capability to model and approximate any function—whether simple or intricate—given proper training.

### Concept:

The power of neural networks as function approximators lies in their remarkable ability to learn intricate relationships between inputs and outputs. During the training process, neural networks iteratively adjust their weights and biases to minimize the discrepancy between the predicted output and the actual target. By incorporating sufficient hidden layers and neurons, these networks can effectively capture complex patterns and subtle nuances within data, making them highly versatile and well-suited for a variety of tasks, including image recognition, natural language processing, and time-series forecasting.

### *How It Works:*

- Input Layer: The input layer allows data to enter the network and feed it into the layers that follow.
- Hidden Layers: These intermediate layers, made up of neurons, perform complex computations on the inputs by utilizing weighted sums and activation functions. As the number of hidden layers increases, the network becomes capable of capturing and modeling increasingly intricate relationships and patterns in the data.
- Output Layer: The final layer produces the network's prediction, which is then compared to the actual value during training to compute the loss function.
- Training: Using backpropagation and optimization methods such as stochastic gradient descent (SGD), the network iteratively adjusts its weights and biases, refining its approximation to minimize errors and enhance performance.

The universal approximation theorem states that a sufficiently complex neural network has the capacity to approximate any function. However, it does not provide any assurance regarding the efficiency with which this approximation can be achieved. In practice, the accuracy of the approximation is influenced by several critical factors, including the network's architecture, the volume of training data, and the effectiveness of optimization techniques. Moreover, real-world scenarios often present noisy or incomplete data, which introduces additional complexities that can hinder the network's ability to achieve precise function approximation.

### Limitations:

While neural networks possess the theoretical capability to approximate any function, practical challenges often emerge. The network's ability to model complex functions is significantly influenced by factors such as its architecture (e.g., the number of layers and neurons), the selection of activation functions, and the quality of the training process. Additionally, overfitting may arise when the network becomes excessively complex, capturing not just the genuine patterns in the data but also the noise. Therefore, while neural networks are highly effective function approximators, achieving successful generalization requires meticulous design, regularization, and rigorous validation to avoid potential pitfalls.

## Summary

This chapter provides an in-depth exploration of key concepts in machine learning, beginning with linear models such as Support Vector Machines (SVMs), Perceptrons, and Logistic Regression, which are commonly used for classification tasks. It then progresses to the realm of neural networks, examining the limitations of shallow networks in capturing complex patterns and highlighting the superior capability of deep networks to learn intricate, non-linear relationships. The chapter further explains the neural network training process, focusing on the critical roles of loss functions, backpropagation for adjusting weights, and Stochastic Gradient Descent (SGD) for optimizing the learning process efficiently. Concluding with a discussion on neural networks as universal function approximators, the chapter emphasizes their potential to approximate any continuous function with sufficient layers and neurons, showcasing their extraordinary power for modeling complex data.

## Exercise Questions

- What is the main difference between a Perceptron and a Support Vector Machine (SVM)?
- How does Logistic Regression differ from Linear Regression, especially in terms of output?
- Explain the concept of a margin in the context of Support Vector Machines.
- What is the significance of the activation function in a neural network? Provide an example.
- What is a shallow neural network, and how does it differ from a deep neural network?
- Describe the process of backpropagation in neural networks. Why is it important for training?
- What role do loss functions play in training a neural network? Give examples of common loss functions.
- Explain the difference between Batch Gradient Descent and Stochastic Gradient Descent.
- What does it mean for a neural network to be a universal function approximator?
- In practical machine learning, why might a neural network with too many layers lead to overfitting? How can this be mitigated?

CHAPTER - 7

# Concepts in Deep Learning and Neural Network

## History of Deep Learning

The history of deep learning has its origins in the broader domain of artificial intelligence (AI) and neural networks, evolving over several decades through significant theoretical advancements, groundbreaking algorithmic innovations, and continuous technological progress (see Figure 7.1).

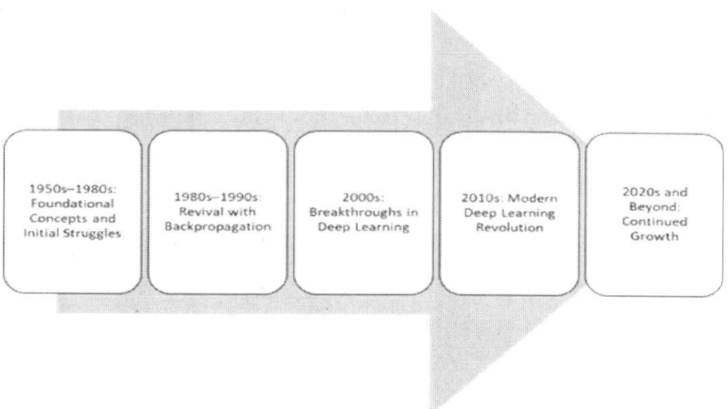


**Figure 7.1: History of Deep Learning.**

- Below is a detailed account of its evolution:

1. 1950s–1980s: Foundational Concepts and Initial Struggles

## Origins of Neural Networks:

The idea of mimicking the human brain through artificial neurons was pioneered in the 1940s by Warren McCulloch and Walter Pitts. They developed a revolutionary mathematical model of neural activity, laying the cornerstone for neural networks. In 1958, Frank Rosenblatt further advanced this concept by introducing the Perceptron, a pioneering neural network that could learn and identify linearly separable patterns, marking a significant milestone in the field's evolution.

### Challenges with Multilayer Networks:

- Insufficient training algorithms made it challenging for researchers to extend the perceptron to multilayer architectures.
- In their 1969 book Perceptrons, Marvin Minsky and Seymour Papert criticized the shortcomings of single-layer perceptrons, which resulted in less money and interest in neural network research

2. 1980s–1990s: Revival with Backpropagation

### Backpropagation Algorithm:

In the 1980s, Geoffrey Hinton, David Rumelhart, and Ronald Williams revolutionized the field of neural networks with the popularization of the backpropagation algorithm. This innovative method allowed for the efficient training of multilayer neural networks by minimizing errors through gradient descent. Their breakthrough unlocked the potential for neural networks to tackle more complex problems, sparking a resurgence of interest and development in the field of artificial intelligence.

### Emergence of Deeper Architectures:

Researchers began delving into deeper networks; however, computational limitations and the vanishing gradient problem—where gradients become exceedingly small during backpropagation in deep networks—significantly impaired their effectiveness.

3. 2000s: Breakthroughs in Deep Learning

### Rise of Computational Power:

Advancements in computing hardware, especially the development of Graphics Processing Units (GPUs), have significantly accelerated the training of deep neural networks, making it faster and more efficient. The availability of vast datasets, such as ImageNet, which contains millions of labeled images, further revolutionized model training by providing rich, high-quality data for improved learning and performance.

### Algorithmic Innovations:

In the mid-2000s, Geoffrey Hinton and his collaborators pioneered unsupervised pre-training techniques, such as Deep Belief Networks (DBNs), which revolutionized the training of deeper neural networks. Furthermore, the introduction of Rectified Linear Units (ReLU) as activation functions effectively tackled the vanishing gradient problem, significantly enhancing the efficiency of training deep learning models.

4. 2010s: Modern Deep Learning Revolution

## Breakthrough Models:

The triumph of AlexNet in the 2012 ImageNet competition heralded the dawn of the modern deep learning era, showcasing the transformative power of convolutional neural networks (CNNs) in image recognition. Following this breakthrough, architectures such as VGGNet, ResNet, and Inception introduced groundbreaking innovations in network design, significantly advancing both the accuracy and efficiency of deep learning models.

## Generative Models and GANs:

Generative Adversarial Networks (GANs), introduced by Ian Goodfellow in 2014, have transformed the landscape of generative tasks, empowering the creation of highly realistic images, videos, and other multimedia content with unprecedented precision and creativity.

## Applications Across Domains:

Deep learning has evolved far beyond image recognition, making significant strides in fields such as natural language processing (e.g., transformers, BERT), speech recognition, healthcare, autonomous vehicles, and numerous other cutting-edge applications.

5. 2020s and Beyond: Continued Growth

## Transformer Architectures and Large Language Models:

Transformer-based models, such as GPT and BERT, have significantly expanded the horizons of deep learning, especially in the realms of language comprehension and generation. Furthermore, breakthroughs in self-supervised and semi-supervised learning have lessened the reliance on vast labeled datasets, enabling more efficient and scalable models.

## Integration with Other Technologies:

Deep learning is progressively being integrated with reinforcement learning (such as AlphaGo) and generative models, enabling a wide range of applicationsfrom innovative creative tasks to tackling intricate challenges across science and engineering fields.

## Factors Driving Deep Learning Success

- Big Data: The vast availability of both labeled and unlabeled datasets has revolutionized machine learning, enabling more robust and accurate models.

- Advanced Algorithms: Breakthrough techniques, such as batch normalization, dropout, and state-of-the-art optimizers like Adam, have significantly enhanced the performance and stability of deep learning models.
- Hardware Advancements: The development of powerful hardware, including GPUs, TPUs, and the widespread use of cloud computing, has drastically reduced training times, making large-scale models more feasible and efficient.
- Community and Open-Source Tools: Platforms like TensorFlow and PyTorch have democratized access to deep learning, empowering developers, researchers, and organizations worldwide with cutting-edge tools and resources for innovation.

Deep learning has emerged as a fundamental pillar of artificial intelligence, and its relentless advancement is catalyzing transformative shifts across industries. Fueled by continuous research and innovation, the field is well-positioned to address increasingly complex challenges in the future, unlocking new possibilities and solutions.

## A Probabilistic Theory of Deep Learning

The probabilistic theory of deep learning aims to elucidate the effectiveness of deep neural networks by leveraging principles of probability and statistics (Figure 7.2). This theoretical framework offers valuable insights into the underlying mechanisms of generalization, learning dynamics, and the overall behavior of models. Below is an explanation of the core ideas:

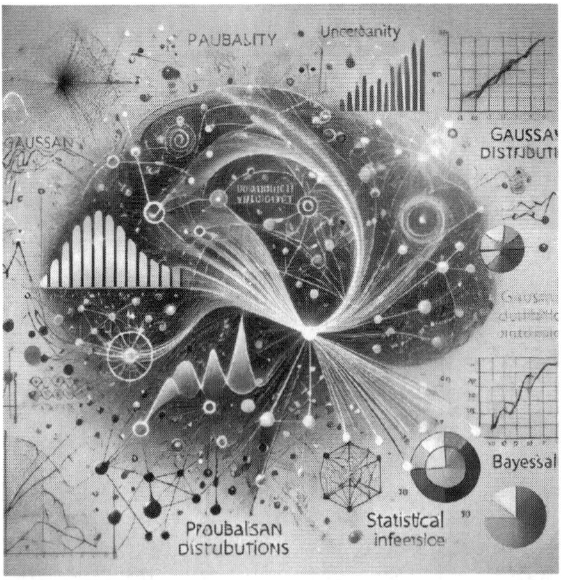


**Figure 7.2: Probabilistic Theory.**

## 1. Deep Learning as Probabilistic Inference

Deep learning can be understood as a process of probabilistic inference aimed at modeling the underlying probability distribution of data. Neural networks, especially deep architectures, serve as powerful and flexible function approximators, mapping inputs to outputs while effectively capturing the inherent uncertainty within the data.

- Bayesian Perspective: From a Bayesian perspective, deep learning seeks to determine the posterior distribution $P(\theta|X,Y)$ denotes $\theta$the model parameters, X represents the input data, andY corresponds to the outputs..
- Maximum Likelihood Estimation (MLE): Training a neural network typically involves optimizing the likelihood of the observed data, aiming to identify the parameter values that most accurately represent and explain the underlying patterns within the data.

## 2. Representation Learning

Deep networks excel in hierarchical representation learning, with each successive layer progressively capturing increasingly abstract features, enabling the model to learn complex patterns and relationships at various levels of abstraction.

*This is connected to probabilistic principles:*

- Low-Level Features: The initial layers capture fundamental patterns, such as edges in images, which align with high-probability areas of simple distributions.
- High-Level Features: Deeper layers uncover intricate patterns and relationships, effectively capturing the dependencies that characterize the joint probability distribution$P(X)$.

## 3. Generalization and Overfitting

The probabilistic theory elucidates generalization, which refers to a network's ability to perform effectively on unseen data, by leveraging concepts such as uncertainty, distribution, and probabilistic modeling:

- Implicit Regularization: Techniques such as dropout, weight decay, and even the design of neural network architectures themselves serves as forms of regularization. These methods help prevent overfitting by discouraging the development of overly complex models that would otherwise only fit the training data, ensuring better generalization to unseen data.
- Bayesian Neural Networks (BNNs): By treating weights as random variables and utilizing posterior distributions, Bayesian Neural Networks (BNNs) provide a rigorous framework for modeling uncertainty, effectively mitigating overfitting and enhancing the model's generalization capabilities.

### 4. Noise and Stochasticity in Deep Learning

The stochastic nature of the training process, exemplified by techniques like Stochastic Gradient Descent (SGD), can be interpreted through a probabilistic lens:

- Noisy Optimization: Stochastic Gradient Descent (SGD) introduces randomness by updating weights through random mini-batches. This inherent noise functions as a regularizer, enabling the model to avoid getting stuck in local minima and facilitating a more thorough exploration of the loss surface.
- Probabilistic Sampling: Data augmentation and dropout techniques implicitly form ensembles by effectively sampling from a variety of model configurations during the training process.

### 5. Deep Learning and Information Theory

The Information Bottleneck Principle offers a probabilistic explanation of how deep networks learn:

- Compression: Networks condense input information into efficient representations by eliminating unnecessary details, emphasizing key features that are essential for producing the desired output.
- Trade-Off: The key to effective generalization lies in striking the right balance—retaining sufficient information to accurately predict outcomes while minimizing unnecessary complexity.

### 6. Limitations and Challenges

While probabilistic theory provides a foundation, challenges remain:

- Non-Convex Optimization: The training of neural networks involves non-convex loss surfaces, which makes theoretical assurances challenging.
- Black-Box Nature: Deep network interpretation is still difficult, particularly in high-dimensional spaces, even with probabilistic models.

## Applications of Probabilistic Theory

- Utilized for tasks that call for quantifying uncertainty, like autonomous driving or medical diagnosis.
- Variational Autoencoders (VAEs) and Generative Adversarial Networks (GANs) are instances of such models that are backed by probabilistic frameworks.
- Using probability distribution estimation to make use of unlabeled data.

The probabilistic theory of deep learning provides a basis for analyzing neural networks' behavior and directing future developments by bridging the gap between theoretical knowledge and their empirical success.

## Back propagation and regularization

Backpropagation is a fundamental algorithm commonly used for training neural networks. It calculates the gradient of the loss function in relation to the network's weights and biases, enabling the adjustment of these parameters to minimize the error and improve the model's performance.

### *How it Works:*

- Forward Pass: By comparing predictions with actual targets, data moves through the network to determine the output and the corresponding loss.
- Backward Pass: The error is propagated backward through the network by applying the chain rule of calculus, enabling the computation of the gradient of the loss function with respect to each weight.
- Weight Updates: Gradients are utilized to update the weights in a neural network, typically through an optimization algorithm such as Stochastic Gradient Descent (SGD), which iteratively adjusts the weights to minimize the error and improve the model's performance.

**Mathematical Basis:** The partial derivatives of the loss $L$ with respect to each parameter $\theta$ are calculated:

$$\frac{\partial L}{\partial \theta} = \frac{\partial L}{\partial y} \cdot \frac{\partial y}{\partial z} \cdot \frac{\partial z}{\partial \theta}$$

Here, $y$ represents the activation output, and z represents the input to the activation.

### Regularization

Regularization techniques help prevent overfitting by imposing penalties on excessive model complexity or by enforcing constraints on parameter values, thereby ensuring the model maintains its ability to generalize effectively to new, unseen data.

### Types of Regularization:

- L1 Regularization (Lasso): Applies a fine based on the weights' absolute values:

$$L_{\text{reg}} = L + \lambda \sum |w|$$

Encourages sparsity, forcing some weights to become zero.

- L2 Regularization (Ridge): Adds a fine based on the weights' squared value:

$$L_{\text{reg}} = L + \lambda \sum w^2$$

Discourages large weights, spreading the influence across multiple features.

- Dropout: During training, a random fraction of neurons is set to zero, effectively preventing feature co-adaptation and promoting more robust learning.
- Early Stopping: Stops training when the validation error begins to rise, effectively preventing overfitting and ensuring better model generalization.

## Integration of Back Propagation and Regularization

Regularization terms can be seamlessly integrated into the loss function during backpropagation, ensuring that weight updates account for both error minimization and the imposed regularization constraints, thereby promoting a more balanced and robust model.

***For example:***

$$L_{\text{total}} = L + \text{Regularization term}$$

By integrating backpropagation with regularization, neural networks strike an optimal balance between accurately fitting the training data and preserving their ability to generalize effectively to unseen data.

## Batch Normalization

Batch Normalization (BatchNorm) is a vital deep learning technique that significantly enhances the training efficiency and overall performance of neural networks. It works by normalizing the inputs to each layer within a mini-batch, effectively mitigating the problem of internal covariate shift, which arises from the changing distribution of activations during training. This normalization process not only stabilizes the training dynamics but also accelerates convergence, enabling neural networks to learn more effectively and robustly.

### *How Batch Normalization Works?*

BatchNormalization (BatchNorm) works by standardizing the inputs of each layer within a mini-batch, ensuring that they have a mean of zero and a variance of one. This normalization process helps improve model training stability and accelerates convergence by reducing internal covariate shift. For an input $x$, it calculates the normalized value $x^\wedge$ as follows:

$$\hat{x} = \frac{x - \mu}{\sqrt{\sigma^2 + \epsilon}}$$

Here:

- $\mu$ is the mean of the mini-batch.
- $\sigma^2$ is the variance of the mini-batch.
- $\epsilon$ is a small constant added for numerical stability.

After normalization, BatchNorm scales and shifts the normalized values using two learnable parameters, $\gamma$ (scale) and $\beta$ (shift):

$$y = \gamma\hat{x} + \beta$$

This step guarantees that the network maintains its ability to learn diverse representations, even after undergoing normalization.

## Benefits of Batch Normalization

- Faster Convergence: By reducing internal covariate shift, BatchNorm significantly accelerates the training process. It facilitates faster convergence of neural networks by allowing the use of higher learning rates, all while mitigating the risk of instability.
- Improved Generalization: Batch Normalization exerts a regularizing effect similar to noise injection, effectively mitigating overfitting. This built-in regularization often obviates the need for additional techniques, such as dropout, to prevent overfitting in deep learning models.
- Reduced Sensitivity to Initialization: Neural networks incorporating BatchNorm are less reliant on precise parameter initialization, which streamlines the training process and enhances overall model performance.
- Versatility Across Architectures: BatchNorm is extensively utilized in Convolutional Neural Networks (CNNs), Generative Adversarial Networks (GANs), and various other deep learning architectures to significantly improve model stability, accelerate convergence, and enhance overall performance.

## Challenges of Batch Normalization

- Small mini-batches may result in inaccurate estimates of the mean and variance, which can compromise the effectiveness of normalization and lead to suboptimal model performance.
- In sequential data, such as time-series or natural language, BatchNorm can interfere with temporal dependencies. Alternatives like Layer Normalization or Group Normalization are often more suitable for Recurrent Neural Networks (RNNs).
- During inference, the normalization statistics are derived from the population mean and variance calculated during training, which may not

always align with the distributions of unseen data, potentially affecting model accuracy.

## Applications of Batch Normalization

A crucial element in modern deep learning architectures is Batch-Norm, including:

- Image Classification: Batch Normalization (BatchNorm), commonly used in Convolutional Neural Networks (CNNs) such as ResNet and VGG, enhances model accuracy and significantly speeds up the training process by stabilizing learning and reducing internal covariate shift.
- Natural Language Processing (NLP): Employed in Transformer models and various other architectures to enhance learning stability and improve training efficiency.
- Generative Models: In Generative Adversarial Networks (GANs), Batch Normalization (BatchNorm) plays a crucial role in stabilizing the training process, promoting smoother convergence, and effectively mitigating the risk of mode collapse.

# VC Dimension and Neural Nets-Deep vs. Shallow Networks

## VC Dimension and Neural Networks

The Vapnik–Chervonenkis (VC) Dimension serves as a key metric for assessing the capacity or expressiveness of a machine learning model, specifically its ability to generalize effectively to previously unseen data. In the context of neural networks, the VC dimension is closely tied to the architecture's complexity, including factors like the number of neurons, layers, and connections. It provides valuable insight into how well a network can classify data across varying levels of complexity and helps to determine the model's potential to perform on diverse, real-world tasks.

## Aspects of VC Dimension in Neural Networks

- Definition: The VC dimension of a model refers to the largest set of points that the model is capable of "shattering." A set is considered shattered if the model can correctly classify every possible labeling of those points. In other words, a model with a higher VC dimension has the capacity to represent more intricate and complex relationships between the data.
- Complexity and Overfitting: A higher VC dimension indicates a greater capacity for learning, but it also raises the likelihood of overfitting, where the model excels on training data yet struggles to generalize to unseen data. To counteract this, regularization techniques are crucial in controlling model complexity and improving its ability to generalize effectively.

- Implications for Neural Networks: Neural networks with a greater number of layers and neurons typically exhibit a higher VC dimension. However, this increased complexity doesn't necessarily lead to improved generalization. Achieving optimal performance requires a balance between model complexity, ample training data, and the implementation of effective regularization techniques.

## Deep vs. Shallow Networks

The key distinction between deep and shallow networks lies in their architectural design, computational complexity, and their capacity to tackle complex problems.

## Shallow Networks

- Architecture: Shallow networks typically comprise one or two hidden layers, making their structure more straightforward and less demanding in terms of computational resources.
- Learning Capability: These networks are highly effective for straightforward tasks like linear classification, basic regression, and handling low-dimensional data. However, they face challenges when tackling problems that involve intricate patterns or complex relationships.

## Advantages:

- Simple to understand and train, making them user-friendly for implementation.
- Efficient in terms of computational power and memory usage, reducing resource demands.
- Highly effective with smaller datasets and relatively straightforward tasks, ensuring reliable performance.

**Limitations:** Shallow networks often require an impractically large number of neurons to solve complex problems, rendering them inefficient for handling such tasks effectively.

## Deep Networks

- Architecture: Deep neural networks consist of multiple hidden layers, which can range from tens to even hundreds. This layered structure enables them to effectively capture and model hierarchical representations of data, allowing for more complex and nuanced patterns to be learned.
- Learning Capability: Deep neural networks are highly effective at tackling complex tasks such as image recognition, speech processing, and AI-driven gaming. By learning hierarchically, they extract fundamental features such as edges in imagesat the initial layers, and progressively

integrate these into more abstract, high-level representations, such as objects or scenes, as they move through deeper layers. This layered learning process allows them to handle intricate patterns and nuances, making them ideal for tasks that require advanced perception and decision-making.

## Advantages:

- Capable of modeling complex and hierarchical patterns with precision.
- Delivering cutting-edge performance across domains such as computer vision, natural language processing (NLP), and time-series analysis.

## Limitations:

- Computationally demanding and highly memory-intensive, requiring significant resources.
- Depend on vast datasets and meticulous parameter tuning to avoid overfitting.
- Susceptible to training difficulties, such as vanishing or exploding gradients, which can hinder performance.

**Comparison Table: Deep vs. Shallow Networks, as mention in Table 7.1.**

**Table 7.1: Deep vs. Shallow Networks.**

| Aspect | Deep Neural Networks (DNNs) | Shallow Neural Networks |
|---|---|---|
| Layers | Have multiple hidden layers (often > 2) | Typically have a single hidden layer |
| Depth | Deep structure with many layers, enabling complex feature extraction | Shallow structure with few layers, less complexity |
| Learning Capacity | High learning capacity, able to model intricate patterns | Limited learning capacity, struggles with complex patterns |
| Training Time | Longer training time due to more parameters and layers | Faster training time due to fewer parameters and layers |
| Performance | Better performance on complex tasks like image recognition, NLP | Suitable for simpler tasks like linear regression or basic classification |
| Computational Cost | Higher computational cost (memory and processing power) | Lower computational cost |

| Aspect | Deep Neural Networks (DNNs) | Shallow Neural Networks |
|---|---|---|
| Interpretability | Harder to interpret and understand due to complex architectures | Easier to interpret and understand |
| Overfitting Risk | Higher risk of overfitting without proper regularization | Lower risk of overfitting due to fewer parameters |
| Use Cases | Used for complex tasks like image recognition, speech processing, etc. | Used for simpler tasks or when data is less complex |

## Detailed Explanation of Points in Para Form

- **Architecture**: Shallow networks feature a simpler architecture, typically consisting of one or two hidden layers. These networks are computationally efficient and relatively easy to design, making them well-suited for solving low-complexity problems. In contrast, deep networks are characterized by a greater number of hidden layers, which allow them to learn hierarchical features. This layered structure equips deep networks to tackle more complex problems by capturing intricate patterns and relationships within the data.
- **Learning Capability**: Shallow networks excel at handling simple tasks but struggle to capture intricate patterns within the data. In contrast, deep networks are designed to decompose complex problems into more manageable components, utilizing multiple layers to develop a comprehensive and nuanced understanding of the input data.
- **Training Complexity**: Shallow networks are relatively simple to train due to their limited number of parameters. In contrast, deep networks necessitate sophisticated optimization techniques, such as Batch Normalization and the Adam optimizer, to effectively tackle challenges like vanishing gradients and ensure stable training.
- **Applications**: Shallow networks are typically employed in smaller-scale applications, such as low-dimensional regression tasks or linear classification problems. In contrast, deep networks excel in domains that require high precision and advanced pattern recognition, including self-driving cars, voice assistants, and the creation of deepfakes.

## Convolutional Networks

Convolutional Neural Networks (CNNs) are a specialized class of neural networks tailored for processing structured, grid-like data, such as images and videos. These networks are highly effective in tasks like image classification, object detection, and segmentation, owing to their ability to automatically learn spatial hierarchies of features directly from the raw data. Inspired by the human brain's visual processing system, CNNs are structured with multiple layers, each designed to detect increasingly complex patterns, enabling them to capture intricate visual information at various levels of abstraction.

## Components of CNNs

### 1. Convolutional Layer

The convolutional layer serves as the foundational component of Convolutional Neural Networks (CNNs). It applies a series of filters, also known as kernels, to the input data in order to extract essential features. Each filter performs element-wise multiplication with a specific region of the input, and the resulting values are aggregated to form a feature map. This process enables CNNs to identify fundamental patterns such as edges, textures, and more intricate structures within images. Parameters like stride and padding regulate the movement of filters across the input and manage boundary pixels, ultimately impacting the size and quality of the generated feature maps.

### 2. Activation Function

After the convolution operation, an activation function is applied to introduce non-linearity into the network, allowing it to capture and model complex relationships. The Rectified Linear Unit (ReLU) function is commonly employed, which replaces negative values in the feature map with zeros. This non-linearity is crucial as it enables the network to learn and approximate intricate, non-linear patterns, enhancing its ability to effectively handle and understand real-world data.

### 3. Pooling Layer

Pooling layers are employed to decrease the spatial dimensions of feature maps while preserving the most critical information. This is accomplished through techniques such as max pooling, which selects the maximum value within a specified window, or average pooling, which calculates the mean value. By reducing dimensionality, pooling layers not only lower computational complexity but also help prevent overfitting and enhance the network's robustness to small translations in the input data.

### 4. Fully Connected Layer

In the final stages of a Convolutional Neural Network (CNN), the extracted features are flattened into a one-dimensional vector and fed into fully connected layers. These layers establish connections between every neuron and those in both the preceding and subsequent layers, effectively integrating the extracted features for the ultimate classification or regression task. The output from the last fully connected layer is typically passed through a softmax or sigmoid activation function, transforming it into probabilities that correspond to class labels or predictions.

## 5. Dropout

Dropout is a powerful regularization technique employed to mitigate overfitting during the training process. It works by randomly disabling a portion of neurons in each iteration, preventing the network from becoming overly dependent on specific neurons. This process forces the model to develop more diverse and generalized features, ultimately enhancing its ability to perform better on unseen data and increasing its overall robustness.

## Working of CNNs

Convolutional Neural Networks (CNNs) begin by taking an input, typically an image, represented as a grid of pixel values. Through a series of convolutional and pooling layers, the network gradually extracts a hierarchy of features, starting with simple, low-level patterns like edges and textures, and advancing to more complex, high-level concepts such as shapes and objects. These extracted features are then flattened and forwarded to fully connected layers, where they are processed for tasks like classification or regression. The final output layer delivers the model's prediction, such as the probability that the image belongs to a particular category (as illustrated in Figure 7.3).

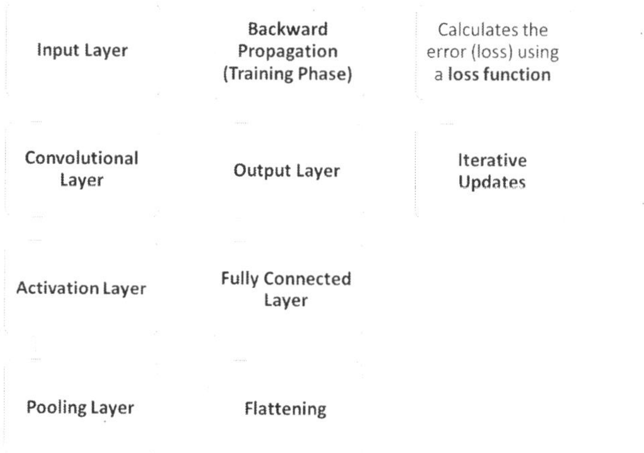


**Figure 7.3: Working Flow.**

## Applications of CNNs

Convolutional Neural Networks (CNNs) have diverse and impactful applications across various fields. In image classification, they accurately identify and categorize images, such as recognizing animals, objects, or scenes. In object detection, CNNs go a step further by not only detecting but also localizing and classifying multiple objects within an image, playing a crucial role in technologies like autonomous vehicles and surveillance systems. For image segmentation, CNNs perform pixel-level labeling, enabling precise delineation of objects or regions, making them invaluable in domains like medical imaging. In facial recognition, CNNs are widely used to identify individuals, enhancing security systems and enabling features in social media platforms. Furthermore, CNNs extend beyond visual tasks, contributing significantly to natural language processing by analyzing text embeddings to recognize patterns for tasks such as sentiment analysis.

### Advantages of CNNs

Convolutional Neural Networks (CNNs) provide substantial advantages owing to their architecture. By autonomously learning pertinent features directly from raw input data, they eliminate the need for manual feature extraction. The incorporation of convolutional layers not only minimizes the number of trainable parameters but also enhances computational efficiency, even in the presence of their complex structure. Additionally, CNNs excel at recognizing spatial hierarchies of patterns, which makes them exceptionally well-suited for image processing and related tasks.

### Limitations of CNNs

Despite their many strengths, Convolutional Neural Networks (CNNs) face several challenges. They require extensive labeled datasets to achieve optimal performance, which are not always readily available. Furthermore, training deep CNNs is computationally demanding, necessitating powerful hardware and substantial processing time. Additionally, while CNNs excel in tasks involving spatial data, such as image processing, they may encounter difficulties when handling non-spatial data, like tabular datasets.

## Generative Adversarial Networks (GAN)

Generative Adversarial Networks (GANs) are a sophisticated class of machine learning models that comprise two neural networks: the Generator and the Discriminator. These networks are trained concurrently in a dynamic, competitive framework. The Generator's goal is to produce synthetic data that is indistinguishable from genuine data, while the Discriminator's task is to accurately differentiate between real and fake samples. This adversarial interaction fuels the Generator's continuous improvement, as it strives to refine its outputs with each iteration.

### Working

Generative Adversarial Networks (GANs) function through a dynamic adversarial interaction between two neural networks: the Generator and the Discriminator. The Generator begins with a random input (a latent vector) and transforms it into synthetic data, such as images or text, that closely resembles real-world examples. On the other hand, the Discriminator evaluates both real data from the training set and the generated synthetic data, classifying them as either real or fake. The Generator's objective is to produce data so convincingly realistic that the Discriminator cannot tell the difference from authentic data, while the Discriminator's goal is to enhance its ability to accurately identify counterfeit data.

This adversarial interplay drives mutual improvement, with the Discriminator being periodically updated to refine its classification accuracy, while the Generator is adjusted to make it more difficult for the Discriminator to spot fake data. Loss functions like binary cross-entropy guide this optimization process. As the networks continue to compete, the Generator becomes increasingly proficient at creating high-quality, lifelike data, while the Discriminator's ability to distinguish between real and fake data diminishes. Ultimately, this results in a Generator that is capable of generating highly realistic data for applications like image synthesis, style transfer, and data augmentation.

## 1. Generator

The Generator is a neural network crafted to generate synthetic data that closely resembles the distribution of real-world data. It begins with a random input, known as the latent vector, and transforms this noise into outputs, such as images, text, or other data formats. The main objective of the Generator is to produce data that can convincingly fool the Discriminator into classifying it as authentic. Through repeated iterations, the Generator refines its ability to generate realistic samples, minimizing the Discriminator's capacity to distinguish between genuine and fake data.

## 2. Discriminator

The Discriminator is a neural network that serves as a binary classifier, tasked with distinguishing between authentic data from the dataset and synthetic data produced by the Generator. Its primary goal is to optimize its ability to accurately differentiate real samples from fake ones. As the Generator evolves and becomes more proficient, the Discriminator must continuously improve its detection capabilities, creating an adversarial feedback loop that drives the refinement of both networks, making this dynamic a highly effective training mechanism.

## 3. Training Process

The training of GANs involves alternating between updating the Generator and Discriminator.

- Generator Training: The Generator improves by receiving feedback from the Discriminator on the authenticity of its generated samples. It then fine-tunes its parameters to reduce the Discriminator's ability to distinguish between real and fake outputs, thereby enhancing the realism of its creations.
- Discriminator Training: The Discriminator is trained to optimize its ability to accurately distinguish between real and fake data. It employs binary cross-entropy loss to enhance its classification performance and minimize errors in the process.

## 4. Loss Functions

- Adversarial loss functions are used by GANs to maximize the discriminator and generator.
- Generator Loss: It aims to reduce the probability that the discriminator will correctly identify generated data as fraudulent.
- Discriminator Loss: Aims to increase the likelihood of accurately identifying authentic and fraudulent samples.

## 5. Applications of GANs

GANs have diverse applications in multiple domains:

- Image Synthesis: Developing lifelike visuals for media, gaming, and art.
- Data Augmentation: Developing artificial datasets to enhance model training.
- Style Transfer: Converting pictures into other formats or styles (photo to painting, for example).
- Super-Resolution: Increasing the resolution of images to improve their quality.
- Text-to-Image Generation: Using textual descriptions to generate images.

## 6. Challenges in GANs

GANs face several challenges, including:

- Mode Collapse: The Generator focuses on a restricted subset of data and generates limited variations.
- Training Instability: The adversarial training procedure may not converge because it is extremely sensitive to hyperparameters.
- Evaluation Metrics: It is difficult and subjective to determine the generated samples' quality.

**Table 7.2: Components and Functions in GANs.**

| Component | Function |
|---|---|
| Generator (G) | Generates synthetic data that resembles real data by taking random noise as input. |
| Discriminator (D) | Distinguishes between real data (from the training set) and fake data (generated by the generator). |
| Noise Vector (z) | A random input vector that the generator uses to produce synthetic data. |
| Loss Function | Measures how well the generator and discriminator are performing. The generator tries to minimize its loss, while the discriminator aims to maximize its loss. |

| | |
|---|---|
| Adversarial Training | A two-player minimax game where the generator tries to improve its data generation and the discriminator tries to become better at distinguishing real from fake data. |
| Optimizer | Typically, algorithms like Adam or SGD used to adjust the parameters of both the generator and discriminator to improve performance. |
| Epochs | The number of times the entire training dataset is passed through the network during training. |
| Latent Space | A high-dimensional space that the generator samples from to create the synthetic data. |

Generative Adversarial Networks (GANs) are a cutting-edge tool in machine learning and generative modeling, consistently advancing the frontier of synthetic data generation and unlocking innovative creative applications (Table 7.2).

## Semi-supervised Learning

Semi-supervised learning is an advanced machine learning approach that integrates both labeled and unlabeled data during the training process. This technique is particularly valuable in situations where acquiring labeled data is costly or labor-intensive, but abundant unlabeled data is accessible. The core principle of semi-supervised learning is to use the small set of labeled data to guide the model's learning, while leveraging the larger pool of unlabeled data to enhance the model's performance and generalization capabilities. It is especially beneficial in fields where labeled data is hard to obtain, such as medical image analysis or large-scale natural language processing tasks.In semi-supervised learning, the model initially trains on the limited labeled data to establish a basic understanding of the task. The model then uses the unlabeled data to predict labels or uncover underlying patterns, grouping similar data points together. These predicted labels, referred to as pseudo-labels, are incorporated into subsequent training iterations, effectively expanding the dataset. Over time, the model refines its predictions and improves accuracy by learning from both the labeled and pseudo-labeled data. This iterative process strengthens the model's ability to learn more meaningful features, enhancing its overall performance even with a small number of labeled examples. Semi-supervised learning has found widespread application in areas like image classification, speech recognition, natural language processing, and medical diagnostics, where large volumes of unlabeled data are readily available, but labeled data remains scarce and expensive to obtain.

**Table 7.3: Semi-Supervised Learning.**

| Aspect | Description |
|---|---|
| Definition | A machine learning approach that uses a small amount of labeled data combined with a large amount of unlabeled data to improve learning accuracy. |

| Aspect | Description |
|---|---|
| Key Characteristics | - Uses both labeled and unlabeled data.<br>- Bridges the gap between supervised and unsupervised learning.<br>- Helps when labeling data is expensive or time-consuming. |
| Advantages | - Reduces the need for large labeled datasets.<br>- Improves model performance compared to purely unsupervised learning.<br>- Useful for real-world problems where labeled data is scarce. |
| Disadvantages | - Can be sensitive to incorrect assumptions about the unlabeled data.<br>- May still require some labeled data.<br>- The performance depends on the quality of both labeled and unlabeled data. |
| Common Algorithms | - Self-training<br>- Co-training<br>- Graph-based methods<br>- Generative models (e.g., Variational Autoencoders) |
| Applications | - Speech and image recognition<br>- Medical diagnosis<br>- Fraud detection<br>- Web content classification |
| Example Scenario | A spam detection system that starts with a small set of manually labeled emails and improves its classification ability by learning from a large set of unlabeled emails. |

## Summary

This chapter provides an in-depth exploration of key concepts in deep learning and neural networks, tracing their evolution and grounding them in probabilistic theories. It highlights the pivotal role of techniques such as backpropagation, regularization, and batch normalization in optimizing neural networks. Additionally, the chapter emphasizes the significance of the VC Dimension in evaluating the capacity of neural models. A comparison between deep and shallow networks underscores the superior ability of deep networks to capture intricate patterns and relationships. The chapter also delves into the workings of convolutional neural networks (CNNs), renowned for their effectiveness in image processing, and generative adversarial networks (GANs), which excel at generating realistic data. Finally, it covers the concept of semi-supervised learning, which leverages both labeled and unlabeled data to enhance learning efficiency, particularly in situations where labeled data is limited.

## Exercise Questions:

- What is the history and evolution of deep learning?
- How does a probabilistic theory contribute to deep learning?
- What are the key principles of backpropagation in neural networks?
- Explain the role of regularization in neural network training.
- What is batch normalization, and how does it improve neural network performance?
- How is the VC Dimension used to evaluate neural networks?
- What are the primary differences between deep and shallow networks?
- How do Convolutional Neural Networks (CNNs) work, and what are their key applications?
- What is the mechanism behind Generative Adversarial Networks (GANs)?
- How does semi-supervised learning benefit from both labeled and unlabeled data?

CHAPTER - 8

# Linear Methods and CNNS

## Linear (PCA, LDA) and Manifolds

### Principal Component Analysis (PCA)

Principal Component Analysis (PCA) is a powerful linear dimensionality reduction technique designed to transform a dataset into a new set of coordinates. These new coordinates, known as principal components, are arranged in descending order based on the variance they capture from the original data. By identifying the directions (principal components) that maximize data variance, PCA effectively simplifies the dataset, retaining its most significant features while minimizing complexity. This allows for a more efficient representation of the data without sacrificing crucial information.

*The working of PCA involves the following steps:*

- **Standardizing the Data:** If the data has different scales, it's essential to normalize or standardize it so that each feature contributes equally to the analysis.
- **Covariance Matrix:** PCA computes the covariance matrix to understand the relationships between different features in the data.
- **Eigenvalues and Eigenvectors:** It calculates the eigenvalues and eigenvectors of the covariance matrix, where the eigenvectors represent the directions of maximum variance (principal components) and eigenvalues represent the magnitude of that variance.
- **Projection:** The data is then projected onto the selected eigenvectors (principal components), resulting in a lower-dimensional representation of the data.
- Applications of PCA include face recognition, image compression, and exploratory data analysis where reducing the dimensions of high-dimensional data helps to find hidden patterns.

## Linear Discriminant Analysis (LDA)

Linear Discriminant Analysis (LDA) is another dimensionality reduction technique but with a different objective than PCA. While PCA focuses on maximizing variance, LDA tries to maximize the separability between different classes in the data. It is a supervised method, meaning it takes class labels into account.

*The working of LDA involves:*

- **Standardizing the Data:** When data features are on different scales, it's crucial to normalize or standardize the data, ensuring that each feature contributes equally to the analysis without one dominating the others due to its scale.
- **Covariance Matrix:** Principal Component Analysis (PCA) first computes the covariance matrix, which helps identify the relationships and correlations between different features in the dataset.
- **Eigenvalues and Eigenvectors:** PCA then calculates the eigenvalues and eigenvectors of the covariance matrix. The eigenvectors define the directions of maximum variance (the principal components), while the eigenvalues represent the magnitude of the variance along these directions, indicating the importance of each principal component.
- **Projection:** The data is projected onto the selected eigenvectors (principal components), reducing the dataset's dimensionality while retaining its most significant variance, allowing for a simplified yet accurate representation of the original data.
- **Applications of PCA:** PCA is widely used in areas like face recognition, image compression, and exploratory data analysis, where dimensionality reduction helps uncover hidden patterns and makes complex data easier to analyze and interpret.

## Manifold Learning

Manifold learning encompasses a collection of techniques designed to reduce high-dimensional data to lower-dimensional representations while maintaining its intrinsic structure. This approach is grounded in the principle that high-dimensional data often resides on a lower-dimensional manifold within the higher-dimensional space. Unlike linear methods such as Principal Component Analysis (PCA) and Linear Discriminant Analysis (LDA), manifold learning methods do not rely on linear assumptions but instead focus on uncovering and preserving the nonlinear relationships inherent in the data.

*Popular manifold learning techniques include:*

- **Isomap:** Isomap integrates concepts from multidimensional scaling (MDS) and graph theory to uncover the underlying manifold of data, effectively preserving geodesic distances—the shortest paths between points on a curved surface—within the dataset.

- Locally Linear Embedding (LLE): LLE focuses on maintaining the local geometric structure of the data, aiming to represent each data point as a linear combination of its neighboring points, thus preserving neighborhood relationships.
- t-Distributed Stochastic Neighbor Embedding (t-SNE): t-SNE is a powerful technique commonly used for visualizing high-dimensional data, emphasizing the preservation of local pairwise similarities when reducing the dimensionality of the data to a more comprehensible, lower-dimensional space.
- Applications of manifold learning: Manifold learning techniques have broad applications in fields such as image recognition, speech processing, and dimensionality reduction, particularly for datasets characterized by complex, nonlinear relationships.

Principal Component Analysis (PCA) and Linear Discriminant Analysis (LDA) are both linear dimensionality reduction techniques, each with distinct goals: PCA seeks to maximize variance in the data, while LDA aims to enhance class separability in Table 8.1. In contrast, manifold learning methods are specifically designed to handle data that exists on a non-linear manifold, making them particularly valuable for complex datasets where linear techniques like PCA and LDA may fall short in capturing the underlying structure.

## Metric Learning

Metric learning is a specialized machine learning technique that aims to learn an optimal distance or similarity metric between data points. The objective is to develop a function that quantifies the degree of similarity or dissimilarity between instances, which is particularly useful in tasks such as clustering, classification, and nearest-neighbor search. Unlike conventional machine learning approaches, where distances or similarities between instances are predefined, metric learning dynamically learns these relationships directly from the data itself (as illustrated in Figure 8.1).

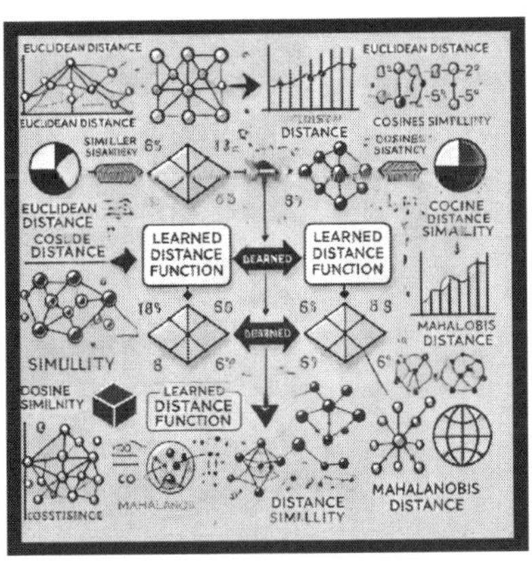


**Figurc 8.1: Metric Learning.**

**Table 8.1: PCA, LDA, and Manifold Learning.**

| Aspect | PCA (Principal Component Analysis) | LDA (Linear Discriminant Analysis) | Manifold Learning |
|---|---|---|---|
| Purpose | Dimensionality reduction by identifying the principal components (directions of maximum variance) in the data. | Supervised dimensionality reduction to find a linear combination of features that best separate classes. | Non-linear dimensionality reduction to uncover hidden structure in the data that might not be linear. |
| Type of Learning | Unsupervised | Supervised | Unsupervised |
| Assumptions | Assumes that data lies along linear subspaces and focuses on maximizing variance. | Assumes normality within each class, and equal covariance among classes. | No specific assumptions about the data distribution; it looks for intrinsic geometry of the data. |
| Input Data | Works on data with no class labels (unlabeled data). | Requires labeled data to create class distinctions. | Works with unlabeled data to explore non-linear structure. |
| Goal | Reduce dimensionality by projecting data along the most significant axes (components). | Maximize class separability while reducing dimensions. | Uncover lower-dimensional representation that preserves the data's manifold structure. |
| Technique | Projects the data into new axes based on eigenvectors of the covariance matrix (linear transformation). | Finds a projection that maximizes the ratio of between-class variance to within-class variance. | Uses techniques like Isomap, t-SNE, or Locally Linear Embedding (LLE) to preserve manifold structure. |
| Output | Principal components, sorted by the amount of variance they explain in the data. | A linear transformation that maximizes class separability. | A lower-dimensional embedding of the data. |

| | | | |
|---|---|---|---|
| Applicability | Suitable for data reduction in high-dimensional spaces, like image compression or feature extraction. | Used when class labels are available and the goal is to find optimal features for classification tasks. | Useful for complex data where the intrinsic structure is non-linear, like in speech or image data. |
| Computation Complexity | Computationally less expensive, often linear in terms of the number of features. | Can be computationally intensive when the number of classes or features is high. | May be more computationally expensive depending on the method (e.g., t-SNE can be slow for large datasets). |
| Example Methods | Eigenvalue decomposition, Singular Value Decomposition (SVD). | Fisher's Linear Discriminant. | Isomap, t-SNE, Locally Linear Embedding (LLE), etc. |

The above Table8.2 provides a comparative view of these methods, highlighting their differences in terms of objectives, approaches, and applications.

## Concepts in Metric Learning:

**Similarity and Dissimilarity:** Metric learning operates by defining a distance metric that quantifies the degree of similarity or dissimilarity between pairs of data points. A smaller distance indicates higher similarity, while a larger distance signifies greater dissimilarity.

**Learning the Metric:** The goal of metric learning algorithms is to learn a distance function that enables the model to distinguish between similar and dissimilar pairs of data points. This is achieved by adjusting the weight of features in the feature space, ensuring that similar data points are closer together, and dissimilar ones are positioned farther apart.

**Distance Functions:** Common distance functions used in metric learning include Euclidean distance, cosine similarity, and Mahalanobis distance. The model fine-tunes the parameters of these functions to optimize its performance for a given task.

**Training with Pairwise Constraints:** Metric learning typically involves training the model using pairs of data points labeled as either similar or dissimilar. These pairwise constraints serve as the foundation for learning the appropriate distance metric. For instance, a pair of similar images may be labeled "same" or "positive," while dissimilar images would be labeled "different" or "negative."

## Applications of Metric Learning

- Face Recognition: Metric learning plays a crucial role in face verification and identification, aiming to quantify the similarity between two facial images and determine whether they correspond to the same individual.
- Image Retrieval: In image retrieval systems, metric learning enhances the accuracy of the retrieval process by learning an optimal distance metric that measures the similarity between a query image and a database of images.
- Recommendation Systems: Metric learning can be leveraged in recommendation systems to predict user preferences by learning a similarity metric that captures the relationships between users and items, enabling personalized suggestions.
- Clustering and Classification: By learning a well-defined distance function, metric learning enhances clustering and classification tasks by positioning similar data points closer together in the feature space, thus improving the quality of groupings and predictions.

## Types of Metric Learning Algorithms:

### 1. Contrastive Loss Function

The contrastive loss function is designed to train models by minimizing the distance between similar pairs of data and maximizing the distance between dissimilar pairs. This approach is commonly employed in Siamese networks, where the model learns a shared metric to compare and assess the similarity between two input samples, enhancing its ability to distinguish between related and unrelated data.

2. **Triplet Loss**

Triplet loss is a widely-used metric learning strategy that incorporates three data points: an anchor, a positive example (similar to the anchor), and a negative example (dissimilar to the anchor). The model is trained to reduce the distance between the anchor and the positive example while increasing the distance between the anchor and the negative example, thus learning a more meaningful and discriminative feature space.

3. **Mahalanobis Distance**

Mahalanobis distance is a robust, generalized distance metric that accounts for correlations and dependencies among features in the data. By learning a Mahalanobis distance function, metric learning can tailor the distance measure to the specific structure of the dataset, making it particularly effective for tasks such as clustering, classification, and anomaly detection, where feature relationships play a critical role.

## Challenges in Metric Learning

**Scalability:** Training an effective metric on large datasets with numerous data points and example pairs can be computationally demanding, requiring significant resources.

**Selecting Negative Samples:** One of the key challenges in metric learning is the careful selection of negative samples (dissimilar pairs). If these negative samples are poorly chosen, it can degrade the model's performance and hinder its ability to generalize.

**Overfitting:** A major risk in metric learning is overfitting, where the model might learn an overly specific distance metric that performs well on the training data but fails to generalize to unseen data.

## Autoencoders and Dimensionality Reduction in Networks

Artificial neural networks called autoencoders are mainly employed for unsupervised learning tasks like denoising, feature extraction, and dimensionality reduction.

- They consist of an encoder and a decoder:

## Encoder:

Input data is converted into a lower-dimensional representation by the encoder. It condenses the initial input into a "bottleneck" or latent space that contains the input's most crucial characteristics.

### Decoder:

The decoder reconstructs the original data from its compressed representation, aiming to reproduce the input as accurately as possible. The core concept of autoencoders is that the network learns to represent the data in a more compact form with fewer dimensions than the original input, which is beneficial for tasks like data compression and noise reduction. This dimensionality reduction process is similar to Principal Component Analysis (PCA), but it offers greater flexibility through non-linear transformations. Once trained, the autoencoder can also be applied to various tasks, including anomaly detection, data generation, and more.

### Types of Autoencoders:

**Denoising Autoencoders (DAE):** These autoencoders are designed to reconstruct clean data from noisy inputs. The objective is to learn a resilient and robust feature representation by training the model to recover meaningful information despite the presence of noise or corruption in the data.

**Sparse Autoencoders:** Sparse autoencoders apply a sparsity constraint to the hidden layer, ensuring that only a small number of neurons are activated at any given time. This mechanism encourages the model to learn more efficient, sparse, and interpretable features, enhancing its ability to capture relevant patterns in the data.

**Variational Autoencoders (VAE):** VAEs are generative models that not only learn a representation of the data but also capture a distribution over the latent space, enabling the generation of new samples from this learned distribution. By incorporating a probabilistic framework, VAEs aim to approximate the posterior distribution of the latent variables, adding a probabilistic element to the autoencoder architecture.

### Applications

Autoencoders are powerful tools for dimensionality reduction, offering significant advantages for tasks like data visualization and improving the efficiency of subsequent machine learning models. By training the autoencoder on normal data and analyzing the reconstruction error on new, unseen data, anomalies can be identified through deviations in reconstruction quality. Additionally, autoencoders can be trained to filter out noise from images, making them ideal for applications where clean, high-quality data is required from noisy or corrupted inputs.

## Convolutional Neural Networks (CNN)

Convolutional Neural Networks (CNNs) are a specialized class of deep neural networks that have demonstrated exceptional performance in tasks such as image and video recognition, image classification, and natural language processing. These networks are engineered to automatically learn spatial hierarchies of features by employing convolutional layers followed by pooling layers, enabling them to capture intricate patterns and structures in data with remarkable efficiency.

## Components of CNNs:

- **Convolutional Layers**

These layers apply filters (or kernels) to the input image, performing a convolution operation to detect key features such as edges, textures, and shapes. Each filter is specialized in identifying a particular feature that is relevant to the task, allowing the network to progressively capture more abstract information as layers deepen.

- **Pooling Layers**

Pooling layers reduce the spatial dimensions of the output from the convolutional layers, which minimizes computational complexity and memory usage while preserving the most critical features. Max pooling, which selects the highest value from each region, is commonly employed to retain the most significant information.

- **Fully Connected Layers**

Once the convolution and pooling layers have extracted relevant features, the processed output is passed through fully connected layers for classification or regression tasks. These layers integrate all the learned features and make the final prediction or decision based on the combined information.

- **Activation Functions**

Non-linear functions, such as ReLU (Rectified Linear Unit), are applied after each convolution to introduce non-linearity into the model. This allows CNNs to model complex, real-world patterns by enabling the network to learn intricate relationships within the data.

- **Training CNNs**

CNNs are trained using backpropagation and optimization algorithms, such as stochastic gradient descent (SGD). During training, the filters are updated by adjusting their weights to minimize the difference between the predicted output and the actual ground truth, effectively refining the model's ability to make accurate predictions.

## Applications:

- Image Classification: CNNs are frequently used for image classification tasks, such as recognizing scenes or objects in pictures.
- Object Detection: CNNs can detect objects in an image and surround them with bounding boxes.
- Video Analysis: CNNs are useful for tasks like action recognition and video summarization because they can be used for frame-by-frame video analysis.

**Table 8.2: Autoencoders and Convolutional Neural Networks (CNNs).**

| Feature | Autoencoders | Convolutional Neural Networks (CNNs) |
|---|---|---|
| Purpose | Data compression, denoising, and feature learning | Image classification, object detection, segmentation, etc. |
| Architecture | Encoder-Decoder structure | Multiple layers of convolutions, pooling, and fully connected layers |
| Main Application | Dimensionality reduction, anomaly detection, image denoising | Image recognition, facial recognition, video analysis, etc. |
| Training Objective | Minimize reconstruction error (e.g., MSE) | Minimize classification error (e.g., cross-entropy loss) |
| Layers Involved | Encoder (compresses data) and Decoder (reconstructs data) | Convolutional layers, pooling layers, and fully connected layers |
| Data Type | Used for unsupervised learning tasks, mostly on structured and unstructured data | Primarily used for image and video data (structured data) |
| Feature Extraction | Learns efficient encoding and feature representation from input data | Learns hierarchical feature representations through convolutions |
| Output | Reconstructed input data | Predicted labels or class probabilities |
| Training Complexity | Usually simpler, less computationally intensive | Often more computationally expensive, especially for large datasets |
| Used For | Data compression, denoising, generating new data | Image classification, video processing, autonomous vehicles |

Table 8.2 highlights the core differences and applications between Autoencoders and CNNs, along with their key components and advantages.

***Autoencoder Example:***

## Problem: Image Denoising

**Scenario:** Imagine you have a collection of noisy images, and your goal is to reconstruct the original, clean image from these corrupted inputs. An Autoencoder can be trained to effectively remove this noise and recover the original image.

## Working:

**Input:** A noisy image is passed through the Encoder, which consists of a series of layers designed to compress the image into a more compact representation.

**Latent Space Representation:** The encoder generates a low-dimensional, compressed version of the noisy image, capturing its essential features while discarding the noise.

**Decoder:** The compressed image is then passed through the Decoder, which attempts to reconstruct the original image from the reduced representation.

**Output:** The output is the denoised image. During training, the network learns by minimizing the difference between the noisy input and the reconstructed, clean output.

**Application:** Denoising autoencoders have practical applications in various fields, such as removing noise from medical images (e.g., MRI scans), enhancing satellite imagery, and improving image compression processes.

***Convolutional Neural Network (CNN) Example:***

## Problem: Object Classification in Images

**Scenario:** The goal is to build a model capable of classifying images of animals into distinct categories such as "cat," "dog," and "bird."

## Working Process:

**Input Image:** The image of an animal (for example, a dog) is input into the model, where it is passed through multiple convolutional layers. These layers apply various filters to detect fundamental features such as edges, textures, and colors.

**Pooling:** Following each convolutional operation, pooling layers are applied to downsample the image, reducing its dimensionality. This process helps retain only the most essential features while discarding irrelevant information.

**Fully Connected Layers:** After undergoing several rounds of convolution and pooling, the extracted high-level features are flattened into a vector. This vector is then passed through fully connected layers, which help in making predictions based on the identified patterns.

**Output:** The final output layer utilizes a softmax function to generate probabilities for each class (e.g., "dog," "cat," or "bird"). The model predicts the class that has the highest probability.

**Applications:** Convolutional Neural Networks (CNNs) are extensively used in various computer vision tasks, such as image classification (e.g., recognizing animals or medical images), object detection, and video analysis. CNNs are integral to systems like facial recognition, autonomous driving, and medical diagnostics, such as the analysis of X-ray or MRI images.

## AlexNet

AlexNet is a pioneering deep convolutional neural network (CNN) specifically designed for image classification. It garnered widespread acclaim after winning the 2012 ImageNet Large Scale Visual Recognition Challenge (ILSVRC), delivering a remarkable leap in performance compared to prior models. Developed by Alex Krizhevsky, Ilya Sutskever, and Geoffrey Hinton, this groundbreaking achievement is widely regarded as the catalyst for the rapid advancement of deep learning, particularly in the realm of computer vision.

### Features and Architecture

AlexNet consists of several important architectural components that differentiate it from traditional machine learning methods (Figure 8.2):

**Figure 8.2: Features and Architecture.**

**Input Layer:** AlexNet accepts input images of size 224x224x3, where each image consists of three RGB channels. These images are resized to a consistent fixed size, ensuring uniformity across the model's training data, which is essential for maintaining consistent performance during learning.

**Convolutional Layers:** AlexNet contains five convolutional layers designed to extract essential features from the input images. As the data progresses through these layers, the number of filters (kernels) increases, enabling the network to learn increasingly complex and abstract features from the raw pixel data.

**ReLU Activation:** A pivotal innovation in AlexNet is the use of the Rectified Linear Unit (ReLU) as the activation function. Unlike traditional functions such as sigmoid or tanh, ReLU mitigates the vanishing gradient problem, accelerating the model's training by allowing it to learn faster and more effectively, while enhancing its overall performance.

**Pooling Layers:** AlexNet incorporates max-pooling layers to downsample the feature maps and reduce their spatial dimensions. This not only helps to decrease the computational load but also aids in minimizing overfitting. The max-pooling operation is performed with a stride of 2, ensuring that the most important features are retained while reducing redundant information.

**Fully Connected Layers:** After the convolutional layers, AlexNet uses three fully connected layers to process and interpret the high-level features extracted from the images. The final fully connected layer generates the network's output, with one neuron corresponding to each class in the classification task, determining the final predicted label.

**Dropout:** To prevent overfitting, AlexNet uses the dropout technique as a regularization strategy. During training, random neurons are set to zero, forcing the model to not rely too heavily on any particular neuron, which improves generalization and robustness.

**Softmax Layer:** The output of the last fully connected layer is passed through a softmax layer, which transforms the output into a probability distribution across all possible classes. This layer helps the network make a final, probabilistic decision on which class the input image belongs to, based on the learned features.

## Innovations in AlexNet

*Several key innovations contributed to the success of AlexNet:*

- ReLU Activation: By utilizing the ReLU activation function instead of traditional alternatives like sigmoid or tanh, AlexNet effectively mitigated the vanishing gradient problem, resulting in faster convergence and improved performance during training.
- GPU Acceleration: As one of the pioneering models to leverage Graphics Processing Units (GPUs) for training deep neural networks, AlexNet significantly reduced training time, particularly when handling large-scale datasets such as ImageNet.
- Data Augmentation: To enhance the diversity of the training data, AlexNet employed data augmentation techniques, including image flipping, cropping, and brightness adjustments. These strategies contributed to better generalization, enabling the model to perform more robustly on unseen data.
- Dropout: The dropout technique was implemented to combat overfitting by randomly deactivating a subset of neurons during each training iteration, ensuring the model learned more generalized features.

## Training the Model

AlexNet was trained on the ImageNet dataset, a vast collection of millions of labeled images spanning thousands of categories. The sheer size of this dataset, combined with the complexity of the classification task, enabled the effective training of a deep neural network. To optimize the network's weights, Stochastic Gradient Descent (SGD) was employed. By incorporating a momentum term into the optimization process, the convergence rate was accelerated, significantly enhancing the efficiency of training.

**Loss Function:** The model calculates the difference between the true label and the predicted output using cross-entropy loss. Reducing this loss is the aim of training.

## Impact and Legacy

The success of AlexNet had a profound impact on the development of deep learning, particularly in computer vision:

**a) Revolutionizing Computer Vision with Deep Learning:** AlexNet demonstrated the superior performance of deep neural networks compared to traditional machine learning models like support vector machines (SVMs) and decision trees. This breakthrough propelled deep learning to the forefront, quickly establishing it as the dominant method for image classification and a wide range of related tasks.

**b) Laying the Groundwork for Future Architectures:** Building on the success of AlexNet, a multitude of advanced deep learning architectures have been introduced and further refined, including VGG, GoogLeNet, and ResNet. These models expand upon AlexNet's foundational principles, pushing the limits of what neural networks can achieve in complex computational tasks.

**c) Expanding into Diverse Applications:** The techniques pioneered by AlexNet have become integral across various industries, including medical image analysis, autonomous vehicles, facial recognition systems, and augmented reality, demonstrating their vast potential beyond image classification.

## Applications of AlexNet

- Image Classification: Identifying and categorizing objects in images.
- Object Detection: Detecting and locating multiple objects within an image.
- Face Recognition: Identifying individuals in images or videos.
- Medical Imaging: Analyzing X-rays, MRIs, and other medical images to detect diseases.
- Autonomous Vehicles: Using image data from cameras for navigation and object detection in self-driving cars.

## VGG

VGG, an acronym for Visual Geometry Group, is a deep convolutional neural network architecture created by the Visual Geometry Group at the University of Oxford. Presented in the 2014 paper "Very Deep Convolutional Networks for Large-Scale Image Recognition," VGG quickly garnered attention for its simplicity and exceptional performance in the ImageNet Large Scale Visual Recognition Challenge (ILSVRC). Renowned for its profound depth, the architecture leverages small convolutional filters to enhance feature learning, ultimately achieving state-of-the-art results in its era.

## Features of VGG Architecture

VGG is characterized by its simplicity and structured design. The primary features include:

**Small Filter Sizes:** VGG employs 3x3 convolutional filters consistently throughout the entire network. These smaller filters are effective at capturing fine-grained features, while simultaneously reducing computational complexity in comparison to larger filters.

**Depth:** With 16 to 19 weight layers, VGG stands as one of the pioneering architectures to investigate the performance advantages of very deep networks, demonstrating how increased depth can enhance model capacity.

**Fixed Structure:** The architecture follows a well-defined and repetitive structure, consisting of convolutional layers followed by max-pooling layers. This predictable pattern streamlines both the design and implementation process of the network.

**Non-Linearity with ReLU:** Each convolutional layer is paired with a ReLU activation function, introducing essential non-linearity into the network. This enables the model to learn more complex, abstract patterns in data. While the initial layers capture fundamental features such as edges and textures, the deeper layers are capable of learning higher-level abstractions and intricate patterns.

## Architecture Variants

The VGG family has several variants, with the most notable being VGG-16 and VGG-19:

- VGG-16: Consists of 16 weight layers (13 convolutional layers and 3 fully connected layers).
- VGG-19: A deeper version with 19 weight layers (16 convolutional layers and 3 fully connected layers).

Despite having different numbers of convolutional layers, both models adhere to the same design principles, making VGG-19 marginally more computationally costly than VGG-16.

## Advantages of VGG

- VGG is simple to comprehend and apply due to its consistent architecture and consistent use of tiny filters.
- VGG is appropriate for transfer learning tasks because of its deep architecture, which allows it to learn robust and hierarchical features.
- VGG is frequently utilized as a feature extractor for a range of computer vision applications, including image segmentation and object detection.

## Limitations of VGG

While VGG has been highly influential, it is not without its challenges:

- Computationally Intensive: As the network depth increases, the number of parameters grows exponentially, resulting in significantly higher memory and computational demands. For instance, VGG-16 contains over 138 million parameters, highlighting its resource-intensive nature.
- Extended Training Time: The vast size of the network leads to prolonged training durations, even when leveraging high-performance GPUs, making the process time-consuming and resource-heavy.
- Limited Efficiency Optimization: Later architectures like ResNet and Inception introduced key optimizations that minimized redundancy and reduced computational load, addressing the inherent inefficiencies found in VGG networks.

## Applications of VGG

- Despite its limitations, VGG has proven to be versatile and effective for numerous applications:
- VGG's powerful feature representation makes it exceptionally well-suited for tasks that involve classifying images into predefined categories.
- VGG functions as a foundational model for advanced object detection frameworks such as Fast R-CNN and Faster R-CNN.
- Thanks to its versatile feature extraction capabilities, VGG is commonly fine-tuned for specific domain applications, adapting to various specialized tasks.
- VGG is widely utilized in medical imaging tasks, including cancer detection and identifying anomalies in X-rays and MRIs.

Today, VGG is a key player in transfer learning, owing to its structured architecture and exceptional ability to generate robust feature representations. Its influence is deeply embedded in many state-of-the-art models, making it an indispensable cornerstone of convolutional neural network (CNN) development.

## Inception &ResNet

## Inception Networks

Inception Networks, first introduced as GoogLeNet in 2014, were designed to enhance computational efficiency while maintaining high accuracy in tasks like image classification. The core innovation behind this architecture is the Inception module, which processes input data using filters of different sizes (such as 1x1, 3x3, and 5x5) in parallel. This enables the network to capture both fine-grained details and broader contextual information within a single layer. The outputs from these diverse filter operations are then concatenated, allowing the network to handle multi-scale features more effectively. A key feature of Inception Networks is the use of 1x1 convolutions for dimensionality reduction. These operations reduce the number of feature maps before applying larger filters, which lowers computational complexity without compromising performance. Additionally, the modular design of Inception Networks supports parallel processing, where each branch independently processes data, leading to more efficient and redundant-free feature extraction.

Inception Networks also incorporate auxiliary classifiers at intermediate layers, improving gradient flow during training and mitigating the vanishing gradient problem that can arise in deeper architectures. This strategy ensures better convergence and more efficient training for deep networks. Successive iterations of Inception, such as Inception v2, v3, and v4, introduced further optimizations, including factorized convolutions and more streamlined modules. These networks have achieved state-of-the-art performance on benchmarks like ImageNet, while remaining computationally efficient. Their ability to balance accuracy with efficiency has made Inception Networks a preferred choice for various computer vision tasks, including image classification, object detection, and transfer learning.

## ResNet (Residual Networks)

ResNet, introduced by Microsoft in 2015, tackles the challenge of training very deep neural networks by integrating residual connections, also referred to as skip connections. These connections allow the network to bypass one or more layers, creating direct links between the input and output. This design alleviates the vanishing gradient problem by ensuring that gradients can propagate through the network without diminishing, even in extremely deep architectures. At the heart of ResNet is the concept of the residual function. Rather than learning a direct mapping of the input $(x)$, the network learns the residual, defined as $(x) = H(x) - x$. This simplification of the learning process facilitates the optimization of deeper networks, as the residual function is often easier to train.Each residual block in ResNet generally comprises two or three convolutional layers, contributing to a modular and stackable architecture. ResNet demonstrates remarkable scalability, with variants such as ResNet-18, ResNet-34, ResNet-50, and ResNet-152, where the numbers correspond to the total number of layers. The deeper configurations deliver exceptional performance on complex tasks while maintaining computational stability. This scalability and efficiency make ResNet highly adaptable for a wide range of applications.

The key advantages of ResNet include its ease of training and improved accuracy, enabling the successful training of networks with hundreds of layers—something previously hindered by gradient-related issues. The architecture has set new benchmarks in fields such as image recognition, object detection, and semantic segmentation. Furthermore, its powerful generalization capabilities have inspired the development of subsequent architectures like DenseNet and EfficientNet.

## Comparison of Inception and ResNet

Inception and ResNet represent two distinct and influential approaches to deep learning architecture design. Inception Networks emphasize computational efficiency by processing inputs at multiple scales within each Inception module. This multi-scale processing allows the model to capture a wide range of features while minimizing redundancy through advanced dimensionality reduction techniques. In contrast, ResNet focuses on depth, utilizing residual connections to facilitate the stable training of extremely deep networks. This innovation enables ResNet to achieve exceptional accuracy, particularly in tasks that require large-scale data processing. While Inception excels in computational efficiency and multi-scale feature extraction, ResNet is renowned for its ability to effectively train very deep networks. Both architectures have significantly impacted the field of deep learning, driving advancements in computer vision and inspiring the development of many subsequent designs (Table 8.3).

**Table 8.3: Comparison between Inception and ResNet.**

| Feature | Inception | ResNet |
|---|---|---|
| **Introduced by** | Google (Szegedy et al.) | Microsoft (He et al.) |
| **Year** | 2014 (Inception-v1), later versions followed | 2015 |
| **Architecture Type** | Multi-path (parallel convolutions) | Deep Residual Learning (skip connections) |
| **Key Innovation** | Inception modules with multiple kernel sizes | Residual connections (skip connections) |
| **Depth** | Comparatively shallower, but with complex modules | Very deep (up to 1000+ layers) |
| **Computation Efficiency** | Optimized via 1x1 convolutions and factorized filters | Efficient gradient flow due to skip connections |
| **Gradient Vanishing Issue** | Less prominent due to batch normalization | Addressed via residual connections |
| **Performance on ImageNet** | High accuracy with fewer parameters | State-of-the-art performance, deeper networks |
| **Parameter Efficiency** | More efficient due to factorization and filter sizes | More parameters due to depth, but better training stability |
| **Variants** | Inception-v1, v2, v3, v4, Xception | ResNet-18, 34, 50, 101, 152, ResNeXt |
| **Suitability** | Best for computationally constrained environments | Best for very deep networks with stable training |
| **Used In** | GoogleNet, Xception, EfficientNet | ImageNet classification, object detection, GANs |

# Training a Convent

## Training a Convolutional Neural Network (ConvNet)

Training a ConvNet involves several crucial steps that ensure the network effectively learns patterns in the data to make accurate predictions. Here's a detailed explanation:

### 1. Data Preprocessing

Before training a model, raw input data (e.g., images) must undergo various preprocessing steps. These include resizing images to match the network's input dimensions, normalizing pixel values within a specified range (e.g., 0 to 1), and augmenting the data to artificially expand the dataset. Techniques such as flipping, rotation, and cropping are employed to enhance the model's robustness and mitigate overfitting.

### 2. Weight Initialization

Convolutional layers in a network are initialized with weights that are gradually adjusted during training to minimize prediction errors. Proper weight initialization is crucial to avoid challenges like vanishing or exploding gradients. Methods like Xavier and He initialization ensure that weights are distributed effectively, preserving stable gradient flow throughout the network layers.

### 3. Forward Propagation

During forward propagation, input data is processed through the network layer by layer. Convolutional layers extract spatial features, pooling layers reduce the data's dimensionality, and fully connected layers map these features to output predictions. The output is then compared with the ground truth to compute the loss, quantifying the prediction error.

### 4. Loss Function

The loss function quantifies the difference between predicted and actual values. For classification tasks, categorical cross-entropy is commonly used, while for regression tasks, mean squared error (MSE) is often preferred. The choice of loss function depends on the specific task and problem being solved.

### 5. Backpropagation

Backpropagation computes the gradient of the loss function with respect to each weight in the network. By utilizing the chain rule, the error signal is propagated back through the layers, allowing the network to adjust weights and reduce the loss effectively.

### 6. Optimization

Optimization algorithms, such as Stochastic Gradient Descent (SGD) or its more advanced variants like Adam or RMSprop, are used to update the weights during training. These algorithms rely on gradients calculated during backpropagation to efficiently minimize the loss function. Learning rate scheduling is employed to balance convergence speed and training stability.

### 7. Regularization Techniques

Regularization strategies, including dropout and L2 regularization, are applied to prevent overfitting. Dropout randomly deactivates a portion of neurons during training, forcing the model to learn more robust and generalized features. L2 regularization introduces a penalty term to the loss function, discouraging excessively large weights and encouraging a more generalized model.

### 8. Batch Normalization

Batch normalization normalizes the inputs to each layer within a mini-batch, promoting faster and more stable training. This process ensures that the network's activations maintain a consistent scale, which helps accelerate learning and stabilize the training process.

### 9. Hyperparameter Tuning

The process of hyperparameter tuning involves adjusting key parameters, such as learning rate, batch size, number of epochs, and the network architecture, all of which have a profound impact on model performance. Techniques like grid search or random search are commonly used to identify the optimal configuration for these parameters.

### 10. Validation and Testing

During training, a separate validation set is used to monitor the model's performance. After training is complete, the model is tested on previously unseen data to evaluate its generalization capabilities. Performance metrics such as accuracy, precision, recall, and F1-score provide valuable insights into the model's effectiveness and robustness.

## Challenges in Training ConvNets

- Overfitting: A network might function well with training data but poorly with fresh data.
- Gradient Issues: When deep networks backpropagate, they may run into vanishing or exploding gradients.
- Computational Cost: ConvNet training on big datasets demands a lot of processing power.

Image classification, object detection, and other tasks can be successfully trained using ConvNets by carefully planning the architecture, selecting suitable training methods, and keeping an eye on performance.

## Weights initialization

Weight initialization plays a crucial role in the training process of neural networks. Proper initialization not only accelerates the convergence rate but also enhances the stability of training, ensuring that the model reaches an optimal solution. On the other hand, improper initialization can result in issues such as vanishing or exploding gradients, which can severely hinder the training process, making it both inefficient and, in some cases, infeasible.

- Below is a detailed explanation of weights initialization:

### 1. The Role of Weights in Neural Networks

In neural networks, the transformation of input data at each layer is determined by weights. They stand for the direction and strength of neuronal connections. The optimization algorithm modifies these weights during training in order to minimize the loss function. The network may not learn efficiently if the weights are not initialized correctly, producing predictions that are either inaccurate or suboptimal.

### 2. Challenges with Poor Initialization

The network may become unstable due to the explosion of gradients during backpropagation caused by weights initialized with very large values. On the other hand, gradients might disappear if weights are started with extremely low values, which would result in few updates and sluggish convergence. These problems are especially noticeable in multi-layered, deep networks.

***For instance:***

- Exploding Gradients: Lead to numerical instability and divergence.
- Vanishing Gradients: Slow down or halt learning in deep layers.

### 3. Types of Weight Initialization Methods

Several methods have been developed to address the challenges of weight initialization:

**Random Initialization:** Weights are given random values. Simple, it frequently needs scaling to prevent vanishing or exploding gradients.

**Xavier Initialization:** Distributes weights in a way that maintains the activation variance across layers. This works especially well with tanh and sigmoid activation functions.

$$W \sim \mathcal{U}\left(-\sqrt{\frac{1}{n}}, \sqrt{\frac{1}{n}}\right)$$

Where,

- $n$ is the number of neurons in the previous layer.

**He Initialization:** Though made for ReLU activations, it is comparable to Xavier. For layers with ReLU-like activations, it guarantees that gradients are scaled appropriately.

$$W \sim \mathcal{N}\left(0, \sqrt{\frac{2}{n}}\right)$$

## 4. Importance of Proper Scaling

When weights are scaled appropriately, the signals (activations) moving through the network don't grow out of control or go to zero as they move through the layers.

***For example:***

- To ensure consistency across layers, the variance is modified in Xavier Initialization.

The rectifying nature of ReLU is taken into account by an extra factor in He Initialization, which guarantees that positive activations are scaled appropriately.

## 5. Bias Initialization

Initializing biases is important in training, even though weights are frequently the main focus. Usually, biases are set to zero because this preserves the network's symmetry and enables the optimization process to identify the proper offsets.

## 6. Practical Considerations

In modern architectures, proper weight initialization is often combined with:

- Batch Normalization: By normalizing layer inputs, it eliminates the need for flawless weight initialization.
- Pre-trained Models: To start the current model, use weights from networks that have been trained on big datasets.
- Custom Initialization: Depending on the properties of the data, unique initialization schemes may be created for particular tasks.

## Batch normalization

Batch Normalization (BatchNorm) is a widely adopted technique in neural networks that normalizes the inputs to a layer over a mini-batch of data. Introduced by Sergey Ioffe and Christian Szegedy in 2015, BatchNorm effectively addresses issues such as internal covariate shift, accelerates training, enhances model stability, and facilitates the use of higher learning rates, thereby contributing to more efficient and robust deep learning models. Below is a detailed explanation of Batch Normalization and its impact:

## The Need for Batch Normalization

As data progresses through a deep neural network, the distribution of inputs to each layer can change due to updates made in the previous layers during training. This phenomenon, referred to as internal covariate shift, can significantly slow down the training process and even cause instability. Batch Normalization (BatchNorm) addresses this issue by standardizing the inputs to each layer, ensuring that the distribution remains consistent throughout training, which accelerates convergence and enhances stability.

## How Batch Normalization Works?

BatchNorm normalizes the activations of a layer using the mean and variance of a mini-batch. It modifies the inputs as follows:

**Normalization:** Subtract the batch mean and divide by the batch standard deviation to ensure zero mean and unit variance:

$$\hat{x}_i = \frac{x_i - \mu_B}{\sqrt{\sigma_B^2 + \epsilon}}$$

Where $\mu_B$ and $\sigma_B^2$ are the mean and variance of the batch, and $\epsilon$ is a small constant to prevent division by zero.

**Scaling and Shifting:** After normalization, BatchNorm introduces trainable parameters $\gamma$ (scale) and $\beta$ (shift):

$$y_i = \gamma \hat{x}_i + \beta$$

These parameters allow the network to learn the optimal scale and shift, restoring representational capacity when needed.

## BatchNorm in Practice

BatchNorm can be used in a layer before the activation function but after the linear transformation. It is utilized in many different models, ranging from fully connected layers in dense networks to convolutional layers in CNNs.

***For example:***

- In CNNs: Feature maps across channels are subjected to BatchNorm, which independently normalizes each channel's statistics.
- In RNNs: For handling sequential data, specialized versions of BatchNorm are utilized.

## Alternatives to BatchNorm

To address the limitations of BatchNorm, other normalization techniques have been developed:

- Layer Normalization (LN): Suitable for RNNs, it normalizes across features rather than the batch.
- Instance Normalization (IN): Frequently employed in style transfer, it focuses on normalization within a single sample.
- Group Normalization (GN): Channels are grouped for normalization, which works well for small batches.

## Benefits of Batch Normalization

- Accelerated Training: By normalizing activations, BatchNorm mitigates the sensitivity to weight initialization, enabling the use of higher learning rates and significantly speeding up convergence.
- Mitigated Overfitting: BatchNorm serves as a natural regularizer by injecting noise from batch statistics, thereby reducing the reliance on other regularization techniques, such as dropout.
- Stable Gradient Flow: By normalizing activations, BatchNorm ensures that gradients remain stable, preventing issues like vanishing or exploding gradients, which is particularly beneficial in deep neural networks.
- Enhanced Generalization: Networks trained with BatchNorm typically exhibit superior generalization capabilities, performing better on unseen data.

## Hyper Parameter Optimization

Hyperparameter optimization plays a crucial role in machine learning and deep learning by fine-tuning parameters that control both the learning process and the model architecture, ultimately maximizing performance. Unlike model parameters, which are learned directly from the training data, hyperparameters are set prior to training and significantly influence how the model learns, its complexity, and its capacity to generalize to new, unseen data. Proper hyperparameter tuning is key to achieving optimal model accuracy and efficiency.

## Importance of Hyperparameter Optimization

The performance of a model can be highly sensitive to the selection of hyperparameters. Carefully tuned hyperparameters can accelerate convergence, enhance accuracy, and promote better generalization. In contrast, suboptimal choices may lead to problems such as underfitting, where the model fails to capture the underlying patterns in the data, or overfitting, where the model becomes too specialized in memorizing the training data and struggles with new, unseen data. The process of hyperparameter optimization seeks to strike a balance between these competing trade-offs, ensuring the model remains both effective and resilient across a range of real-world scenarios.

## Techniques for Hyperparameter Optimization

- There are several techniques for optimizing hyperparameters:

Grid Search performs an exhaustive search across a defined set of hyperparameter values. Though it is comprehensive and straightforward, it becomes computationally costly and time-consuming, especially in high-dimensional hyperparameter spaces.

Random Search, on the other hand, tests randomly chosen combinations of hyperparameters. It is typically more efficient than Grid Search and can often identify optimal configurations more quickly by exploring a broader range of possibilities.

Bayesian Optimization leverages probabilistic models to intelligently predict the most promising hyperparameter values based on previous evaluations. This approach is computationally efficient and excels when dealing with continuous hyperparameter spaces, optimizing performance with fewer evaluations.

Evolutionary Algorithms are inspired by natural selection and iteratively evolve hyperparameter combinations over multiple generations. These algorithms are highly effective for exploring complex, high-dimensional, and non-differentiable hyperparameter spaces, offering a robust solution for challenging optimization tasks.

## Challenges in Hyperparameter Optimization

One of the key challenges in hyperparameter optimization is its significant computational cost, as training deep learning models is both time-consuming and resource-intensive. Moreover, the interdependencies among hyperparameters further complicate the optimization process, with the effectiveness of one hyperparameter often hinging on the values of others. Additionally, the high-dimensional nature of hyperparameter spaces intensifies the complexity, necessitating the use of sophisticated algorithms capable of efficiently navigating these spaces without resorting to exhaustive search methods.

## Tools and Best Practices

To optimize the process more efficiently, advanced tools such as Optuna, Ray Tune, and Hyperopt automate hyperparameter tuning through sophisticated algorithms. Best practices involve prioritizing the most influential hyperparameters, tracking learning curves to detect overfitting or underfitting, and utilizing transfer learning to fine-tune hyperparameters from pretrained models. Additionally, Automated Machine Learning (AutoML) platforms simplify experimentation and deployment, accelerating the entire process. Hyperparameter optimization plays a pivotal role in both machine learning and deep learning pipelines. By strategically selecting hyperparameters, practitioners can drastically improve model performance, ensuring quicker convergence, higher accuracy, and enhanced generalization for real-world applications.

## Summary

This chapter delves into essential concepts in linear methods and Convolutional Neural Networks (CNNs). It starts by exploring dimensionality reduction techniques, including Principal Component Analysis (PCA) and Linear Discriminant Analysis (LDA), before advancing to metric learning and autoencoders for network-based dimensionality reduction. The section on CNN architectures provides an in-depth look at iconic models such as AlexNet, VGG, Inception, and ResNet, examining their groundbreaking innovations and transformative influence on the field of deep learning. Finally, the chapter concludes by discussing CNN training methodologies, focusing on critical elements such as weight initialization, batch normalization, and hyperparameter optimization to enhance model performance and generalization.

## Exercise Questions:

- Explain the difference between PCA and LDA. Provide examples where each would be preferred.
- What is metric learning, and how does it differ from traditional classification tasks?
- Discuss the role of autoencoders in dimensionality reduction and give an example application.
- Compare and contrast AlexNet and VGG architectures, focusing on their layer structures.
- How does the inception module in Inception networks address computational efficiency and feature extraction?
- What are the key innovations introduced by ResNet, and why are skip connections important?
- Explain the significance of weight initialization in training deep neural networks. Provide examples of common initialization methods.
- Describe how batch normalization improves training stability and speeds up convergence.
- What are some techniques for hyperparameter optimization? Which would you choose for a high-dimensional hyperparameter space, and why?
- Discuss how convolutional networks have transformed image classification tasks. Provide examples of real-world applications.

CHAPTER - 9

# Optimization in Deep Learning

## Optimization in Deep Learning

Optimization in deep learning involves fine-tuning the parameters (weights and biases) of a neural network to minimize a loss function, which measures the discrepancy between the predicted outputs and the actual targets. This optimization process is iterative and relies on gradient-based algorithms that compute the derivatives of the loss function with respect to the network's parameters. By following these gradients, the model adjusts its parameters in a direction that reduces the loss. Common optimization algorithms such as Stochastic Gradient Descent (SGD), Adam, and RMSprop each employ unique strategies to update parameters, improving the efficiency and stability of the learning process.However, deep learning optimization is a complex task due to the high-dimensional, non-convex nature of neural networks. Challenges such as vanishing or exploding gradients, slow convergence, and the risk of getting stuck in local minima or saddle points can hinder the training process. To overcome these issues, techniques like batch normalization, learning rate scheduling, gradient clipping, and momentum-based methods are employed. Additionally, adaptive optimizers like Adam dynamically adjust learning rates for each parameter, further enhancing model performance.Advanced optimization techniques, such as regularization methods (e.g., L1/L2 regularization, dropout) and weight decay, help mitigate overfitting and improve the model's generalization ability. These strategies ensure that the network not only excels on training data but also performs reliably on unseen data, which is essential for real-world deployment and application.

## Non-convex Optimization for Deep Networks

Non-convex optimization plays a crucial role in training deep neural networks, as the loss functions are inherently non-convex due to the intricate architectures and nonlinear activation functions. Unlike convex optimization, which guarantees a single global minimum, non-convex optimization presents significant challenges.

The loss landscape is riddled with local minima, saddle points, and flat regions, creating a complex terrain that makes it difficult for optimization algorithms to find the optimal solution efficiently.

## Challenges in Non-Convex Optimization

### 1. Multiple Local Minima

In non-convex landscapes, optimizers may encounter several local minima, which are points where the gradient equals zero, but the loss does not reach its global minimum. However, research indicates that in high-dimensional spaces, many of these local minima have loss values that are close to the global minimum, making them sufficiently effective for practical applications despite not being the absolute best.

### 2. Saddle Points

Saddle points are locations where the gradient is zero, but the point is neither a local minimum nor maximum. These regions can significantly hinder optimization, as the optimizer struggles to escape them, especially in high-dimensional spaces where the complexity of the landscape increases.

### 3. Flat Regions and Plateaus

Some parts of the loss surface are characterized by very small gradients (flat regions), which slow down the optimization process. This issue is particularly problematic in deep neural networks, where activation functions may become saturated, causing a stagnation in progress.

## Strategies to Address Non-Convex Optimization

- Gradient-Based Optimization Algorithms:

Popular algorithms such as Stochastic Gradient Descent (SGD), Adam, and RMSprop are widely employed to optimize non-convex loss surfaces. These algorithms leverage advanced techniques like momentum and adaptive learning rates, enabling them to effectively navigate complex and challenging optimization landscapes.

- Weight Initialization Techniques

Proper initialization of network weightssuch as Xavier or He initializationis crucial in preventing issues like vanishing or exploding gradients. These methods help avoid getting stuck in flat regions early in the training process, leading to more efficient convergence.

- Regularization Methods

Techniques like dropout, weight decay, and batch normalization are not only effective in reducing overfitting but also play a key role in smoothing the loss surface. This results in more manageable optimization and improves model generalization.

- Learning Rate Scheduling

Gradually reducing the learning rate throughout the training process enables the optimizer to make finer, more precise updates as it approaches local minima or flat regions. This strategy helps improve the model's convergence behavior.

- Gradient Clipping

To prevent exploding gradients, particularly in recurrent neural networks, gradient clipping limits the magnitude of gradients during backpropagation. This technique ensures that the training process remains stable and avoids excessive updates.

- Second-Order Optimization Methods

Although computationally intensive, second-order methods like Newton's Method and quasi-Newton techniques can enhance convergence. These methods leverage curvature information of the loss surface to provide more accurate and efficient updates, often leading to faster convergence.

## Insights from Theory and Practice

Despite the inherent challenges, empirical evidence demonstrates that neural networks trained using gradient-based methods often identify solutions that generalize effectively, even when they do not converge to the global minimum. This phenomenon can be attributed to the nature of high-dimensional parameter spaces, where many suboptimal minima are sufficiently effective. Additionally, stochastic techniques like Stochastic Gradient Descent (SGD) play a crucial role in facilitating the escape from poor minima and saddle points by introducing noise into the optimization process. By leveraging a combination of innovative strategies and techniques, non-convex optimization in deep learning networks has achieved remarkable success, driving significant advancements in fields such as computer vision, natural language processing, and reinforcement learning.

**Table9.1: Overview of Non-Convex Optimization for Deep Networks.**

| Aspect | Details |
|---|---|
| **Definition** | Non-convex optimization involves optimizing a function that is not convex, meaning the function may have multiple local minima and maxima. |
| **Significance in Deep Networks** | Deep neural networks are typically trained using non-convex optimization due to their complex architectures, leading to many local minima and saddle points in the loss function. |
| **Challenges** | - **Local Minima & Saddle Points**: The presence of multiple local minima and saddle points makes it harder to find the global optimum. |

| | |
|---|---|
| **Optimization Techniques** | - **Stochastic Gradient Descent (SGD)**: A popular optimization method used for deep networks, helping avoid local minima. It works by updating weights based on mini-batches of data.<br>- **Momentum**: Enhances SGD by adding previous gradients to help accelerate convergence.<br>- **Adam Optimizer**: Uses adaptive learning rates based on estimates of first and second moments of gradients. |
| **Types of Non-Convexity** | - **Flat Local Minima**: Regions where the loss is suboptimal but the network performs well on the task.<br>- **Sharp Minima**: Regions with steep gradients, potentially overfitting the data.<br>- **Saddle Points**: Points where the gradient is zero but the point is not a minimum or maximum. |
| **Global vs Local Minima** | In deep networks, the goal is often to find a "good enough" local minimum, which leads to effective generalization, rather than aiming for the global minimum. |
| **Convergence** | - Convergence in non-convex problems is often slower and more unpredictable. However, heuristics and empirical evidence suggest deep networks often converge to good minima that provide reasonable generalization. |
| **Overcoming Challenges** | - **Initialization Strategies**: Using proper weight initialization methods (e.g., Xavier, He initialization) to avoid getting stuck in poor local minima.<br>- **Regularization**: Techniques like L2 regularization, dropout, and batch normalization help in improving generalization. |
| **Empirical Results** | Despite the non-convexity of the loss function, deep networks often perform well in practice. They tend to converge to regions with good performance due to the inherent structure and optimization techniques used. |
| **Practical Considerations** | Non-convex optimization in deep networks is challenging but tractable using advanced techniques like momentum, adaptive learning rates, and parallelization. Additionally, recent advances in neural architecture design and optimization have made the training of deep networks more efficient despite non-convexity. |

The above Table9.1 summarizes key aspects and strategies for non-convex optimization in deep learning.

## Stochastic Optimization

Stochastic optimization plays a pivotal role in deep learning by optimizing model parameters when dealing with large-scale datasets. Unlike traditional optimization techniques, which depend on complete data, stochastic optimization introduces an element of randomness to approximate solutions, significantly enhancing both efficiency and scalability. This becomes particularly crucial in deep learning, where the sheer size of datasets and the complexity of models often render deterministic methods computationally impractical. One of the most widely used stochastic optimization techniques is Stochastic Gradient Descent (SGD). In contrast to standard gradient descent, which computes the gradient over the entire dataset in each iteration, SGD evaluates the gradient using a randomly selected subset of data, referred to as a mini-batch. This reduces computational overhead and accelerates model parameter updates. Additionally, the randomness in SGD helps the algorithm escape local minima, thereby improving the likelihood of finding better solutions. However, this stochastic nature can cause oscillations around the optimal minimum, necessitating careful tuning of hyperparameters such as the learning rate and batch size.

Several variants of SGD, such as Momentum, RMSprop, and Adam, address some of its limitations. Momentum improves convergence speed by incorporating a fraction of the previous update, helping to smooth out noisy oscillations. RMSprop adapts the learning rate for each parameter based on the recent magnitudes of gradients, thus preventing excessively large updates. Adam combines the advantages of both Momentum and RMSprop, offering adaptive learning rates and faster convergence, which has made it one of the most popular optimizers in deep learning. Despite its strengths, stochastic optimization is not without challenges, including sensitivity to hyperparameters and the potential instability of convergence. Excessive randomness can lead to suboptimal solutions, necessitating strategies such as learning rate scheduling or regularization to strike a balance between exploration and stability. Nevertheless, stochastic optimization remains a foundational technique in deep learning, enabling the efficient training of neural networks and unlocking their potential across diverse applications like image recognition, natural language processing, and more.

## Generalization in Neural Networks

Generalization refers to a neural network's capacity to effectively process and perform on new, unseen data, extending beyond the specific examples encountered during training. Essentially, it gauges the model's ability to identify and learn the underlying patterns and relationships within the data, rather than simply memorizing the training set. Achieving strong generalization is crucial for deploying neural networks in real-world applications, where the test data may differ significantly from the training data, as illustrated in Figure 9.1.

## Concepts of Generalization

Overfitting and Underfitting:Overfitting occurs when a model becomes excessively tailored to the training data, learning not only the underlying patterns but also the noise and specific details. As a result, it struggles to generalize to new, unseen data, leading to poor performance on test sets. While overfitted models exhibit low training error, they often show high test error. On the other hand, underfitting arises when a model is too simplistic, failing to capture the data's underlying structure, which results in both high training and test errors.

Capacity of Neural Networks:Neural networks with an excessive number of parameters possess the ability to represent a vast range of functions, including those that are overly complex or fit the noise present in the data. Achieving an optimal balance between model complexity and the size of the dataset is essential to prevent overfitting. This balance ensures that the model has enough capacity to learn meaningful patterns without becoming overly specialized to the training data.

**Figure 9.1: Generalization in Neural Networks.**

## Techniques to Improve Generalization

**Regularization:** Techniques like L1 and L2 regularization incorporate a penalty term into the loss function, discouraging the model from becoming overly complex by limiting the magnitude of its weights. Dropout, another effective technique, randomly deactivates a subset of neurons during training, compelling the network to learn redundant representations, which enhances its robustness.

**Data Augmentation:** By artificially enlarging the training dataset with variations such as rotations, flips, or added noise, data augmentation enables the network to learn invariant features, leading to better generalization across diverse inputs.

**Batch Normalization:** Normalizing the activations of intermediate layers helps mitigate internal covariate shifts, fostering more stable training and enhancing the model's ability to generalize.

**Early Stopping:** By continuously monitoring the model's performance on a validation set and halting training when performance plateaus, early stopping prevents overfitting, ensuring the model does not start learning irrelevant patterns late in training.

**Learning Rate Scheduling:** Dynamically adjusting the learning rate throughout training (e.g., gradually reducing it) allows the model to fine-tune its parameters more effectively, aiding in the search for a better local optimum and ultimately improving generalization.

### Role of Data and Architecture

**Data Quality and Diversity:** Ensuring high-quality and diverse datasets is crucial for effective generalization. A lack of variability or the presence of biases in the training data can result in models that struggle to perform well on unseen data, ultimately limiting their effectiveness.

**Architectural Choices:** Thoughtful architectural design plays a key role in enhancing generalization. For instance, employing convolutional layers for image data or recurrent layers for sequential data allows models to capitalize on domain-specific inductive biases, leading to better performance and adaptability.

### Evaluation of Generalization

Generalization is commonly assessed through methods such as train-test splits or cross-validation. When both training error and test error are low, it signals strong generalization. Furthermore, techniques like leave-one-out cross-validation can provide deeper insights into the model's robustness and overall performance.

## Spatial Transformer Networks

Spatial Transformer Networks (STNs) are a specialized class of neural networks aimed at improving the spatial invariance of deep learning models. They empower neural networks to dynamically learn and apply spatial transformations to feature maps, such as scaling, cropping, rotation, and other affine transformations, allowing the model to focus on the most relevant regions of input data. This capability proves especially valuable in tasks like image classification, object detection, and recognition, where precise spatial alignment of features plays a crucial role in enhancing overall performance.

### Components of Spatial Transformer Networks

- Localization Network

The localization network is a specialized neural network designed to predict the parameters necessary for spatial transformations. For instance, it might predict six parameters for an affine transformation. Typically, this network is a convolutional neural network (CNN) when working with image data, though its architecture can be adapted to suit other types of data.

- Grid Generator

The grid generator utilizes the transformation parameters predicted by the localization network to create a coordinate grid in the input image space. For example, an affine grid generator maps output coordinates to corresponding input coordinates by applying an affine transformation, aligning the grid with the predicted spatial changes.

- Sampler

The sampler is responsible for interpolating the input data values at the grid points generated by the grid generator. Common interpolation methods include bilinear sampling, which is differentiable, enabling the network to backpropagate errors effectively during training.

### *How STNs Work?*

- Input Transformation

The input data, such as an image, is fed into the localization network, which processes it to generate transformation parameters. These parameters typically include values for scaling, rotation, or other geometric adjustments, represented in the form of transformation matrices.

- Grid Generation

Using the predicted transformation parameters, the grid generator computes a new set of coordinates. These coordinates define the positions where the input data will be sampled after applying the transformation, ensuring alignment with the predicted changes.

- Data Sampling

The sampler then applies the transformation by interpolating the pixel values at the newly calculated coordinates. This results in a transformed version of the input data, which is then forwarded to the next layers of the network for further processing.

## Advantages of Spatial Transformer Networks

- Spatial Invariance

STNs eliminate the need for explicit pre-processing by enabling networks to manage input data variations, including shifts in scale, rotation, or translation.

- End-to-End Learning

STNs easily integrate into neural networks, enabling end-to-end training in contrast to conventional techniques that call for manual feature engineering.

- Reduced Model Complexity

STNs can make learning easier for downstream layers by dynamically changing inputs, which improves performance while using fewer parameters.

## Applications of STNs

- Image Classification: Spatial alignment of features significantly enhances classification accuracy, particularly in datasets with diverse perspectives or varying scales.
- Object Detection and Recognition: Spatial Transformer Networks (STNs) normalize object appearances, bolstering the robustness of detection and recognition tasks.
- Medical Imaging: STNs aid in aligning medical images with anatomical landmarks, thereby improving the precision of diagnoses and analysis.
- Robotics and Autonomous Systems: STNs play a crucial role in guiding robots and autonomous systems to identify and focus on relevant elements of the environment, such as obstacles or targets.

## Challenges and Limitations

- Adding STNs to a model introduces extra computational complexity due to the localization network and sampling process.
- The transformations learned by the STNs are limited by the parameterization (e.g., affine transformations may not capture all spatial variations).
- Training STNs can be unstable if the localization network struggles to predict accurate transformation parameters.

## Recurrent Networks

Recurrent Neural Networks (RNNs) are a specialized class of artificial neural networks engineered to process and analyze sequential data. Unlike traditional feedforward networks, RNNs feature feedback connections that loop back on themselves, enabling them to retain and leverage a hidden state. This unique architecture allows RNNs to excel in tasks where the sequence and context of inputs play a critical role, such as time-series forecasting, natural language processing, and speech recognition.

## Features of RNNs

**Sequential Processing:** Recurrent Neural Networks (RNNs) process data in a stepwise manner, sequentially analyzing each element while retaining memory of previous inputs within their hidden states. This ability enables RNNs to effectively capture temporal dependencies between elements in the sequence.

**Shared Parameters:** RNNs use the same set of weights and biases across all time steps, which minimizes the number of parameters and enhances the network's efficiency when dealing with sequential data.

**Hidden States:** At each time step, the network updates its hidden state by incorporating both the current input and the previous hidden state. This mechanism allows the RNN to retain crucial information from earlier time steps, effectively enabling it to "remember" and leverage context over time.

## Working of RNNs

### Input Layer

At each time step $t$, an input vector is fed into the network. This input could be a word in a sentence, a frame in a video, or a data point in a time series.

### Hidden Layer

The hidden layer computes a new hidden state $ht$ based on the current input and the previous hidden state $ht-1$. This computation is represented as:

$$h_t = f(W_h \cdot h_{t-1} + W_x \cdot x_t + b)$$

Here:

- $W_h$: Weights for the hidden state
- Wx: Weights for the input
- b: Bias
- f: Activation function (commonly tanh or ReLU)

### Output Layer

The output $y_t$ at each time step is computed from the hidden state:

$$y_t = g(W_y \cdot h_t + c)$$

Here:

- $W_y$: Output weights
- c: Output bias
- g: Activation function (commonly softmax for classification tasks)

### Backpropagation Through Time (BPTT)

Errors are propagated backward through the network during RNN training. A technique known as Backpropagation Through Time (BPTT) extends this process over several time steps.

## Advantages of RNNs

**Context Awareness:** Recurrent Neural Networks (RNNs) excel in processing sequential data by leveraging context from previous inputs, making them particularly effective for tasks that demand a deep understanding of temporal dependencies.

**Compact Architecture:** By reusing weights across time steps, RNNs efficiently reduce the parameter count, in contrast to fully connected feedforward networks, leading to more streamlined models.

**Versatility:** RNNs are highly adaptable and can be applied across a wide spectrum of domains, including natural language processing, speech recognition, video analysis, and other forms of sequential data, showcasing their broad applicability.

## Challenges of RNNs

**Vanishing and Exploding Gradients:** During the training process, gradients may either diminish to almost zero (vanishing gradients) or escalate exponentially (exploding gradients), severely hindering the model's ability to learn and effectively process long sequences.

**Difficulty in Capturing Long-Term Dependencies:** Standard RNNs face significant challenges in preserving information over extended time frames, limiting their capacity to handle tasks that require the retention of long-term dependencies.

**Training Complexity:** The Backpropagation Through Time (BPTT) algorithm is computationally intensive and can become inefficient, especially when dealing with long sequences, leading to slow and resource-heavy training processes.

## Variants of RNNs

To address the limitations of vanilla RNNs, several advanced architectures have been developed:

- Long Short-Term Memory (LSTM):

LSTMs enhance traditional RNNs by introducing three key gates—input, forget, and output—which regulate the flow of information. This structure enables LSTMs to effectively capture long-range dependencies in sequential data.

- Gated Recurrent Unit (GRU):

GRUs streamline the LSTM architecture by combining certain gates, reducing computational complexity while retaining similar performance. This makes GRUs a more efficient option for many tasks.

- Bidirectional RNNs:

Bidirectional RNNs process sequences in both forward and backward directions, enabling them to capture dependencies from both past and future contexts. This feature improves the model's ability to understand complex sequence dynamics.

- Attention Mechanisms:

Attention mechanisms improve RNNs by allowing the model to focus on specific parts of the input sequence. This selective focus enhances performance in tasks like machine translation, summarization, and other sequence-to-sequence applications.

Recurrent Neural Networks (RNNs) are a potent tool for modeling sequential data, offering significant advantages in retaining contextual information. Despite challenges such as vanishing gradients, innovations like LSTMs, GRUs, and attention mechanisms have greatly enhanced RNNs' ability to capture long-term dependencies and have expanded their use across a variety of domains.

## LSTM - Recurrent Neural Network Language Model

Long Short-Term Memory (LSTM) networks are an advanced variant of Recurrent Neural Networks (RNNs) specifically engineered to address the challenge of long-term dependencies in sequential data. While traditional RNNs face difficulties with the vanishing gradient problem, which hampers their ability to capture relationships in long sequences, LSTMs tackle this limitation with a distinct architecture. This architecture enables the efficient flow of gradients across extended time steps, allowing LSTMs to excel in complex tasks such as language modeling, text generation, and machine translation.

## Key Features of LSTM

### Cell State

The cell state in Long Short-Term Memory (LSTM) networks functions as a memory unit that preserves and transfers information across time steps. Serving as the primary channel for information flow, it is updated or adjusted at each time step through specialized gates. This architecture empowers LSTMs to selectively retain or discard information according to its relevance to the task, facilitating the efficient management of both short-term and long-term dependencies.

### Gates

*LSTMs use three types of gates to manage information flow:*

- The forget gate controls which portions of the cell state should be discarded by evaluating the current input and the previous hidden state.
- The input gate governs the addition of new information to the cell state, determining what should be updated.
- The output gate decides which parts of the cell state influence the current output. These gates utilize sigmoid and tanh activation functions to effectively manage the flow of information.

**Gradient Flow**

A key strength of LSTMs lies in their capacity to tackle the vanishing gradient problem. By leveraging the cell state as a conduit for gradients, LSTMs maintain stable gradient values across multiple time steps. This stability enables the network to effectively capture long-range dependencies, making it ideal for tasks that require understanding of extended sequences, such as language translation and speech recognition.

## Architecture of LSTM

At each time step t, the LSTM processes the input $x_t$, previous hidden state $h_{t-1}$, and previous cell state $C_{t-1}$, computing the following (Figure 9.2):

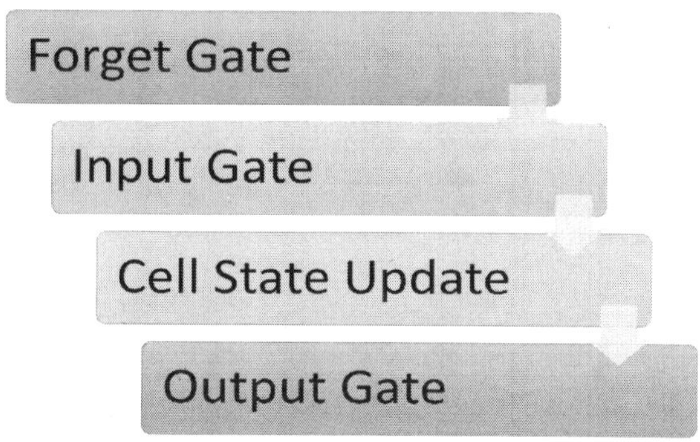


**Figure 9.2: Architecture.**

- Forget Gate

Determines which parts of the cell state should be forgotten:

$$f_t = \sigma(W_f \cdot [h_{t-1}, x_t] + b_f)$$

- Input Gate

Updates the cell state with new information:

$$i_t = \sigma(W_i \cdot [h_{t-1}, x_t] + b_i)$$

$$\tilde{c}_t = \tanh(W_c \cdot [h_{t-1}, x_t] + b_c)$$

- Cell State Update

Combines the old state and new candidate values:

$$c_t = f_t \cdot c_{t-1} + i_t \cdot \tilde{c}_t$$

- Output Gate

Computes the output for the current time step:

$$o_t = \sigma(W_o \cdot [h_{t-1}, x_t] + b_o)$$

$$h_t = o_t \cdot \tanh(c_t)$$

Here:

- σ: Sigmoid activation function
- tanh: Hyperbolic tangent activation function
- W and b: Weight matrices and biases for each gate

## LSTM in Language Models

In language models, Long Short-Term Memory (LSTM) networks are designed to predict the next word or sequence of words based on the given context. They process input sequences of word embeddings, which are dense, numerical representations of words, and maintain a dynamic hidden state that evolves as the sequence progresses. At each time step, this hidden state is passed through a fully connected layer with a softmax activation function, generating probability distributions for the potential next words. This capability makes LSTMs a fundamental building block for various natural language processing tasks, such as machine translation, text generation, and autocomplete systems.

## Advantages of LSTM in Language Modeling

LSTMs excel at capturing long-range dependencies in sequences, making them exceptionally well-suited for understanding and predicting natural language. Their unique architecture allows them to selectively focus on the most relevant parts of the input, effectively ignoring extraneous information. This capability is particularly beneficial for tasks like machine translation and text summarization, where context is critical for accurate outcomes. Additionally, LSTMs' adaptability to process sequences of varying lengths makes them highly versatile, allowing them to be applied across a broad spectrum of natural language processing tasks.

## Challenges

Although LSTMs offer significant advantages, they also present several challenges. Their computational complexity is elevated due to the numerous parameters needed for the gating mechanisms, making them resource-intensive during training. Furthermore, LSTMs are highly susceptible to overfitting, especially when working with small datasets, necessitating the use of regularization techniques such as dropout to prevent this issue. While LSTMs effectively mitigate the vanishing gradient problem, they still struggle with extremely long sequences, which can lead to significant memory and computational difficulties.

## Word-Level RNNs & Deep Reinforcement Learning

Word-level RNNs are a specialized variant of Recurrent Neural Networks specifically tailored to process text data at the word level. These models are extensively utilized in various natural language processing (NLP) tasks such as text generation, language translation, and sentiment analysis. Unlike character-level RNNs, which operate at the granularity of individual characters, word-level RNNs handle sequences of entire words, allowing them to capture more intricate linguistic structures and semantic nuances for enhanced text comprehension.

### Concepts in Word-Level RNNs

**Input Representation:** In natural language processing, words are initially converted into numerical representations using word embeddings like Word2Vec, GloVe, or FastText. These embeddings map each word to a dense vector within a continuous vector space, capturing semantic meaning and relationships. For example, words such as "king" and "queen" would be represented by similar vectors, reflecting their semantic similarity and relational context.

**Sequential Processing:** Word-level Recurrent Neural Networks (RNNs) process text sequentially, one word at a time, while maintaining a hidden state that encodes the context from the preceding words in the sequence. For instance, in the sentence "The cat sat on the mat," the RNN updates its hidden state at each step, allowing it to predict the next word by considering the entire context of the sentence.

**Output Generation:** At each time step, the RNN generates an output, which can either be a probability distribution over the vocabulary to predict the next word (as in text generation tasks) or a classification label (such as sentiment polarity in sentiment analysis). This output is produced through a fully connected layer followed by a softmax activation function.

**Training Word-Level RNNs:** Training a word-level RNN involves minimizing a loss function, such as cross-entropy, which measures the difference between the predicted and actual next words. To optimize the model's performance, backpropagation through time (BPTT) is applied, updating the network's weights and improving its ability to predict word sequences effectively.

### Advantages of Word-Level RNNs

- **Linguistic Awareness:** By operating at the word level, these RNNs more effectively capture both syntactic and semantic relationships, offering a deeper understanding compared to character-level models.
- **Efficiency:** Word-level models process long sequences more quickly, requiring fewer time steps than their character-level counterparts, making them more efficient.

- **Contextual Understanding:** These models excel in tasks that demand a strong understanding of word-level context, such as machine translation and text summarization, ensuring high-quality results.

## Challenges

- **Expansive Vocabulary Requirements:** Handling a large vocabulary necessitates substantial computational power and memory resources.
- **Challenges with Out-of-Vocabulary (OOV) Words:** Words that were not encountered during training can complicate prediction accuracy. Subword techniques such as Byte Pair Encoding (BPE) offer a solution to mitigate this issue.
- **Difficulty with Long-Term Dependencies:** While word-level Recurrent Neural Networks (RNNs) perform well with short-to-medium sequences, they often face difficulties in capturing long-term dependencies. Models like Long Short-Term Memory (LSTM) networks and Gated Recurrent Units (GRUs) are more adept at addressing these challenges.

## Deep Reinforcement Learning (Deep RL)

Deep Reinforcement Learning (DRL) merges the foundational concepts of reinforcement learning (RL) with the power of deep learning, empowering agents to make decisions in complex, high-dimensional environments. Unlike supervised learning, where models are trained on labeled data, DRL involves learning through a process of trial and error. Agents interact with their environment, continuously refining their decision-making by receiving feedback in the form of rewards or penalties based on their actions. This dynamic process enables the agent to learn optimal strategies for navigating intricate tasks.

## Components of Deep RL

**Agent and Environment:** The agent engages with an environment by observing its current state, taking actions, and receiving rewards that reflect the effectiveness of those actions. The agent's ultimate goal is to optimize its cumulative rewards over time, improving its decision-making process through experience.

**Policy:** A policy defines the strategy that governs the agent's actions in response to the environment's state. It can be deterministic, where a specific action is chosen for each state, or stochastic, where actions are selected based on a probability distribution, introducing an element of randomness in decision-making.

## Value Function

The expected cumulative reward from a specific state or state-action pair is estimated by the value function. It helps the agent make decisions that will result in greater rewards.

### Deep Neural Networks

The policy or value function is approximated by deep learning models, such as LSTMs or Convolutional Neural Networks (CNNs). The agent can handle complex inputs like text, images, or time-series data thanks to these models.

### Popular Algorithms in Deep RL

- **Deep Q-Networks (DQN):** DQN integrates the power of Q-learning with deep learning techniques to approximate the optimal action-value function. This approach is highly effective for problems involving discrete action spaces, such as those found in Atari games, where it excels in decision-making tasks.
- **Policy Gradient Methods:** These methods focus on directly optimizing the policy by adjusting model parameters in the direction that maximizes expected rewards. Algorithms like REINFORCE and Actor-Critic are prominent examples of this approach, which allows for more flexible and continuous policy improvement.

### Proximal Policy Optimization (PPO):

A popular algorithm that maintains stable training while striking a balance between exploration and exploitation. PPO works well in continuous action spaces and is reliable.

### Applications of Deep RL

- **Game Playing:** Reinforcement Learning (RL) has been instrumental in developing AI agents that exceed human capabilities in complex games such as Go, Chess, and Dota 2.
- **Robotics:** Deep Reinforcement Learning (DRL) empowers robots to autonomously learn and execute tasks, including walking, object manipulation, and performing intricate industrial operations.
- **Autonomous Vehicles:** RL plays a critical role in enabling self-driving cars to make real-time decisions and navigate through dynamic, unpredictable environments.
- **Recommendation Systems:** RL is leveraged to personalize user experiences, tailoring content and product recommendations on platforms like Netflix and Amazon based on individual preferences.
- **Finance:** RL is revolutionizing financial strategies by optimizing portfolio management and refining algorithmic trading techniques to enhance profitability.

### Challenges

- **Exploration-Exploitation Tradeoff:** Striking thc right balance between exploring new actions (exploration) and optimizing rewards based on familiar actions (exploitation) presents a complex and nuanced challenge in reinforcement learning.

- **Sample Inefficiency:** Reinforcement learning often requires a significant amount of interaction with the environment, which can be both time-consuming and resource-intensive, making it less efficient in terms of sample usage.
- **Stability and Convergence:** Reinforcement learning models are susceptible to instability and may fail to converge effectively unless fine-tuned with precise hyperparameters.
- **Scalability:** Scaling reinforcement learning to environments with extremely high-dimensional states or intricate dynamics continues to be a formidable obstacle.
- **Word-Level RNNs and Deep Reinforcement Learning:** Word-level Recurrent Neural Networks (RNNs) and Deep Reinforcement Learning represent two influential paradigms in modern AI. While Word-Level RNNs enhance capabilities in natural language processing, Deep RL is revolutionizing the way agents learn to make decisions and take actions in complex, dynamic environments.

## Computational & Artificial Neuroscience

Computational neuroscience is dedicated to unraveling the brain's function by mathematically modeling neural processes and simulating them computationally. This field investigates how biological neurons encode, process, and transmit information, with key areas such as neural coding and neural dynamics. Neural coding examines patterns of action potentials (spikes) to decode sensory and cognitive information, while neural dynamics explores how neurons interact over time to produce behaviors. Advanced models like the Hodgkin-Huxley equation and integrate-and-fire models describe the electrical and chemical activities of neurons, providing insights into processes such as memory formation and sensory perception.In contrast, artificial neuroscience draws inspiration from biological systems to create computational models, notably Artificial Neural Networks (ANNs). These networks emulate the structure and function of the brain, solving complex problems across diverse domains, including image recognition, speech processing, and robotics. With breakthroughs like deep learning, ANNs now feature multiple hidden layers, allowing them to tackle increasingly intricate tasks. Neuromorphic computing, a subfield of artificial neuroscience, focuses on developing hardware systems that replicate the architecture and efficiency of biological brains. Examples include IBM's TrueNorth and Intel's Loihi chips, which push the boundaries of brain-inspired computation.

While computational neuroscience seeks to understand the underlying mechanisms of the brain, artificial neuroscience applies this knowledge to develop intelligent systems. For instance, principles of plasticity, such as Hebbian learning and spike-timing-dependent plasticity (STDP), have influenced algorithms in artificial models. Additionally, platforms like TensorFlow and PyTorch empower researchers to create artificial systems inspired by computational neuroscience, bridging the gap between biological and synthetic intelligence. This dynamic interplay between fields drives remarkable progress in both neuroscience and artificial intelligence, with computational neuroscience shedding light on phenomena like decision-making and learning, while artificial neuroscience translates these insights into practical applications in autonomous vehicles, personalized medicine, and brain-computer interfaces. This convergence is essential for future breakthroughs in brain-inspired AI and cognitive modeling (Table 9.2).

**Table9.2: Comparison of Computational and Artificial Neuroscience.**

| Feature | **Computational Neuroscience** | **Artificial Neuroscience** |
|---|---|---|
| **Definition** | The study of brain function through mathematical models, simulations, and theoretical analysis. | The development of AI systems inspired by biological neural processes. |
| **Focus Area** | Understanding how the brain processes information and neural dynamics. | Creating AI models that mimic neural functions to achieve human-like intelligence. |
| **Key Techniques** | Mathematical modeling, simulations, neural networks, and brain mapping. | Deep learning, neural networks, reinforcement learning, and bio-inspired computing. |
| **Primary Goal** | To explain how real neurons and networks operate in biological systems. | To build efficient AI systems that replicate cognitive abilities. |
| **Use of Data** | Uses biological data (EEG, fMRI, neural recordings) for validation. | Uses large-scale datasets for training AI models. |
| **Application Domains** | Neuroscience, medicine, cognitive science, and psychology. | Machine learning, robotics, AI, automation, and computer vision. |
| **Degree of Biological Fidelity** | High fidelity to real biological systems and neurophysiology. | Inspired by biology but often simplified for computational efficiency. |
| **Examples** | Hodgkin-Huxley model, Integrate-and-Fire models, and Blue Brain Project. | Deep learning architectures (CNNs, RNNs), GPT models, Neuromorphic computing. |
| **Limitations** | Complex and computationally expensive; real-time brain modeling is difficult. | Lacks full biological realism; AI models are often black boxes with limited interpretability. |

## Summary

This chapter provides an in-depth exploration of key concepts in optimization and advanced architectures within deep learning. It begins by addressing the challenges posed by non-convex optimization, focusing on strategies to overcome local minima and saddle points that commonly arise in deep networks. The chapter further investigates stochastic optimization techniques, such as SGD and Adam, highlighting their effectiveness in training large-scale models. The significance of generalization in neural networks is thoroughly discussed, with an emphasis on methods to improve model performance on previously unseen data. Spatial Transformer Networks are introduced as a solution for dynamic data transformation, enhancing the adaptability of neural networks. Additionally, the chapter explores recurrent neural networks, with a focus on LSTMs to capture long-term dependencies in sequential data, and word-level RNNs for tasks like language modeling. The role of deep reinforcement learning in decision-making processes is also examined, alongside the integration of computational and artificial neuroscience principles to inspire brain-like models. This comprehensive coverage connects advanced optimization techniques with the latest advancements in neural network architectures and applications.

## Exercise Questions

- Explain the challenges of non-convex optimization in deep networks and how techniques like momentum and second-order methods address them.
- What are the differences between stochastic gradient descent (SGD) and Adam optimizers? Discuss their respective advantages.
- Define generalization in neural networks and list three strategies to improve generalization in deep learning models.
- Describe the architecture and working of Spatial Transformer Networks. How do they handle dynamic input transformations?
- What makes LSTMs more effective than standard RNNs for handling long-term dependencies in sequential data?
- Explain the concept of word-level RNNs. How are they used for language modeling and text generation?
- Discuss the importance of reinforcement learning in training agents for real-world decision-making tasks. Provide examples.
- How do concepts from computational neuroscience inspire artificial neural networks? Give two examples.
- Compare deep and shallow networks in terms of representation power and training efficiency.
- Design a scenario where Spatial Transformer Networks could significantly enhance the performance of a deep learning model. Explain your reasoning.

CHAPTER - 10

# Applications of Deep Learning

Deep learning, a subset of machine learning, has become one of the most powerful tools in artificial intelligence (AI) over the past decade. This technology is inspired by the human brain's neural networks and uses multiple layers of algorithms to analyze and model complex patterns in data. Deep learning is distinguished by its ability to learn from large volumes of data, improving accuracy and performance as the system processes more information. The proliferation of deep learning techniques has revolutionized industries, enabling new solutions to problems that were once difficult to solve using traditional methods.One of the most prominent applications of deep learning is in the field of computer vision. By training deep neural networks on vast datasets of images, deep learning models can recognize and classify objects, faces, and even emotions. This has opened doors to innovations in industries like healthcare, where deep learning assists in diagnosing medical images such as X-rays and MRIs. In addition, computer vision applications extend to autonomous vehicles, where deep learning is crucial for enabling self-driving cars to interpret their surroundings and make decisions in real-time.

Another major application is in natural language processing (NLP). Deep learning techniques, such as recurrent neural networks (RNNs) and transformers, have significantly advanced the way machines understand and generate human language. This has led to the development of highly sophisticated AI systems that can perform tasks like language translation, sentiment analysis, and chatbots. In industries like customer service, deep learning-powered chatbots are providing instant, human-like interactions, thereby improving customer experience and reducing the need for human intervention. Speech recognition is yet another area where deep learning is making significant strides. Modern speech recognition systems, powered by deep learning models, have become increasingly accurate at transcribing spoken words into text. These systems are now used in virtual assistants like Siri and Alexa, enabling voice commands to control devices and perform tasks. The technology also plays a pivotal role in transcription services, accessibility tools for the hearing impaired, and customer support systems that rely on voice interaction.

The field of recommendation systems has also greatly benefited from deep learning. Streaming platforms, such as Netflix and Spotify, use deep learning to analyze user preferences and suggest content that aligns with individual tastes. By processing vast amounts of data about user behavior and preferences, deep learning models generate highly personalized recommendations, increasing user engagement and satisfaction. These systems are also used in e-commerce, where platforms like Amazon recommend products based on past behavior and similar user interests.Finally, deep learning is revolutionizing the field of autonomous robotics. From drones to industrial robots, deep learning algorithms are being employed to enable machines to learn from their environment and perform complex tasks autonomously. In manufacturing, deep learning allows robots to adapt to changes in the production line, improving efficiency and precision. In agriculture, robots powered by deep learning are being deployed for tasks such as crop monitoring, pest control, and harvesting. This technology is driving forward the next generation of intelligent robots capable of performing in dynamic, real-world environments.Deep learning's applications are transforming industries and solving complex problems that were previously considered insurmountable. Whether in healthcare, entertainment, or manufacturing, deep learning is opening up new opportunities and improving the way we interact with technology. As the technology continues to evolve, its impact is likely to expand, paving the way for even more groundbreaking innovations in the future.

## Images Segmentation

Image segmentation is a fundamental process in computer vision that involves dividing an image into distinct, meaningful segments or regions. These segments often represent objects, features, or other significant components of the image, enabling more precise analysis and interpretation. With its broad range of applications, image segmentation plays a vital role in fields such as medical imaging, autonomous driving, and object recognition (Figure 10.1).

**Figure 10.1: Images Segmentation.**

## Types of Image Segmentation

### 1. Semantic Segmentation:

This technique assigns a specific class label to each pixel in an image. For instance, in a street scene, the pixels are categorized into classes such as road, cars, pedestrians, and buildings. However, it does not differentiate between distinct instances of the same object.

### 2. Instance Segmentation

In contrast to semantic segmentation, instance segmentation not only labels each pixel but also recognizes and separates individual instances of objects within an image. For example, in an image with several cars, instance segmentation identifies each car as a distinct entity.

### 3. Panoptic Segmentation:

Panoptic segmentation merges both semantic and instance segmentation approaches. It offers pixel-level classification while also distinguishing between individual instances of objects, providing a comprehensive understanding of the image.

## Working of Image Segmentation

**Preprocessing:** The image undergoes initial preprocessing, which may involve resizing, normalization, or augmentation techniques aimed at enhancing key features to improve the quality and accuracy of segmentation results.

**Feature Extraction:** Advanced deep learning models, such as Convolutional Neural Networks (CNNs), are employed to extract high-level features from the image, including edges, textures, and patterns, which are essential for differentiating and identifying various regions within the image.

**Segmentation Algorithm:** Sophisticated segmentation algorithms, such as U-Net, Mask R-CNN, or Fully Convolutional Networks (FCNs), are applied to partition the image into meaningful segments. These models generate pixel-wise prediction maps, assigning specific labels to each pixel to represent distinct regions.

**Post-processing:** post-processing techniques, like Conditional Random Fields (CRFs) or smoothing filters, are utilized to refine the segmentation results, enhancing overall accuracy while resolving boundary uncertainties and inconsistencies.

## Applications

- Medical Imaging

Plays a crucial role in the segmentation of tumors, organs, and tissues in CT, MRI, or X-ray scans, facilitating accurate diagnosis and informed treatment planning.

- Autonomous Driving

Vital for comprehending road environments by detecting and segmenting lanes, vehicles, pedestrians, and obstacles, ensuring safe and efficient navigation.

- Satellite Imaging

Supports land use analysis, urban development, and environmental monitoring by segmenting regions such as forests, water bodies, and urban areas for more precise planning and decision-making.

- Agriculture

Helps monitor crop health and soil conditions by segmenting and analyzing vegetation areas, contributing to more effective and sustainable farming practices.

- Augmented Reality (AR)

Powers real-time object identification and segmentation, enhancing interactive and immersive AR experiences for users.

## Challenges in Image Segmentation

- Images containing complex or overlapping objects often pose challenges for precise segmentation.
- Certain classes within an image may dominate, making it difficult for models to accurately segment smaller or less frequent classes.
- Real-time applications, such as autonomous vehicles, necessitate fast and precise segmentation, which in turn requires substantial computational power.

**Table 10.1: Popular Image Segmentation Models.**

| Model | Description | Applications |
|---|---|---|
| **U-Net** | Encoder-decoder architecture with skip connections, commonly used in biomedical segmentation. | Medical Imaging |
| **Mask R-CNN** | Extends Faster R-CNN by adding a branch for pixel-level segmentation. | Object Detection and Segmentation |
| **FCN** | Fully Convolutional Network replaces fully connected layers with convolutional layers for segmentation. | Scene Understanding |
| **DeepLab** | Uses atrous convolution for multi-scale context and dense predictions. | Semantic and Instance Segmentation |

Image segmentation is continually advancing, driven by breakthroughs in deep learning and enhanced computational power, enabling the delivery of exceptionally accurate and efficient outcomes across a wide range of domains (Table 10.1).

## Object Detection

Object detection is a core task in computer vision, focused on identifying and precisely locating multiple objects within an image or video frame. Unlike image classification, which assigns a single label to an entire image, object detection requires predicting both the class labels and the coordinates of the bounding boxes for each detectable object within the scene. This dual challenge of classification and localization makes object detection a complex yet highly versatile application of deep learning techniques, with wide-ranging uses across industries.

### *How Object Detection Works?*

At its foundation, object detection leverages convolutional neural networks (CNNs) for effective feature extraction. The process begins by feeding an input image into the network, where CNNs analyze and extract both spatial and hierarchical features, creating a detailed feature map. This feature map serves as the foundation for identifying potential object regions. To propose areas of interest, Region Proposal Networks (RPNs) or alternative algorithms are often employed. These proposed regions are then classified into predefined categories, and their bounding boxes are fine-tuned to ensure accurate object localization.

## Advanced Techniques in Object Detection

Modern object detection techniques can be broadly categorized into two types:

- Two-Stage Detectors: Techniques like Faster R-CNN first generate region proposals and then classify each proposed region, ensuring high accuracy. While these models excel in precision, they demand significant computational resources, making them best suited for applications where accuracy is paramount.
- One-Stage Detectors: Models like YOLO (You Only Look Once) and SSD (Single Shot MultiBox Detector) streamline the detection process by performing both region proposal and classification in a single step. This results in faster inference times, making these detectors ideal for real-time applications such as video surveillance and autonomous driving.

Furthermore, recent innovations in object detection have introduced transformer-based models, such as DETR (DEtectionTRansformer). These models eliminate the need for region proposals altogether, simplifying the detection pipeline and improving efficiency.

## Challenges in Object Detection

Despite its success, object detection continues to encounter numerous challenges. Variability in object sizes, shapes, and orientations often complicates accurate detection. Occlusion, where objects overlap or obscure one another, further exacerbates the issue. Moreover, achieving real-time performance on resource-constrained devices, such as smartphones, demands highly optimized models that strike a delicate balance between accuracy and computational efficiency.

## Applications of Object Detection

The versatility of object detection has led to its adoption in numerous fields:

- **Autonomous Vehicles:** Utilizing advanced detection systems to identify pedestrians, other vehicles, and road signs for safe and efficient navigation on the road.
- **Healthcare:** Leveraging image recognition to detect tumours and abnormalities in medical scans, such as X-rays and MRIs, enabling early diagnosis and better patient care.
- **Retail and E-Commerce:** Analyzing customer behavior patterns and optimizing inventory management through real-time surveillance and data analytics.
- **Augmented Reality:** Enhancing user interaction by detecting and responding to real-world objects, creating immersive and dynamic experiences.
- **Security:** Implementing real-time surveillance systems to monitor and identify potential threats or suspicious activities, ensuring heightened safety and security.

## Future Directions

The integration of cutting-edge architectures, such as transformers, alongside breakthroughs in edge computing, is driving the ongoing evolution of object detection. The emphasis has now transitioned towards enhancing model generalization across diverse datasets, improving detection accuracy for small objects, and optimizing performance for deployment on resource-constrained platforms. As a dynamic and rapidly advancing field, object detection remains at the forefront of AI innovation, paving the way for smarter, more intuitive, and interactive technologies.

## Automatic Image Captioning

Automatic image captioning is the process of leveraging artificial intelligence to generate detailed, contextually relevant textual descriptions for images. This process integrates advanced techniques from computer vision, which enables the system to interpret and analyze the visual content of an image, and natural language processing, which allows for the generation of coherent and contextually accurate captions. The ultimate aim is to develop a system capable of producing image descriptions that mirror human-level accuracy, fluency, and understanding.

### *How Automatic Image Captioning Works?*

The process of image captioning typically involves three key components:

- **Image Feature Extraction:** Convolutional Neural Networks (CNNs) are employed to extract high-level features from input images, leveraging popular architectures such as VGG, ResNet, or Inception. These models generate a comprehensive feature vector that encapsulates the key attributes of the image.
- **Language Modeling:** Recurrent Neural Networks (RNNs), often augmented with advanced architectures like Long Short-Term Memory (LSTM) or Gated Recurrent Unit (GRU), are used to generate captions. The network predicts a sequence of words that form a coherent description, based on the extracted image features.
- **Encoder-Decoder Framework:** Modern image captioning systems commonly adopt an encoder-decoder structure:
- **Encoder:** The CNN serves as the encoder, transforming the image into a fixed-size feature vector that encapsulates its essential content.
- **Decoder:** The RNN, or in some cases, a transformer-based model, functions as the decoder, converting the encoded features into a fluent and descriptive sentence.

## Advanced Techniques in Image Captioning

To improve the quality of captions, several advanced techniques have been incorporated:

- Attention Mechanisms: Attention mechanisms enable the model to selectively focus on specific regions of an image as it generates each word in the caption, closely mirroring how humans describe images by sequentially concentrating on the most pertinent areas.
- Transformers: The integration of transformer architectures, such as the Vision Transformer (ViT) and CLIP, has significantly advanced both visual and linguistic understanding in captioning systems, enabling more nuanced and accurate interpretations of images.
- Reinforcement Learning: Reinforcement learning is utilized to fine-tune models by optimizing for evaluation metrics such as BLEU, METEOR, and CIDEr, thereby enhancing the coherence, relevance, and overall quality of generated captions.

## Challenges in Automatic Image Captioning

- Diversity in Visual Content: Images typically encompass a wide range of objects, actions, and contexts, making it challenging to encapsulate all pertinent details within a single caption.
- Ambiguity in Interpretation: Images can be interpreted in multiple ways, influenced by cultural and contextual factors, which makes it difficult to create captions that are universally accepted or understood.

- Complexity of Sentence Construction: Crafting captions that are not only grammatically correct but also contextually precise and smoothly written presents an ongoing challenge.
- Bias in Training Data: Captioning models often inherit inherent biases from the datasets they are trained on, which can result in stereotypical or overly narrow descriptions.

## Applications of Automatic Image Captioning

- Assistive Technologies: Empowering visually impaired individuals by providing real-time audio descriptions that help them navigate and understand their environment through image interpretation.
- Content Management: Streamlining the automation of image tagging and organization, enhancing search engine efficiency and improving visibility across social media platforms.
- E-Commerce: Enriching product descriptions to optimize user experience and boost search engine visibility, leading to increased customer engagement and conversion rates.
- Autonomous Vehicles: Enhancing scene comprehension and enabling precise object recognition to support safe, data-driven decision-making for autonomous systems.
- Education and Entertainment: Elevating educational materials and interactive storytelling by generating immersive descriptive narratives that bring visual content to life for deeper engagement.

## Future Directions

The integration of multimodal AI systems that combine vision, language, and audio holds the potential to significantly enhance the robustness and contextual awareness of image captioning. Moreover, ongoing research is focused on reducing biases, improving cultural adaptability, and enabling real-time captioning on edge devices. Automatic image captioning stands as a prime example of the synergy between vision and language AI, laying the groundwork for more immersive and interactive AI-powered experiences.

## Image Generation with Generative Adversarial Networks

Generative Adversarial Networks (GANs) represent a revolutionary breakthrough in artificial intelligence, transforming the landscape of image generation. First introduced by Ian Goodfellow and his team in 2014, GANs consist of two competing neural networks—the generator and the discriminator—engaged in a dynamic process of adversarial learning. This innovative framework empowers GANs to produce strikingly realistic and diverse images, making a profound impact across industries such as art, design, gaming, and scientific research.

### *How GANs Work?*

The generator produces synthetic images by transforming random noise (latent space vectors) into realistic visuals, while the discriminator assesses whether an image is authentic (from the dataset) or fabricated (from the generator). Both networks are trained concurrently in an adversarial manner:

- The generator learns to produce images that can fool the discriminator.
- The discriminator improves its ability to distinguish between real and fake images.

This adversarial process is framed as a minimax game, where the generator aims to minimize its loss by enhancing the realism of its outputs, while the discriminator seeks to minimize its loss by accurately distinguishing between real and generated images. Through this continuous, iterative interplay, the generator progressively refines its ability to produce highly realistic images.

## Applications of GANs in Image Generation

GANs have become a transformative tool for generating high-quality images. Some key applications include:

- Art and Creativity: GANs have the ability to generate original artworks, seamlessly blend various artistic styles, and fuel the creation of innovative and unique designs.
- Image Super-Resolution: Advanced GANs like SRGAN can significantly enhance the resolution of low-quality images, revealing intricate details and improving overall clarity.
- Image-to-Image Translation: Models such as Pix2Pix and CycleGAN enable the transformation of basic sketches into photorealistic images, apply stylistic changes, and even modify attributes like lighting or time of day.
- Medical Imaging: GANs contribute to the generation of synthetic medical images, enriching datasets and facilitating the analysis of rare or unique cases for more accurate diagnosis and treatment planning.
- Content Creation: GANs drive the creation of highly realistic visual assets for immersive experiences in virtual reality, gaming, and film, pushing the boundaries of digital content.

## Advantages and Challenges

GANs offer significant benefits:

- **Realism:** The generated outputs can closely replicate real-world visuals, capturing intricate details and lifelike features.
- **Diversity:** GANs are capable of producing a vast array of variations, unlocking a wide spectrum of creative possibilities.

- **Scalability:** They can be seamlessly applied across various domains, extending beyond image generation to include tasks like video synthesis and text-to-image transformations.

## However, they also face challenges:

- Training Instability: The adversarial framework of GANs often leads to challenges such as mode collapse, where the generator produces only a narrow range of outputs, limiting diversity.
- High Computational Demand: The training process for GANs is highly resource-intensive, requiring significant computational power and time to achieve optimal performance.
- Ethical Concerns: The potential for GANs to be exploited in creating deepfakes and counterfeit images raises serious ethical issues related to misinformation and misuse.
- Evaluation Metrics: Assessing the quality of GAN-generated outputs is inherently complex, as it involves subjective judgment and lacks universally agreed-upon standards for evaluation.

## The future of GANs in image generation includes:

**Advanced Architectures:** Models like StyleGAN offer more precise control over generated outputs, enhancing the quality and specificity of results.

**Multimodal Integration:** By combining GANs with other AI models, we can significantly broaden their capabilities, enabling applications like generating images directly from textual descriptions.

**Ethical Safeguards:** Efforts are underway to develop advanced tools that can detect GAN-generated images, promoting responsible usage and mitigating potential misuse.

**Table 10.2: GAN Applications and Benefits.**

| Application | Description | Benefits |
|---|---|---|
| **Art and Creativity** | Generates novel artworks and designs, blends styles | Enables unique creative expressions |
| **Super-Resolution** | Enhances low-quality images | Improves clarity and detail |
| **Image Translation** | Converts sketches, styles, and visual attributes | Facilitates design and visual effects |
| **Medical Imaging** | Creates synthetic medical images for rare case analysis | Augments datasets and research |
| **Content Creation** | Develops realistic assets for VR, gaming, and movies | Boosts realism and immersion |
| **Style Transfer** | Applies artistic styles to photos | Personalizes visual outputs |

Generative Adversarial Networks (GANs) have revolutionized the landscape of creativity and artificial intelligence, unlocking endless possibilities to transform industries. However, their widespread adoption also brings forth complex ethical and technical challenges that demand thoughtful evaluation. The groundbreaking potential of GANs continues to drive cutting-edge research and development in the field of AI (see Table 10.2).

## Video to Text with LSTM Models

Converting videos into textual descriptions is essential for various applications, including accessibility, content indexing, and multimedia analysis. This task presents a challenge due to the need to capture both the spatial information within individual video frames and the temporal relationships between those frames to generate coherent, contextually rich text. Long Short-Term Memory (LSTM) networks, a type of recurrent neural network (RNN), are particularly well-suited for this task due to their ability to learn and retain long-term dependencies within sequential data, making them highly effective for video processing. The video-to-text process begins with the extraction of spatial features from each video frame. Convolutional Neural Networks (CNNs), known for their proficiency in detecting visual patterns, are commonly employed to process each frame. These CNNs extract crucial features such as objects, people, and actions within the scene. Since a video consists of a sequence of frames, this stage transforms each frame into a feature vector that encapsulates its content.

Once the spatial features are extracted, they are passed to an LSTM network. The LSTM processes these sequential features, learning to capture the temporal relationships between frames. This ability to understand the flow of events, actions, and transitions over time is fundamental for generating accurate and meaningful textual descriptions. As the LSTM processes each timestep, it updates its internal state, "remembering" the context of previous frames and enabling the generation of coherent sentences that describe what is unfolding in the video. The final step involves passing the learned temporal information to a decoder, which is often another LSTM or a transformer-based model. The decoder uses the sequential data from the LSTM to generate natural language text that describes the video's content. It predicts the next word or phrase based on the hidden state of the LSTM, producing descriptive captions, summaries, or even detailed video annotations. This entire process is trained end-to-end, optimizing the CNN, LSTM, and decoder to work in concert for improved performance.

Video-to-text systems have broad applications. In accessibility, they can provide captions or spoken descriptions for visually impaired users. In education, they can generate summaries of lectures or tutorials, making long videos more digestible. In the media and entertainment industries, video-to-text systems can automatically tag, index, and summarize content, enabling more efficient search and discovery. Additionally, surveillance systems can utilize these models to generate textual reports of events happening in video feeds, facilitating quicker analysis and response.Despite the promise of LSTM-based video-to-text systems, they are not without their challenges. One significant issue is handling long videos, which demand substantial computational resources. Moreover, LSTMs may struggle to capture complex or abstract visual elements, leading to vague or inaccurate descriptions. To overcome these limitations, newer models are incorporating attention mechanisms and transformer architectures, which enhance accuracy, efficiency, and scalability, making video-to-text conversion more robust and adaptable to diverse applications.

## Attention Models for Computer Vision

In recent years, attention mechanisms have become a critical component in improving the performance of computer vision models. Originally popularized by their success in natural language processing (NLP), attention mechanisms are designed to help models focus on the most relevant parts of an input, effectively simulating human-like attention. In computer vision, this idea translates into selectively concentrating on important regions of an image while processing the entire input, allowing the model to make more informed predictions. Attention mechanisms are particularly useful in tasks such as image classification, object detection, and segmentation, where understanding the spatial relationships and important features is vital for accurate performance.

One of the key motivations for using attention in computer vision is to tackle the issue of spatial variability. Images, being high-dimensional data, can contain numerous features, but not all of them are equally important for a given task. Attention models help by dynamically weighting the importance of different regions of the image. This capability is crucial in complex tasks like object detection, where certain objects may be obscured or appear in different sizes and orientations. Attention models help the network "attend" to the most relevant parts of the image, which can improve accuracy and reduce computational cost by ignoring irrelevant regions.The Transformer model, initially developed for NLP tasks, has had a significant impact on computer vision. The Vision Transformer (ViT) leverages self-attention mechanisms to treat image patches as sequences and applies attention to these patches to capture long-range dependencies. Unlike traditional convolutional neural networks (CNNs), which rely on local receptive fields, transformers can capture global contextual relationships between different parts of an image. This makes them particularly effective in handling images with complex patterns and relationships that would otherwise require deeper and more computationally expensive CNN architectures.

One notable extension of attention models in computer vision is the use of spatial attention. Spatial attention models allow the network to focus on specific regions in the image that are crucial for the task at hand. For instance, in image captioning, the model can attend to specific objects or regions within an image, generating a caption that accurately describes the most important elements. By incorporating spatial attention into CNN-based models or transformers, these models can better understand where to focus their processing power, leading to improvements in both accuracy and efficiency.In addition to spatial attention, another important development is the use of channel attention mechanisms. In this approach, the model focuses on different feature channels or levels of abstraction, rather than specific regions of an image. Channel attention mechanisms can be particularly useful in tasks where different feature maps contain varying levels of importance, such as fine-grained classification or multi-object detection. By learning which feature channels are most relevant for the task, these models can filter out noise and improve overall performance.

The combination of both spatial and channel attention has led to the creation of hybrid attention models that perform better across a range of computer vision tasks. These models are capable of dynamically focusing on the most relevant regions and features, enhancing their ability to handle complex visual information. Additionally, as computational resources improve, attention mechanisms are being integrated into more advanced models, enabling real-time and scalable solutions for practical applications in areas like autonomous driving, medical imaging, and augmented reality. As research continues, attention mechanisms are expected to play an increasingly pivotal role in advancing computer vision technologies.

## Summary

This chapter explores a wide array of advanced applications in deep learning, with a particular emphasis on key areas of computer vision. It delves into image segmentation, where deep learning models are employed to partition an image into meaningful components. The chapter also covers object detection, illustrating how models are capable of identifying and pinpointing objects within an image. Another application discussed is automatic image captioning, in which deep learning models generate accurate descriptive text based on the content of an image. Additionally, the chapter examines image generation through Generative Adversarial Networks (GANs), demonstrating how these models can create highly realistic images. The use of Long Short-Term Memory (LSTM) models for converting video sequences into text is also explored, showing how video frames can be transformed into coherent and descriptive language. Finally, the chapter highlights attention mechanisms in computer vision, explaining how these models enable deep learning systems to focus on pertinent regions of an image, enhancing both efficiency and accuracy. Collectively, these applications underscore the transformative and wide-ranging potential of deep learning in addressing real-world visual tasks.

## Exercise Questions:

- Explain the difference between semantic segmentation and instance segmentation. Provide examples of real-world applications for each.
- Describe the architecture of YOLO (You Only Look Once) and explain how it differs from other object detection frameworks like Faster R-CNN.

- How does the combination of CNNs and RNNs work in automatic image captioning? Illustrate with a block diagram.
- What are the roles of the generator and discriminator in a GAN, and how do they interact during training?
- Explain the process of using LSTM models for video captioning. What challenges are associated with this approach?
- What is the role of attention mechanisms in computer vision tasks, and how do they address the limitations of traditional CNNs?
- Compare the use of GANs for image generation with attention models for image classification. Highlight the strengths and limitations of each approach.
- Why is dataset quality crucial for tasks like object detection and image captioning? Discuss the characteristics of an ideal dataset for these tasks.
- Discuss potential advancements in attention models for computer vision. How might they improve tasks like object detection and segmentation?
- Design a system that integrates image segmentation, object detection, and automatic captioning to create a comprehensive scene-understanding application. Outline the key components and their roles.

# Books for Further Reading


- Deep Learning" by Ian Goodfellow, Yoshua Bengio, and Aaron Courville
- "Pattern Recognition and Machine Learning" by Christopher M. Bishop
- "Machine Learning: A Probabilistic Perspective" by Kevin P. Murphy
- "Hands-On Machine Learning with Scikit-Learn, Keras, and TensorFlow" by Aurélien Géron
- "Deep Learning for Computer Vision" by Rajalingappaa Shanmugamani
- "Artificial Intelligence: A Guide to Intelligent Systems" by Michael Negnevitsky
- "Neural Networks and Deep Learning" by Michael Nielsen
- "The Elements of Statistical Learning" by Trevor Hastie, Robert Tibshirani, and Jerome Friedman
- "Python Machine Learning" by Sebastian Raschka and Vahid Mirjalili
- "Reinforcement Learning: An Introduction" by Richard S. Sutton and Andrew G. Barto

# Bibliography


- Abolhasani, M., & Kumacheva, E. (2023). The rise of self-driving labs in chemical and materials sciences. In *Nature Synthesis*. https://doi.org/10.1038/s44160-022-00231-0
- Aggarwal, C. C. (2023). Neural Networks and Deep Learning: A Textbook. In *Neural Networks and Deep Learning: A Textbook*. https://doi.org/10.1007/978-3-031-29642-0
- Al Hajj, G. S., Pensar, J., & Sandve, G. K. (2023). DagSim: Combining DAG-based model structure with unconstrained data types and relations for flexible, transparent, and modularized data simulation. *PLoS ONE*. https://doi.org/10.1371/journal.pone.0284443
- Alharbi, F., & Vakanski, A. (2023). Machine Learning Methods for Cancer Classification Using Gene Expression Data: A Review. In *Bioengineering*. https://doi.org/10.3390/bioengineering10020173
- Alharbi, L. A. (2023). A Systematic Literature Review on AI Algorithms and Techniques Adopted by e-Learning Platforms for Psychological and Emotional States. *International Journal of Advanced Computer Science and Applications*. https://doi.org/10.14569/IJACSA.2023.0140254
- Ali, A., & Mashwani, W. K. (2023). A Supervised Machine Learning Algorithms: Applications, Challenges, and Recommendations. In *Proceedings of the Pakistan Academy of Sciences: Part A*. https://doi.org/10.53560/PPASA(60-4)831
- Almazroi, A. A., Aldhahri, E. A., Bashir, S., & Ashfaq, S. (2023). A Clinical Decision Support System for Heart Disease Prediction Using Deep Learning. *IEEE Access*. https://doi.org/10.1109/ACCESS.2023.3285247
- Ceia-Hasse, A., Sousa, C. A., Gouveia, B. R., & Capinha, C. (2023). Forecasting the abundance of disease vectors with deep learning. *Ecological Informatics*. https://doi.org/10.1016/j.ecoinf.2023.102272
- Chandrika, G. N., Gumudavelli, S. V. R., Kalleru, A., Kambhampati, V., & Kandaggatlta, P. (2023). Comparative Analysis of Machine Learning Algorithms to Forecast Indian Stock Market. *ITM Web of Conferences*. https://doi.org/10.1051/itmconf/20235605009

- Chen, L., Jose, S. T., Nikoloska, I., Park, S., Chen, T., & Simeone, O. (2023). Learning with Limited Samples: Meta-Learning and Applications to Communication Systems. In *Foundations and Trends in Signal Processing*. https://doi.org/10.1561/2000000115
- Dara, O. A., Lopez-Guede, J. M., Raheem, H. I., Rahebi, J., Zulueta, E., & Fernandez-Gamiz, U. (2023). Alzheimer's Disease Diagnosis Using Machine Learning: A Survey. *Applied Sciences (Switzerland)*. https://doi.org/10.3390/app13148298
- Duncan, M. J., Eyre, E. L. J., Clarke, N., Hamid, A., & Jing, Y. (2024). Importance of fundamental movement skills to predict technical skills in youth grassroots soccer: A machine learning approach. *International Journal of Sports Science and Coaching*. https://doi.org/10.1177/17479541231202015
- El Majzoub, A., Rabhi, F. A., & Hussain, W. (2023). Evaluating interpretable machine learning predictions for cryptocurrencies. *Intelligent Systems in Accounting, Finance and Management*. https://doi.org/10.1002/isaf.1538
- Escobar-Ipuz, F. A., Torres, A. M., García-Jiménez, M. A., Basar, C., Cascón, J., & Mateo, J. (2023). Prediction of patients with idiopathic generalized epilepsy from healthy controls using machine learning from scalp EEG recordings. *Brain Research*. https://doi.org/10.1016/j.brainres.2022.148131
- Gheisari, M., Ebrahimzadeh, F., Rahimi, M., Moazzamigodarzi, M., Liu, Y., Dutta Pramanik, P. K., Heravi, M. A., Mehbodniya, A., Ghaderzadeh, M., Feylizadeh, M. R., & Kosari, S. (2023). Deep learning: Applications, architectures, models, tools, and frameworks: A comprehensive survey. In *CAAI Transactions on Intelligence Technology*. https://doi.org/10.1049/cit2.12180
- Gilad, G., & Sharan, R. (2023). From Leiden to Tel-Aviv University (TAU): exploring clustering solutions via a genetic algorithm. *PNAS Nexus*. https://doi.org/10.1093/pnasnexus/pgad180
- Hadad, B., Froim, S., Yosef, E., Giryes, R., & Bahabad, A. (2023). Deep learning in optics—a tutorial. In *Journal of Optics (United Kingdom)*. https://doi.org/10.1088/2040-8986/ad08dc
- Islam, N., Khizar Khan, S., Rehman, A., Aftab, U., & Syed, D. (2023). Stock Prediction for ARGAAM Companies Dataset. *KIET Journal of Computing and Information Sciences*. https://doi.org/10.51153/kjcis.v6i2.150
- Kofi Immanuel Jones, & Swati Sah. (2023). The Implementation of Machine Learning in The Insurance Industry with Big Data Analytics. *International Journal of Data Informatics and Intelligent Computing*. https://doi.org/10.59461/ijdiic.v2i2.47

- Kothadiya, D. R., Bhatt, C. M., Rehman, A., Alamri, F. S., & Saba, T. (2023). SignExplainer: An Explainable AI-Enabled Framework for Sign Language Recognition With Ensemble Learning. *IEEE Access*. https://doi.org/10.1109/ACCESS.2023.3274851
- Kouba, P., Kohout, P., Haddadi, F., Bushuiev, A., Samusevich, R., Sedlar, J., Damborsky, J., Pluskal, T., Sivic, J., & Mazurenko, S. (2023). Machine Learning-Guided Protein Engineering. In *ACS Catalysis*. https://doi.org/10.1021/acscatal.3c02743
- Lyon, R. J., & Rattay, T. (2023). Fundamentals of machine learning. In *Machine Learning and Artificial Intelligence in Radiation Oncology: A Guide for Clinicians*. https://doi.org/10.1016/B978-0-12-822000-9.00018-5
- Marcinkevičs, R., & Vogt, J. E. (2023). Interpretable and explainable machine learning: A methods-centric overview with concrete examples. *Wiley Interdisciplinary Reviews: Data Mining and Knowledge Discovery*. https://doi.org/10.1002/widm.1493
- Masrom, S., Rahman, R. A., Salleh, N. A., Pitaloka, E., Nor, M. A. M., & Zakaria, N. B. (2023). Machine learning prediction of petty corruption intention among law enforcement officers. *Indonesian Journal of Electrical Engineering and Computer Science*. https://doi.org/10.11591/ijeecs.v30.i3.pp1634-1642
- Matura, R., Thakur, R., & Prathimesh. (2023). Comparing the Performance of Different Supervised Learning Algorithms. *Journal of Artificial Intelligence and Capsule Networks*. https://doi.org/10.36548/jaicn.2023.1.005
- Mazhar, T., Haq, I., Ditta, A., Mohsan, S. A. H., Rehman, F., Zafar, I., Gansau, J. A., & Goh, L. P. W. (2023). The Role of Machine Learning and Deep Learning Approaches for the Detection of Skin Cancer. *Healthcare (Switzerland)*. https://doi.org/10.3390/healthcare11030415
- Mendonça, M. O. K., Netto, S. L., Diniz, P. S. R., & Theodoridis, S. (2023). Machine learning. In *Signal Processing and Machine Learning Theory*. https://doi.org/10.1016/B978-0-32-391772-8.00019-3
- Meyers, C., Löfstedt, T., & Elmroth, E. (2023). Safety-critical computer vision: an empirical survey of adversarial evasion attacks and defenses on computer vision systems. *Artificial Intelligence Review*. https://doi.org/10.1007/s10462-023-10521-4
- Narottama, B., Mohamed, Z., & Aissa, S. (2023). Quantum Machine Learning for Next-G Wireless Communications: Fundamentals and the Path Ahead. *IEEE Open Journal of the Communications Society*. https://doi.org/10.1109/OJCOMS.2023.3309268

- Nechi, A., Groth, L., Mulhem, S., Merchant, F., Buchty, R., & Berekovic, M. (2023). FPGA-based Deep Learning Inference Accelerators: Where Are We Standing? *ACM Transactions on Reconfigurable Technology and Systems*. https://doi.org/10.1145/3613963
- Oğuz, A., & Ertuğrul, Ö. F. (2023). A survey on applications of machine learning algorithms in water quality assessment and water supply and management. *Water Supply*. https://doi.org/10.2166/ws.2023.033
- Pillay, A. B., Pathmanathan, D., Abu, A., & Omar, H. (2023). RFE-Based Feature Selection to Improve Classification Accuracy for Morphometric Analysis of Craniodental Characters of House Rats. *Sains Malaysiana*. https://doi.org/10.17576/jsm-2023-5207-01
- Pistilli, F., & Averta, G. (2023). Graph Learning in Robotics: A Survey. *IEEE Access*. https://doi.org/10.1109/ACCESS.2023.3323220
- Qu, T., Guan, S., Feng, Y. T., Ma, G., Zhou, W., & Zhao, J. (2023). Deep active learning for constitutive modelling of granular materials: From representative volume elements to implicit finite element modelling. *International Journal of Plasticity*. https://doi.org/10.1016/j.ijplas.2023.103576
- Rahman, R. A., Masrom, S., Samad, N. H. A., Daud, R. M., & Mutia, E. (2023). Machine learning prediction of video-based learning with technology acceptance model. *Indonesian Journal of Electrical Engineering and Computer Science*. https://doi.org/10.11591/ijeecs.v29.i3.pp1560-1566
- Rubinger, L., Gazendam, A., Ekhtiari, S., & Bhandari, M. (2023). Machine learning and artificial intelligence in research and healthcare. *Injury*. https://doi.org/10.1016/j.injury.2022.01.046
- Serghiou, S., & Rough, K. (2023). Deep Learning for Epidemiologists: An Introduction to Neural Networks. *American Journal of Epidemiology*. https://doi.org/10.1093/aje/kwad107
- Shakya, A. K., Pillai, G., & Chakrabarty, S. (2023). Reinforcement learning algorithms: A brief survey. In *Expert Systems with Applications*. https://doi.org/10.1016/j.eswa.2023.120495
- Shuvo, M. M. H., Islam, S. K., Cheng, J., & Morshed, B. I. (2023). Efficient Acceleration of Deep Learning Inference on Resource-Constrained Edge Devices: A Review. In *Proceedings of the IEEE*. https://doi.org/10.1109/JPROC.2022.3226481
- Trivedi, K. S. (2023). *Machine Learning Fundamental Concepts*. https://doi.org/10.1007/978-1-4842-9221-1_3
- Tsai, P. F., Gao, C. H., & Yuan, S. M. (2023). Stock Selection Using Machine Learning Based on Financial Ratios. *Mathematics*. https://doi.org/10.3390/math11234758

- Vasilev, Y. A., Bobrovskaya, T. M., Arzamasov, K. M., Chetverikov, S. F., Vladzymyrskyy, A. V., Omelyanskaya, O. V., Andreychenko, A. E., Pavlov, N. A., & Anishchenko, L. N. (2023). Medical datasets for machine learning: fundamental principles of standartization and systematization. *Manager Zdravookhranenia*. https://doi.org/10.21045/1811-0185-2023-4-28-41
- Verma, S., Sahu, S. P., & Sahu, T. P. (2023). Stock Market Forecasting with Different Input Indicators using Machine Learning and Deep Learning Techniques: A Review. In *Engineering Letters*.
- Vijayaraj, V., Balamurugan, M., & Oberai, M. (2023). Machine learning approaches to identify the data types in big data environment: An overview. *The Scientific Temper*. https://doi.org/10.58414/scientifictemper.2023.14.3.60
- Wang, J. (2023). An Intuitive Tutorial to Gaussian Process Regression. *Computing in Science and Engineering*. https://doi.org/10.1109/MCSE.2023.3342149
- Whang, S. E., Roh, Y., Song, H., & Lee, J. G. (2023). Data collection and quality challenges in deep learning: a data-centric AI perspective. *VLDB Journal*. https://doi.org/10.1007/s00778-022-00775-9
- Winn, J. (2023). Model-based machine learning. In *Model-Based Machine Learning*. https://doi.org/10.1201/9780429192685
- Yahiaoui, A., Dorbani, S., & Yahiaoui, L. (2023). Machine learning techniques to predict the fundamental period of infilled reinforced concrete frame buildings. *Structures*. https://doi.org/10.1016/j.istruc.2023.05.052
- Yin, J. (2023). Crime Prediction Methods Based on Machine Learning: A Survey. *Computers, Materials and Continua*. https://doi.org/10.32604/cmc.2023.034190